D0825590

"THIS ISN'T THE AMERICA I THOUGHT I'D FIND"

African Students in the Urban U.S. High School

Rosemary Traoré

Robert J. Lukens

University Press of America,® Inc.

Lanham · Boulder · New York · Toronto · Oxford

Copyright © 2006 by
University Press of America,® Inc.
4501 Forbes Boulevard
Suite 200
Lanham, Maryland 20706
UPA Acquisitions Department (301) 459-3366

PO Box 317
Oxford
OX2 9RU, UK

All rights reserved
Printed in the United States of America
British Library Cataloging in Publication Information Available

Library of Congress Control Number: 2006922497
ISBN-13: 978-0-7618-3455-7 (paperback : alk. paper)
ISBN-10: 0-7618-3455-9 (paperback : alk. paper)

⊖™ The paper used in this publication meets the minimum
requirements of American National Standard for Information
Sciences—Permanence of Paper for Printed Library Materials,
ANSI Z39.48—1984

For Anne and Bob, who lead the way

Contents

List of Tables

FOREWORD

I was born in South Georgia to an agrarian family. I was twenty-seven years old when I went to the African continent for the first time. When I landed in Dakar, Senegal, I had an immediate sense of belonging, more than I had ever had in America. Although my family went back seven generations to slavery in the South I had no idea how deeply embedded Africa was in my mind and emotions until I stepped off the jet at the Dakar International Airport. Unquestionably I had come from people who had been separated from the African continent for a long time but there was something psychological, almost physical, in the relationship I had to being on African soil. In a way, the brilliance of the book, *This isn't the America I Thought I'd Find*, that Professors Rosemary Traoré and Robert Lukens have written, is in its understanding of the tremendous loss that both Africans in the Diaspora and on the continent have suffered from not knowing each other.

The transformation of education remains one of the most discussed themes in the lives of ordinary citizens. There has always been a major interest in the transmission of culture, mores, values, and accumulated learning; it is just unfortunate that many African Americans have been cut off, by no effort of our own, from the traditions that would have sustained us by giving hope, vision, confidence, and a historical record that could be appealed to in times of intellectual and cultural distress. By the same token, many Africans from the continent have little appreciation of the depth of their own pain caused by the excision of a large portion of their population from African societies. The reality is that both groups have experienced loss and this experience is one of the commonalities between us. But it is not just the experience of loss but the particular way the loss came to be experienced that has produced this bond between Africans here and Africans there. In Ghana, the Fante people have a special ritual each year for those who were taken away from their land. This type of ritual also occurs in Senegal as people long for the disconnected part to be reconnected.

Traoré and Lukens are ahead of their time in analyzing an increasingly important theme in urban schools. Already there is a preponderance of urban schools with a diversity of students of African origin in the eastern United States. This will become the case in other schools as well, as more and more students from African nations move to the United States. Like the Jamaicans, Haitians, and Central Americans of African origin, the continental Africans are finding that they have some areas of commonality with African Americans. They have both experienced prejudice and racism, or colonialism and segregation. The fact that continental Africans come from countries with a predominant black population does not mean that there is no racism, particularly if whites dominate the economies of those countries, as is sometimes the case. It might also be that the black leaders of those countries are so confused culturally that they carry out what Frantz Fanon understood as the agenda of the Eurocentric world in the midst of blackness. On the other hand, African Americans know very little about the realities of Africa and share with other Americans the idea that Africa is uniformly backwards, primitive, or dangerous. These are bad stereotypes that have to be expelled in order for people to move forward with their relationships.

What we have always believed is that students ought to be exposed to the best traditions the culture could provide for them. In a multicultural, multiethnic, pluralistic society, this particular desire is often met with multiple conflicts and anxieties because of the difficulty of providing a single model of education for a multicultural society. When it comes to students of African origin, it seems that information is the key to everything. In fact, the lack of information is one characteristic of ignorance; it can be compounded by acting on that lack of information as if it is real. Our discourse is increasingly about the content of the transmission. If you are involved in education you are a part of the configuration of knowledge that includes a discussion of the nature of human community.

I have now visited Africa more than 70 times, living in Zimbabwe for a while during the 1980s, and it is clear to me that the rejuvenation of the interaction between African American and African students at urban schools is possible as long as we are able to provide both groups of students with information. Living in another country as an immigrant or long term visitor takes flexibility, courage, and adaptability. Education is at the root of our ability to perform well in such situations.

It is sad that our public schools do not adequately educate our children about Africa. In addition, we know that Africans are not well educated about African Americans either and like the issues that often occur between African Americans and whites it is all about knowledge. An American student once came to my office to interview me for a journalism class. The first question was, "Dr. Asante, do the people in Ethiopia work?" The question startled me. I was at a loss for words. When I recovered I said, "Jennifer, yes, the people in Ethiopia have a great variety of professions and jobs."

This book is at the core of the discussion of teaching in a pluralistic society. Professors Traoré and Lukens' work is on target with the kind of sensitivity, flexibility, and intellectual insight necessary for a truly enlightened approach to understanding one of the not so subtle areas of the transmission of knowledge.

Among the most important aspects of this book is the fact that the authors concentrate on ways to explore with students their sense of self, identity, and relationships within their communities. The book is Afrocentric, which is good, because it allows the African American and African students to speak in their own voices. All progressive books on education will have to allow the subjects to speak for themselves in the future; this is the only real meaning of being Afrocentric in this situation. The reader is introduced to the elements that help to explain how humans learn to live with each other without totally obliterating each other.

In defiance of nay-sayers, and there will be some, these authors have charged ahead to tell us that the removal of stereotypes that we have about each other can alleviate tensions, bad feelings, racial or ethnic problems. It is not that we did not know these things, but we have often applied them to black and white situations rather than black and black situations. One might be tempted to say that the book is harder on the African Americans than the continental African students, but that is only in the context that the educational system in the United States has not provided either African Americans or whites any in-depth treatment of Africa. Of course, we know that Africans often have strange ideas about African Americans. These reactions on both sides merely mask the inadequacy of information. This book goes a long way toward opening our eyes.

What strikes me most, however, about the contents of this book is how it merges a discussion of academic and physical wellness, with mental and cultural developments. It seeks to show us how the tension between tradition and innovation is the space for creativity. If the continental students bring tradition and enter the world of American innovation, they are participating in something that will lead to a synthesis. If the African American students bring their own local traditions and heroes (inventors, resistance leaders, authors, artists, scientists) from the American context and flow into the innovation that comes from a new experience with the African world, there is the possibility of a massive transformation. Indeed, what Professors Traoré and Lukens have done, is to set the bar very high.

Molefi Kete Asante, Ph.D., Professor, Temple University
Author of *Race, Rhetoric and Identity: The Architecton of Soul*

PREFACE

This book is the culmination of a long journey, started many years ago in the suburbs of Philadelphia. It is a collaborative effort that represents the blended perspectives of its authors who followed very different paths to reach the same realizations about the distance we in America still must travel before the ideals on which our nation was founded are made meaningful for every human being who follows her hopes and dreams and aspirations by coming to our shores. The principal context for our analysis is the public education of America's children because we are convinced that in the manner in which we educate our young is evinced the moral compass and the principles that we most esteem and want successive generations to believe and follow.

Political rhetoric is time- and situation-bound and its effects endure only to the extent that the ideas that it encapsulates attain agreement from or resonate within a community. Our educational practices and policies, however, can leave indelible marks on highly impressionable minds; some lessons that children learn will last a lifetime. This reality makes the responsibilities of teaching so much more delicate than politics and should make our reflections upon what we are teaching our children of the utmost significance. It is imperative that we are leading our children into a successful future, lest the American Dream become a delusion. It would be impossible to convey the full impact of our lifelong journey on the choice of research topic on which this book is founded without explaining the myriad experiences that informed both the choice of subject matter to study as well as the characteristics of the group of students to select to participate.[1] Moreover, because a degree of transparency can be beneficial in both politics and teaching, a description of the personal journeys that laid the groundwork for the genesis of this study may elucidate some of the influential individual life experiences that have contributed to the authorial perspectives included in this book.

The Call of the Peace Corps

For some reason that I, Rosemary, cannot characterize clearly, even to myself, I knew at an early age that I would go to Africa one day. As an earnest 8 year old, I had listened avidly to the newly inaugurated John F. Kennedy's challenge to "ask not what your country can do for you but what you can do for your country." I was 11 years old when President Kennedy died, and I knew then that one day I would join the Peace Corps and go to Africa eventually. Why Africa? is the operative question, and forms the underlying predicate for the book you hold in your hand. I first applied to the Peace Corps when I graduated from high school but the Corps required its volunteers to have earned a college degree, preferably in a subject that was conducive to developing a nation's resources. After graduating from college, however, I delayed my application to the Peace Corps and taught for a year and a half in Philadelphia. I had some eye-opening experiences through some tough teaching situations. My first year teaching I had 42 second graders; all but two of my students were Black. At the time, I had the typical mode of liberal thought in the post-Civil Rights era, which was to try to be "color blind," and to me this meant to ignore difference and treat everyone like me. My second year, I taught 3rd grade in a different school.

Both of the schools I taught in during my first years as a professional educator had similar racial compositions. Although I had more tools at my disposal in my second year, I still did not understand how to reach out to the students in ways that mattered to them. By this time I had learned enough to know that I did not know how to teach students to read and without reading every other subject became impossible. I decided to go to graduate school and, again, I decided to delay volunteering with the Peace Corps until after I'd obtained a graduate degree in Education with a specialization in Reading. The day after I took my Master's comprehensive exam I spent a few weeks visiting with my family in Philadelphia before leaving for the Central African Republic to teach English as a Peace Corps Volunteer.

Inherited Influences

Like most people, I'd already had several experiences that influenced the way I view the world, some of them related to racial stereotypes, which had a lasting influence on the way that I perceived my standing in the world. My maternal uncle, Reverend Richard T. McSorley, S.J., had tried vigorously to integrate his parish in Maryland long before integration was encouraged. He had marched with Dr. Martin Luther King, Jr. in Alabama and was arrested many times for his beliefs in equality, justice and non-violent protest against segregation. His doctoral dissertation on prejudice inexplicably was rejected by the University of Ontario (McSorley, 1960).

Later, Father McSorley founded the Center for Peace Studies at Georgetown University where he taught and counseled non-violence for the remainder of his life. He inspired me with the way that he stalwartly argued for peace and justice for more than 50 years and never lost his faith in humanity.

A Taste of Exclusion

While a freshman at Duquesne University in Pittsburgh I met a few young males in the Student Union who were getting ready to perform. We struck up a conversation and they invited me to attend their concert. I followed them upstairs, walked in, sat down and was then approached by someone who asked me to leave. This was 1970 and I was in a performance sponsored by the Black Student Union. I was the only white person in the room. I got up and stood outside for a while thinking that I'd better cherish this moment because I had just been let in on an experience that too many white people never encounter.

I remember thinking at that moment that the students had every right to ask me to leave. They had plenty of legitimate reasons to take their rightful places on the campus and to exclude anyone who had hitherto excluded them on the basis of their race. Although I had been taught that race was just a different skin color, I also learned that it was so much more.

How We Are Not Equal

When I was about in high school, I brought an African American friend home. I still remember his name, and my parents' reaction shocked me. They weren't unpleasant while he was visiting me at my house. Afterwards, however, their comments made it clear that we might be equal, but we were not going to be permitted to date.

I also remember with some fondness, tinged with retrospective sadness, how we had a Black woman who came to clean our home and help out my mom. Her name was Millie. Now that I know how important it is to call an African American woman by Mrs. or Miss, I realize that we never knew that much about her. I never knew anything about her except that she was friendly and loving. I don't remember how long she was with us or how often or much about her at all. But as with so many white families, we had an African American woman clean the floors and do other menial jobs. Of course, my mom had to do it all herself when Millie was no longer there and I have never gotten the hang of it myself. I have resisted doing those menial and mundane jobs as much as I can. The fact that I call them "menial and mundane" says a lot. The point is that Millie wasn't the same as anyone else that I knew. She worked in our home, but she was not part of our family. She was in our home, but we'd never have gone to visit her in hers. I have no idea where she lived. I never knew her last name.

How We Are the Same

This book could not have been written had I not stayed long enough in Africa to have my colonial mindset altered drastically. In 1976, as a young white female, who had just completed a graduate degree, I joined the Peace Corps and taught English in a high school in the Central African Republic. My experiences there were so positive that I extended my tour for a third year. What moved me the most about my experience was the sense of community and connection to nature so present every day from greeting everyone, everywhere, all the time, to waking up at sunup and going to bed at sunset. It was a natural and revelatory way to live life. I treasured the many events I shared with my neighbors and my students' families, from birth to death. There were hours of storytelling, song and dance. There was a spiritual connection that grabbed my soul because life was meant to be shared with each other. When I was sick, people came to sit with me. Food was eaten from a common plate. Good times and bad times were shared. Celebrations were lively and loud. People let me into their lives and in doing so helped to nurture my soul.

Among my first impressions, I became judgmental about everything in my new surroundings, but in time I saw how much sense the African way of life made and fit in my understanding about the world. I felt that in the United States we had lost some of our sense of community, our sharing together, and our interconnectedness with each other and with nature. I re-discovered these again through my African friends and colleagues.

In later years I returned to the African continent many times spending more than 10 years in various countries there. Each return was a journey to that human connection, and the bond that we share as human beings, connected to the earth. I always felt closer to God while I was on African soil. My African friends and colleagues helped me to see what is most important in life—sharing life with each other. This was a far cry from the cutthroat world of corporate greed and insatiable materialism that I found predominant in America.

I was able to see my country and my values through others' eyes. I remember hearing the Africans say "we have time; you have money" and admiring their appreciation and use of time to connect with others. American culture seemed to be missing this understanding of time. Money seemed to be so much more highly valued. Time was such a different concept for Africans. There was always time to listen, time to help, time to sit, time to be with friends and family, and time to help a neighbor. I seemed to always be short of time, but I learned from my African colleagues, students and friends to change my priorities and to take time and to make time for the important matters life presented. The sense of extended family appealed to me and I cherished my relationships with my African neighbors. I was so accustomed to greeting everyone everywhere all the time that when I came home and continued with this pattern while riding the Philadelphia subways, I felt the eyes of suspicion as I attempted to make eye contact and greet everyone around me.

Many things were different about my life in Africa. It was only years later when I studied African Philosophy, African literature, and Afrocentricity that words could be put to describe my experience of the fundamental value differences that I experienced routinely in my 10 years on the African continent.

Teaching in the United States and Teaching in Africa

Before I joined the Peace Corps, I had taught for almost two years in inner city schools. My experiences teaching on the African continent were different in many ways. I had taught Afro-American students and thought that it would have prepared me to teach in Africa. However, in front of me in African classrooms, I discovered students who were eager to learn in a way that my American students were not. Along with the kind of prestige that African children bestowed automatically on teachers came a level of responsibility to teach them to the best of my ability. The young Central African students before me were curious about everything and eager to learn, but it was their sense of celebration that will remain with me forever. If anyone succeeded, they all succeeded and there was cause for celebration. It could be singing, dancing, a party, or applause as marker of the success of any one student. There was a sense that the students were responsible for each other, to each other and to the teacher. The classroom was a bona fide community, with each student being a full-fledged responsible member.

Years later, I trained and supervised Peace Corps Volunteer teachers and watched them become at home in Africa. For those volunteers who stayed and made the necessary adjustments, there was a new appreciation for values so different than their own. It was not just my experience but also the experience of many. It required putting aside the pre-judgments and negative critiques that kept some from seeing the African way as valuable in its own right and seeing skin color not as an obstacle either for them or for their students. Our skin color was not an impenetrable obstacle for the Africans, even though they had been colonized and in many respects and for many years mistreated by whites. They opened their homes and hearts to me and to so many others. I had never experienced such hospitality, such warm receptions, such kindnesses, such thoughtfulness, such caring, and such giving even from those who materially had so little. Sharing seemed to come naturally.

My teaching experience in Africa challenged me to reflect on my first few years of teaching in an inner city school and admit that I had looked at my students through a deficit lens. I had not seen my Afro-American students with as much potential as I now attributed to my African students. This prompted me to examine Afrocentricity as a tool to bring African and Afro-American students together to learn from and about each other. My own stereotyped beliefs and misconceptions about Africa were dispelled by my experiences on the continent. I learned that skin color is of NO significance in reality but of MAJOR significance in the lived reality of people of color in America. Africans and Afro-Americans are so much more than the media would have us think.

Critical to this research study were my experiences with students and teachers in many different African countries including Burkina Faso, Cameroon, the Central African Republic, Côte d'Ivoire (working with Liberian and Sierra Leonian refugees), Djibouti (working with Ethiopian refugees), Gabon, Republic of Guinea (working with Liberian and Sierra Leonian refugees), Liberia, Malawi, Mauritania, and Uganda. While in Africa over the course of 10 years, I visited more than 200 schools, taught more than 500 African students, and trained more than 2,000 teachers in 11 different countries that covered North, East, West and Central Africa.

In one refugee school in Liberia, the teachers in my workshop complained about their seats and how hard it was to concentrate when they were so uncomfortable. It was a "teachable moment." I asked them to consider how hard it might be for their students to sit still as they lectured to them for several hours at a time. The teachers laughed at their own reactions. I had purposely held the workshop in one of their own schools so that they could be put in their students' places and develop some empathy for the students. I remember being humbled by some of the workshop participants who taught without pay and in the most difficult situations out of a commitment to the African youth and a hope for a better future for them, their country and their continent. Their determination to continue to provide an education to the youth in the face of such dire circumstances, brought on by war, inspired me to face many difficult journeys to refugee schools. They taught with little to no resources or support and came to school day after day though rations were insufficient and obstacles were many.

Jackson High: A Point of Entry

It is important to describe my own journey and how I settled upon this specific project and theory to utilize in my research. In this study the researcher is
the primary instrument for data collection and analysis (Merriam, 1998, p. 8).
My first visit to Jackson High School, the inner city school that was the site of
this research, was not part of this study.[2] I initially had planned on going to
Jackson for an entirely different purpose—to observe a friend teach a few
classes so that I could write a letter of recommendation for him. A few weeks
earlier, he had been beaten up at school by a student and my friend had decided
to leave teaching and get another kind of job.

When I first approached Jackson High I was afraid. I thought it looked
ugly. It seemed to be more a menace than an inviting structure. All but one of
the outside doors were locked. When I finally found the entrance, an open door,
I was not sure whether to go in or run away. As I walked the corridors that first
day I couldn't get the incident involving my friend out of my mind. The same
day that my friend was hurt, an administrator had been shot while in the school;
a teacher had been hospitalized and my friend, who is over 6 feet tall and strong,
had been thrown against a wall. Now even he was afraid to stay at this school.
So who was I not to be afraid?

Jackson has approximately 2,000 students. Physically, it resembles a
prison. The high walls, iron fencing, locked doors and metal detectors at the
entrance add to the prison-like ambience. The halls are crowded with students.
People are pushing; people are shouting. Teachers yell; students curse. After
signing in at the front security desk and a brief visit to the office, I was escorted
to his classroom, which had bars on the doors. He taught computer class. The
computers had to be locked in at night, but he also locked himself in the classroom once the class had started. As I sat down to observe his class I discovered
I was feeling very disheartened. This strapping young man had been one of my
best Peace Corps Volunteer teachers and his school environment in Africa was
tough but nothing had prepared him for what he found at Jackson, and he
wanted to get out badly. To my surprise, however, it only took a few minutes
after the class convened for me to realize that there were Africans in the room
because I heard Liberian English and saw an Ethiopian. I heard West African
French and Krio from Sierra Leone. This was music to my ears because of the
many rewarding years I had spent living in Africa. I hurried to the students and
greeted them.

In a conversation over lunch with my friend's colleagues, I heard horror stories about how the African students were being treated by their African American peers. The teachers told me that there had been fights between Africans and
African Americans that had resulted in a student being stabbed. My friend told
me that some of the African students in his class had complained about teasing,
pushing and general harassment.

Later, it occurred to me that rather than having to do my study in Africa I
had found the ideal place to do my research. I believed that I could focus on
what I immediately saw as significant problems in the ways in which these two

groups, Afro-American and African students interacted. With many years of experience in urban schools in the U.S., coupled with many years of experience in schools in Africa, I thought I might have found a way to contribute to a better understanding between these students. I asked myself whether the presence of the African students at Jackson could bring about a connection for the Afro-American students they rubbed shoulders with every day. Instead of a problem, as their presence in the school had been described by many, could it be an opportunity? This was how the principal envisioned my presence and my research. I asked myself what factors contributed to the hostility that was erupting on a regular basis. How did they see each other? What was keeping these two groups of students apart?

Weis (1992) stresses that it would be very beneficial for middle class researchers to undertake much "soul searching when they interpret the actions, words and silences of the poor, blacks, Hispanics and others. What leads one to see certain things about others?" (p. 53). Who I am as researcher in this study was critical and required strenuous and dedicated soul searching. I am a white middle class female. That makes me a noticeable outsider in a study of African and African American students. Even though I have lived in Africa, have an African husband and son, an African last name, speak an African language and feel an affinity with Africans, I am not African. Asante (1990) explains that it is not a requirement to be African to be Afrocentric, nor is being African or African American a guarantee that someone is Afrocentric. An Afrocentric worldview can be developed by immersing oneself in African culture and accepting African values as the norm. Afrocentricity has evolved into a method, approach, perspective for conducting and analyzing any study of people of African descent. Despite the differences that may separate us, the students accepted me as someone committed to encouraging them to be proud of their African heritage and to learning more about it and one another.

As for my role, I was more than the interested listener who traveled sufficiently to make the African students feel at home; I was the facilitator of a process to bring the African and African American students together around their shared heritage with the goal of improving their understanding of one another as Africans. I could facilitate the process because I had studied Afrocentricity, had access to African and Afro-American cultural materials—literature, poetry, history, films and speakers. I had so immersed myself in the site that the students felt I belonged there.

While Rosemary was evolving her ideas about humanity during her extensive stay in Africa as well as other distant parts of the globe, Robert spent much of his educational career acquiring knowledge about human nature through reading the great literary works and developing his clinical skills. He learned about human nature and its evolution through several years as a teacher in a pre-school setting, and later as clinical director of a program providing care for the mentally ill. He comes to the role of co-author having spent the last several years providing legal aid services for those in most need. Some of the ideas expressed in this book are a reflection of this myriad work that has required an understanding of the American values as these tend to play out in the experiences of the disenfranchised, the indigent, and those perceived as different, and therefore underpin the belief it is most important to ask the tough questions about the ramifications of racism in our society.

During our regular meetings together throughout the genesis of the present work both authors probed constantly to answer the questions "What does this research mean to a teacher in school settings outside our urban centers?" and "What is universal about the experience of the students and what can teachers do with this information?" One objection that the authors must confront directly and at the outset is the potentially disaffirming question about how a Caucasian researcher can presume to study African or Afro-American students and even hope to generate some reliable information. As one student directly inquired:

> I gotta ask you a question. How do you feel talking to an African American and you're Caucasian? I mean, you've done your research and you would be expecting like a black person to come in and talk to you like this. I mean I really feel like I'm actually talking to an African American about their culture.

Our response is simple: We do not presume to speak for the students and consequently we have endeavored to allow the students to speak for themselves throughout this book by using numerous quotes from them.

It is time that we break down the barriers of ignorance and prejudice that we have preserved without reason and to come together as people who share a common interest in the future of the world. It is our hope that this book will help you, the reader, journey along with us as we share together the experiences of the African and Afro-American students who participated in this study.

Rosemary Traoré, Havana, Florida, September 2005
Robert Lukens, Philadelphia, Pennsylvania, September 2005

ACKNOLWEDGEMENTS

Many people contributed to the composition of this book, and to the quality of life that accompanied its creation. Our families, teachers, colleagues, students, and friends, past and present, have all inspired us. The ways in which their lives have intersected with ours have made writing this book almost a joy, but most certainly an experience all the richer and more inclusive. Regrettably, not all can be personally recognized here. A few must be singled out, however, because we know that they know that without them there would be no book at all.

To the warm welcome and boundless generosity provided by so many people on the African continent who demonstrate on a daily basis that life can be lived differently, because it can be celebrated even in the midst of great hardship and deprivation. When we are connected to each other, to the earth and its rhythms and to the Creator, one can find joy and a sense of self and purpose. To be in harmony with each other, with the earth and with the Creator provides great satisfaction, something that money can't buy.

We especially want to thank the principal of Jackson High and the ESOL department chair for providing a great deal of support. Special gratitude to Molefi Kete Asante and Abu Abarry for teaching Afrocentricity to those with an immediate affinity for its principles as well as to those whose resistance to these very principles is a measure of the fundamental verities embodied in this way of approaching life.

To Kate Shaw and Thaddeus Mathis who vociferously challenged some of the underlying premises of this study, and to James Davis who accompanied the students on their first trip to the Balch Institute and who provided his unflagging support all along the way.

To Carl Grant for his warm appreciation of our efforts, for graciously reading an early draft, and for providing us with excellent and constructive recommendations on how to improve our effort. To Sandra Wilson, who also edited and critiqued early drafts, as well as Omiunota Ukpokodu who read earlier drafts and provided us with sensible and heartfelt feedback. To Kimberly Lanier for her earnest and much appreciated efforts to improve the quality of this endeavor, and special thanks to Ragas Nang-Yad who fastidiously reviewed the final draft for us. To Mary Noland and Liz Thul for their continued friendship and unexpected encouragements throughout.

We want to thank Alvaro Toepke and Angel Serrano, the writers and producers of the film "The Language You Cry In: The Story of a Mende Song," as well as everyone involved in the making of this glorious production. This film is an excellent tool for everyone to become more familiar with the connection between Africa and America.

To Anne Meiman Hughes for editing and critiquing earlier drafts and for contributing the wonderful artwork that graces this book's cover. Special thanks to Msgr. Patrick Scott and Sr. Rosemary McSorley, SHCJ for their hospitality and sharing their space with us during the final stretch.

To Mohamed, Laye, and Hamed who daily provide the inspiration to continue with these efforts and to persevere in telling this story.

This book is dedicated to all the wonderful students at Jackson who had the courage and generosity to share their lives with us.

Permission is gratefully acknowledged to reprint excerpts from the film "The Language You Cry In: The Story of a Mende Song," copyright 1998. Reprinted by permission of the producers, INKO Producciones.

Foreword copyright 2005, Molefi Kete Asante.

Cover illustration copyright 2005, Anne Meiman Hughes.

INTRODUCTION

This Really Isn't the America Some Thought They'd Find

In many ways, African children are not unique in their experiences as newly arrived students in the schools of the United States. Throughout America's history, immigrant children have experienced many difficulties adjusting to their new life in our schools (Tyack, 1974). Moreover, society has long placed high expectations on our public schools to help resolve this nation's ills no matter how intractable they may otherwise appear[1] (Hochschild & Scovronick, 2003; Ogbu, 2003; Tyack, 2004). However, the expectations often seem highest where the resources are lowest, and inner-city schools must contend with some of the most serious problems facing their communities while frequently having access to the least opportunities to address profound inadequacies throughout the rest of society. Consequently, it has been the fate of our inner-city schools to shoulder the burden to produce effective education strategies in the face of almost overwhelming odds.

With one eye focused poignantly on our present day circumstances, in writing about the state of urban schools in the 1920s, Rousmaniere (1997) pointed out that Jane Addams, the progressive advocate of urban reform, once described education as "nothing less than the 'great savior of the immigrant district'" (p. 57). Although the influx of immigrants to the United States has waxed and waned, high expectations such as these have not dimmed over the intervening decades. According to Ogbu (2003, p. 46), "societies use formal education to equip young people with the knowledge, skills, values, behaviors, and language required to perform in their future workplace as well as in the political and social domains." Moreover, we "expect schools not only to help students reach their potential as individuals but also to make them good citizens who will maintain the nation's values and institutions, help them flourish, and pass them on the next generation" (Hochschild & Scovronick, 2003, pp. 1-2). According to Benjamin Franklin, who, it appears, really was no friend of the "education is for everyone" approach (Waldstreicher, 2004), it was certain that "[n]othing can more effectually contribute to the cultivation and improvement of a country ... than a proper education of youth" (Best, 1962, pp. 152-153). According to Amy Gutmann (1987), selected in 2004 as president of the University of Pennsylvania, an institution founded by Franklin in the 1750s,

[i]nculcating character and teaching moral reasoning do not exhaust the legitimate ends of primary education in a democracy. Citizens value primary education for more than its moral and political purposes. They also value it for helping children learn how to live a good life in the nonmoral sense by teaching them knowledge and appreciation of (among other things) literature, science, history, and sports. These subjects are properly valued not primarily for the sake of imparting cultural coherence to a child's life, but for their place in cul-

tivating a nonmorally good life for children, characterized by a combination of literary appreciation, scientific and historical knowledge, and physical agility. (p. 51)

With so much at stake, our public schools must discover the means to produce the next generation of viable leaders or our nation's democratic future may be seriously jeopardized (Girouz, 2005; Zinn & Macedo, 2004).[2]

Notwithstanding any experiences they may share with other immigrant children who also are newly arrived students in America's classrooms, the young people from the continent of Africa experience inner-city poverty and the failings of our inner-city schools in a way made unique by the color of their skin. Their student peers, a large proportion of whom may be Afro-American,[3] often do not seem to want them around. The African youth get called "jungle boy (or girl)" or other disparaging terms. Although for myriad reasons they are reluctant to complain about such onerous treatment, when prompted they may even admit to harassment, both physical and emotional, with pushing, hitting and name-calling and other acts of aggression perpetrated by their American peers. The African students wonder why their fellow Afro-American "brothers and sisters" so cavalierly treat them as second-class citizens. In similar fashion, the Afro-American students are perplexed because the African students appear to them as acting superior to them. Neither group of students seems comfortable in the presence of the other. More perplexing still is that some of their teachers characterize the strained relationships between the African and Afro-American students as a flagrant indication that Afro-American students are themselves racist, conveniently equating racism with prejudice and ethnocentrism, as if to justify racism by making it seem universal. Others conclude that this may simply represent an example of those at the bottom of the hierarchical ladder of esteem finding someone under them that they can look down upon, or an example of the oppressed acting like oppressors when given the chance.

The relationship between Africans and Afro-Americans can lucidly be characterized in the following manner: "members of the two communities say they live largely disconnected lives, praying, shopping and socializing among their own, sometimes harboring harsh stereotypes of one another" (Boorstein, 2001, A41). Although stereotypes may abound within both groups, there appears to be a serious disconnect between the seemingly self-evident affiliations between Africans and Afro-Americans and the reality of their interactions. Some have proposed that the origin of this disconnect lies in the lack of honest reflection on the historic passive resistance to slave-trading practices among some of the peoples of Africa. For example,

part of the reason for the gap is that a key stretch of the bridge is missing. The slave trade is not a regular part of the curriculum in many schools in Africa, and . . . this is because Africans would prefer not to face their role in the industry. As a result . . . "they don't understand that they do have a connection." (Boorstein, 2001, A 41, quoting John Arthur, sociologist/anthropologist and Ghana native who has researched African immigration to the United States).

Boorstein suggests that bridging this "gap" requires reforming the curriculum used in schools in Africa. Although curriculum changes in African schools could be very helpful, and are long overdue, it is unclear how any of these would impact life in inner-city high schools in the U.S. where a more complex reality seems to be taking place. What becomes obvious after some preliminary study is that there are negative stereotypes about both Africans and Afro-Americans that are being perpetuated by the media and reinforced in our educational system and public school curriculum. However, these stereotypes may not be as permanent as one might assume from observing the current behavior of African and Afro-American students. Results from our study reject the notion that relations between these two groups are permanently damaged; rather, the possibility is real that Africans and Afro-Americans can come together and learn from and about one another, and it is imperative that American educators realize that the time to ensure that this possibility comes to fruition is now. The presence in our schools of students from Africa is an opportunity, in and of itself. African students bring a perspective that if approached as an asset rather than a liability can help all Americans better understand themselves and the world in which we live. Having students from the continent of Africa in our schools offers an opportunity for both the African and Afro-American students to "rekindle memory" and begin to restore the connection to Africa that was severed so many years ago. Memory is power, and the connection between Africans and Afro-Americans has too long been denied. The story of Africa, its culture and worldview, presents an alternative way of seeing the world that can lead to a coming together not only for Afro-Americans and Africans but for all who come to understand Africa.

Labov (1982) writes of the potential benefit of bridging the home culture, school culture, and peer culture. In response to the query "can the positive forces of the home culture be used to good advantage in the school situation?" Labov warned that if we suppress the home culture

> and try to extract one or two individuals from their cultural context, we will continue the pattern of massive educational failure that we now observe in the schools. The other route is to understand the interests and concerns of the youth who come to school and use the understanding in a positive way. (p. 168)

The results of recent research indicate that both African and Afro-American students, once brought together around their shared heritage, are eager to learn more about one another. The heritage that these students share differs dramatically from the common misperceptions many of the Afro-American students hold prior to their active engagement with the African students. The heritage also differs from the one portrayed in many American textbooks about African history. This conclusion coincides with the research of Molefi Kete Asante, among others. Asante is the principal agent of the articulation of Afrocentricity as a model to explain phenomena endemic to the African nations and carried over into the ways of African immigrants in other countries (Gray, 2001, p. 19). Asante (1998) explicitly has stated that when exploring the history of Afro-

Americans, we should view Afro-American history from an African center (p. 2). This concept is particularly relevant in the context of our urban schools.

Much has been written about the importance of a culturally relevant education and the role of critical pedagogy in counteracting the hegemony of the Eurocentric focus of Western education. Although an Afrocentric education has been among reform proposals for many years, there are few studies extant relating to its implementation in schools. For example Alford, McKenry, and Gavazzi (2001) have reported on a program in Ohio that utilizes the African tradition of initiation or rites of passage and promotes Afrocentric values for Afro-American male students using the principles of the Nguzo Saba.[4] Very little research has contemplated the efficacy of connecting African and Afro-American students through their shared heritage. This book explores the implications of using Afrocentric principles to inform group activities designed to bridge the emotional and historical gaps that often provoke discord between African and Afro-American students and how, once re-connected, these two groups can learn to build on their individual and collective strengths to resolve racial and class divisiveness.

To a lamentable degree, public school education in America is failing our Black children.[5] The double sense of "failing" is apt here because there are plenty of significant data about the number of Black students who fail academically each year; and there are discouraging statistics about the number of Black children in public schools who fail or score poorly on standardized exams. The so-called "academic achievement gap" has perplexed some of the finest minds in American education, whether liberal or conservative politically. The "No Child Left Behind" legislation of 2001 is just the latest iteration of knee-jerk reform, this time in the guise of political gerrymander by standards and testing advocates who expect to close the acknowledged achievement gap by penalizing the already fiscally strapped school systems for failing to meet standards that are meaningless when measured against the emotional vitality of the students missing the grade (Comer, 2004). There are increasing research data on the ways in which public schools fail to teach Black children effectively because teachers and school administrators do not understand the unique needs and learning styles of children of African descent, and consequently public schools fail to provide culturally appropriate teachers, methods, curriculum and materials, despite the significant data confirming that these would make a major difference in the lives and education of these youngsters (Delpit, 1995; Gay, 2000; Irvine, 1990, 2000; Kunjufu, 2002; Ladson-Billings, 1994; Murrell, 2002).

Out of a commitment to reach Black children in America's schools has evolved a movement for African-centered education, which would provide students a "learning environment that is more congruent with the lifestyles and values of Afro-American families. A school based on African values, it is believed, would eliminate the patterns of rejection and alienation that engulf so many Afro-American school children, especially males" (Epps, 2000, p. vi). Hale-Benson (1982) argued that Afro-American culture remains "distinct from white Euro-American culture and that the vast majority of the distinguishing characteristics are traceable to elements of African culture retained by African slaves in America" (p. 183). Afrocentricity is the critical element in the most recent research conducted for the empowerment of Afro-American students. Akbar (1998) has called for "educators who structure learning systems in such a way that children learn to respect who they are and see themselves as allies with the environment rather than the oppressive conquerors" (p. 249).

A recent study of two African-centered schools in Milwaukee (Pollard & Ajirotutu, 2000) has raised many questions about the implementation of African-centered education. There are key ingredients to consider in implementing any reform, such as the quality of leadership of the school, support of the staff, shared vision, teacher-training, adequate resources, and so forth. These ingredients have been well-recognized for many years. One major critique of these African-centered efforts, however, is that the focus of Afrocentric education now must move beyond the focus on students' self-esteem and demonstrate measurable results in academic achievement. Irvine (2000) also has argued that educators must not be distracted by African-centered education and lose sight of the innate inequalities that exist in our current educational system which overwhelmingly disadvantage students of color. Also, not just a matter of what to teach but who teaches it, how, where, and with what results.

In a dramatic way, Africans in America are confronted with a culture and a society of white supremacy that co-exist in rising tension with an unacknowledged lie about Black "inferiority." It has never been exactly a rousing "American dream" in the United States for anyone whose skin color is other than white. The Africans find themselves in a situation in which they are judged by the color of their skin or their accents. For instance, no matter how well they have mastered the English language or how many other languages they speak, having a noticeable accent in America puts the African student in a "less-than" category, a position of inferiority from the outset. Or, emanating from just as stereotyped a stance, some white Americans have told newly arrived Africans to retain their accent in order to protect them from being confused with being Afro-American, which would be a clear attempt to evade any prejudice against Africans by others who might mistakenly perceive them as Afro-American (Waters, 1999). But, of course, having an accent did not save Amadou Diallo from the 41 bullets fired at him by New York police officers just for looking like a suspect while reaching for his wallet and identification; this would have been simply tragic if it were an aberration, but unfortunately similar examples too frequently occur to others throughout America, just for being Black.

Respect is an essential component of the African worldview. Ancestors and elders are to be revered, honored, and cherished; elders are recognized to be the keepers of the wisdom of the ancestors. Parents are to be respected and teachers are at the level of the parents in the hierarchy of respect. This makes the task of being a "teacher" in Africa more appealing because teachers generally do not have to earn the respect of the students before they can teach them. Only serious misbehavior or a grievous offense on the part of the teacher could break that trust. In America, teachers no longer automatically command the respect of their students (or sometimes even the parents of their students). In American schools today, teachers must earn the respect of their students; and in some communities the testing of a teacher can be extremely difficult for a teacher who is not accustomed to being challenged or personally attacked.

Teachers who are not themselves the product of urban schools but who venture into teaching in an urban school usually experience a form of "culture shock." Many Peace Corps Volunteers who have taught successfully for two years in schools in Africa have returned home and volunteered to teach in inner-city schools; some have remarked after a few weeks or months that they would "rather have 100 students in Africa, than 20 in an inner-city school in America." Nothing has been more difficult for them to adjust to than dealing with classroom discipline in the inner-city school.[6] Why should this be the experience these highly qualified teachers have when they return to teaching in the States?

What the African students bring is a fresh perspective, a yet untainted belief in the value of an education and a respect for teachers that is long-held and intact. As a result, you may hear teachers say that they would prefer to teach immigrant children because they appear still to have a respect for teachers and learning. They value getting an education and are willing to work to get one. But what can we learn from them and how can we reap the benefits of their presence? One of the most significant contributions to be made by this Afrocentric research is to expose and perhaps annihilate some of the debilitating stereotypes that maintain the differences between Africans and their Afro-American peers. Before arriving, African students expect to be welcomed as part of the American "family" in the same way that they welcome people into their homes, communities and countries. This is the expected treatment of all strangers by Africans almost everywhere in Africa.[7]

This book is about the dramatic shift in perceptions that are possible when an Afrocentric approach is used to encourage dialogue between the African and Afro-American students. Taking a group of Afro-American and African students to the film "The Language You Cry In: The Story of a Mende Song" was the catalyst to creating a bridge between these two groups that best could be characterized, at least for most of the Afro-American students, as an "A-ha!" experience. In the film, a woman in present day Georgia, a descendent of Southern slaves, has learned to sing a song written in a language that she does not understand but with she implicitly feels an emotional connection. She travels to Sierra Leone to meet another woman who has learned the words to the same song, taught to her as a memorial by her grandmother. Although the American woman was not certain about the meaning of the Mende words of this song, having since childhood repeated the words of the song, the American woman discovers that she has long shared a tenuous connection with a past that her counterpart in Sierra Leone also had kept alive. These two women were emotionally reunited despite the civil war in Sierra Leone and the intervening years of hardship and oppression that they both had endured. After viewing this film, one Afro-American student declared that she "knew that we had come from Africa, but this film made it real." Following the group experience including the film and the discussion generated afterward, there was a coming together between these formerly antagonistic students just as there had been a coming together in this film in which two women discover that they share a cultural heritage manifested in the words to a song that originated in a small village in Africa. The coming together of the African and Afro-American students could serve as a model for the implementation of an Afrocentric perspective that is both emotionally elevating and academically enlightening.

In a similar way, one major difficulty for African students is confronting the illusions about America and Americans created by what the Africans have read or seen in movies or on television. In addition, Africans who have spent any time in America and who have either returned or written to family members and friends back in Africa tend to exaggerate the quality of their lives in America. In order to make their family and friends proud of their achievements, they have made their employment sound more impressive, their living conditions more satisfying, and their experiences of Americans have generally been presented in a more positive light than actually lived. Why would this be the case? Failure in America is seen as the fault of an individual. The people back in Africa have usually sacrificed to get them to America so they can't let them down and who would believe it anyway since the media portrayal of America is as the land of plenty. In the minds of most Africans, the streets of America indeed must be paved with gold because people in the sitcoms that we sell overseas never seem to work, have beautiful houses and beautiful clothes, and don't seem to lack for anything. We promote our technology as if it is the answer to all life's woes. To be in America is to be in paradise, one would think.

The stereotypes on both sides of the Atlantic have damaged the relationship between Africans and Afro-Americans before they even meet. The value of Afrocentric research on recently arrived African students is that we may be able to identify the positive contributions that they could make before they become "McDonaldized." What about the African culture could be of value to Americans? Mosha (2000) writes: "My indigenous education invites me to use my intellectual powers as much as possible, at the same time it lets me listen to my heart and the voice that emerges from my deepest identity" (p. 2). Heart, spirit, soul are terms that relate to significant components of our humanity that seem missing at times in our inner-city schools. Even when those in authority are pleasant and conciliatory, and when all of our teachers care equally for all of their students, the school environment itself may not be very inviting. Finding ways to bring the African and Afro-American students together could help make the environment more inviting and therefore more conducive to learning from each other. There is much to be gained in breaking down stereotypes.

The idea that it was the "Africans who sold us into slavery" has long made some Afro-Americans bitter and encouraged them to resist contemplating any rapprochement with their African heritage. The African students were surprised when they first heard that they are to be blamed for slavery. Slavery damaged Africa too; slave traders lied to families and told them that they were taking their children to get a good education or to benefit in some other way. No African who sold someone under such pretenses could ever have imagined the cruel and inhumane treatment by slave traders and some slave owners that resulted. Although the act of enslavement, of bondage, trading, and selling of human beings, existed in Africa independent of the slave trade practiced by Western societies, the degradation and inhumane treatment experienced in their conveyance to America by African people, and which then enveloped their lives as American slaves, was of a different magnitude[8] (Berlin, 1998; Patterson, 1982).

From the fruits of Afrocentric research there could be a healing of the wounds of slavery, a growing strength in the struggle against oppression, a return to values of the heart and spirit, a revival of the role of education in developing coping skills and enrichening the understanding of one's heritage, and so much more. To the question whether it would raise test scores, which is the call to arms in education today, we respond that not unless the tests themselves and the matter they are designed to measure are changed can there be any dramatic, sustainable improvement in closing the achievement gap between discrete groups of youngsters. Not, at least, until the meaning of education, and the projected equal opportunity it ostensibly engenders, is radically modified and it begins to incorporate subject matter heretofore excluded from consideration, including the cultural perspectives of all of the students in the classroom environs. The presence of Africans in America could be of great benefit *to all Americans* if there would be an exchange of history, experiences, and cultural values between us regardless of our background.

The concepts of multiculturalism, Afrocentricity, and meaningful intervention are critical tools that can guide the selection of activities that provide mutually edifying experiences for all of our students. One immediate goal of the book you hold in your hands is to explain how to conduct activities that can help improve the relationships between a group of African and Afro-American students in urban schools, particularly in those environments where relations between these groups already may be problematic. Specifically, Afrocentricity can be used as an ideological and pedagogical/curricular vehicle that has positive effects on the relationships between groups of African and Afro-American students. In learning more about themselves, about their shared backgrounds, the African worldview and about their similarities as African or Afro-American individuals, the students can come to some common ground. From there, they can enlighten others who may get into conflicts or have difficulties with each other despite a common, shared history. A broader goal of this book is to demonstrate the value of culturally relevant teaching and the benefits of understanding and appreciating the role that culture plays in high quality teaching and learning and creating a more just society.

This book focuses on four key elements of an Afrocentric worldview that may help students to connect and to develop better relationships with one another. The four elements are 1) community, 2) the spiritual/material connectedness of all things, 3) a circular understanding of history and time, and 4) the existence and importance of the Creator. In this book, we will discuss African education, African students' experiences in schools in Canada, African-centered education, Afrocentricity, culturally relevant education, critical pedagogy, race and racialization, Nigresence, and Ogbu's cultural-ecological theory of minority school performance, which explores how Africans and Afro-Americans as minority students are influenced by their environment and their history. Although Ogbu's theory has greatly helped us to better understand the effects of culture and history on minority groups, we argue that studying the views and experiences of African students in conjunction with Afro-American students enhances Ogbu's cultural-ecological theory and makes it more relevant to the education provided in today's inner-city schools.

One of the major impediments to obtaining an equal education, comparable in quality and scope to that provided to indigenous students, and which may affect the African and Afro-American students in different ways, is the seemingly benign preference on the part of some teachers in the U.S. for some particular types of immigrant children (Delpit, 1995). As Noguera (2003) notes, in many schools in the U.S. the fact that "students from the broad assortment of groups labeled as 'Asian' outperform White and other groups on a number of academic indicators has reinforced their status as 'model minority'" (p. 43). This trend regrettably is confirmed by the research on teacher preference discussed in the literature. In assessments of how they fare in comparison to other groups, "foreign-born black children have done better than native-born black children" (Rong & Preissle, 1998, p. 139). This preference may be understandable, given the constraints on teachers and the pressures they are under to produce objective results through improved student performance on standardized tests. In moments of forthrightness, some teachers will tell you that many immigrant children appreciate the chance to get an education, while some American children take it for granted. One recurring complaint from teachers is that American children think they already know it all, or expect to be entertained, or just don't want to learn. Indeed, one major concern expressed by Rong and Preissle is that "many [immigrants] may lose their cultural heritage through assimilation, many may become vulnerable to identifying with the anti-school culture of inner-city communities, in which case not only may they suffer oppression as individuals, but their local communities and our national society will lose a potential for transformation" (p. 144). This concern almost certainly stems from the conviction that immigrants have something very valuable to contribute to America, and America's strength as a democracy derives from its capacity to evolve by finding progressive ways to include newcomers into the vibrancy of its educational, political, and economic institutions (Gutmann, 1987, 2003; Gerstle, 2001; Hochschild & Scovronick, 2003; Jacobson, 1998; King, 2000; Tyack, 2004).

> Inner-city communities benefit from having immigrants of color because such groups tend to stimulate the substandardized urban schools with their strong motivation for education, their different ideas on parenting and schooling, and different attitudes and psychology toward racial discrimination and how to challenge social and financial disadvantages. (Rong & Preissle, 1998, p. 144)

While these benefits may be ephemeral, the experience for many Afro-Americans living on the edge in our country is that immigrants are a threat to their jobs and what little status they may have acquired. Wages in the United States seem at first glance to be huge to many immigrants compared to what they could earn in their country. It is only over time spent in the United States that they too recognize that the cost of living is also huge. One Liberian woman described her plight: "I thought I had found the promised land when I got my first job, only to find myself a slave once again." It is the vast misunderstanding of America as the land of golden opportunity that most bewitches many immigrants (Waters, 1999). Parents in Africa will struggle for many years, saving funds through regular self-denial of their own needs, just to have the chance to emigrate to America. When they have children, the thought of a better education for their children may be sufficient to justify years of hardship. Sadly, the reality of life in the U.S. often does not pan out as promised. For many immigrants in this country, thwarted expectations about the possibilities of achieving the American Dream often lead to disillusionment and a reversal of fortune (Jacobson, 1998).

Structure of the Book

In Chapter 1, we explore the various ways in which African students are misunderstood and underappreciated by their American counterparts and how others perceive the seemingly divergent needs of these students from those of their American peers.

Chapter 2 provides a comparison of pre-American and post-American school entry from the point of view of several highly motivated, intelligent, and resourceful African students who were overwhelmed at the difference in educational quality, and how the lowered expectations in American schools were thwarting their efforts to accomplish all they had aspired to for many years while attending school in Africa. This chapter also investigates the African students' experiences of frustration with the student and teacher attitudes towards Africa and Africans, the negative reactions to their having an accent or having difficulty with English, their desire to work together with their peers on common activities, to help each other. We also will explore the students' experiences with segregated spaces at school for ESOL and their inability to be accepted by their Afro-American peers. The voices of the students convey frankly their perceptions of the prevalent stereotypes about Africans, by Afro-Americans, and about Afro-Americans by African students. Moreover, the students report on how they relate to each other and begin to take the stereotypes apart, to see through them and their underlying mistaken premises about the other group.

In Chapter 3, we outline some of the circumstances in which African students first encounter America. This includes an explanation of what information about America and Afro-Americans they have accrued prior to arriving in the United States, and a description of the backgrounds from which they originate, with a particular focus on their educational experiences in their home countries.

Chapter 4 delineates some of the salient misconceptions about America that many African students initially develop through the media representations in their home country. America as the "Land of the Free and the Home of the Brave" and the "Land of Opportunity" were perhaps once relevant catchphrases to attract emigrants to this country, but these no longer apply for a significant proportion of the immigrant population. Unmet expectations can generate disappointment and frustration for anyone who embarks on a pilgrimage to America with the hope of a better future, particularly when the stark reality of life in America becomes evident almost from the moment they deplane in this country. In this chapter we discuss the various ways in which the African students felt disconnected at school, both intellectually and emotionally, and the ways in which they coped with this disconnect. We will present some detailed descriptions of the effects of negative stereotypes about Africa that interfere with an authentic experience by Afro-American students of the cultural heritage they should share with the African student, as well as the misconceptions about Afro-Americans that confound the authentic experience by the African students of their Afro-American peers. The African students we encountered had a lot to say about what they expected when they arrived in the United States, how those expectations originated, and why they feel so disappointed now that they have experienced firsthand the difficulties of life in America for a person of color.

Chapter 5 profiles the select group of Afro-American students who participated in a study about perceptions of the differences between educational experience in Africa and America. The students describe their reasons for electing to discuss these issues, their concerns and their sources of information about Africa and Africans and their previous exposure to students from the continent.

Chapter 6 explores the relationship between African origin and its link with the perceived racism that the African students encounter in their interactions with their Afro-American peers as well as in their interactions with their teachers and other school personnel. To understand the confusion expressed by African students related to their initial lack of affinity with Afro-Americans, it is important to set the framework of American-style racism in the context of the experiences of Africans and Afro-Americans pertaining to several hundred years of slavery.

In Chapter 7 we provide a theoretical and practical discussion of the principles of Afrocentricity that can be used to bring together students who at first glance seem divided by longstanding misperceptions and unfair, negative stereotypes.

In Chapter 8, we argue that the key to incorporating multicultural values in American classrooms where African and Afro-American students interact is to have an understanding of the principles underlying Afrocentricity and the African worldview and to use these principles to inform activities that will reconnect the students to their shared histories. While the administrations at other schools that experience these same issues of adversarial relations between student groups may call in mediation counselors or conflict resolution experts, the success of this study suggests that a shared history, shared cultural approach, was more appropriate and more effective because it provided a valuable learning experience for all the students. A major lesson learned from these students was that they could not make sustained changes in their behavior without having even more students made aware of their interconnections with each other. The students who participated in this study themselves requested permission to work with the entire student body in small groups to educate them about what they had learned. Surprisingly, they took this step in order to put peer pressure on their side, to use it to ameliorate the tensions between the African and Afro-American students. In this way, the lessons they took with them from their interactions together became self-perpetuating in the best sense of any real learning or growth experience.

In Chapter 9, we endeavor to explain why conflict resolution may result in superficial emolument but that sharing stories and experiences may provide a more lasting interconnection that can resolve many of the tensions that arise recurrently between divergent groups of students in our schools. We offer some advice on how to engage groups of students in the kinds of interactive processes that made this study such a success at one particular, inner-city high school. The Appendix contains some suggested materials for educating young people in America about Africa and about the contributions made to this country by persons of African descent.

CHAPTER 1

"The Darkest Thing About Africa Is America's Ignorance of It"[1]

In almost every corner of our nation, "diversity" is one of the hot topics of the day.[2] Students from many nations around the globe are joining America's classrooms almost constantly. As Rong and Preissle (1998, p. 154) have pointed out, "every day, more than 1,000 children from foreign countries enter our schools and walk into our classrooms." A substantial number of these children emigrate from Africa. The arrival of students from various countries on the continent of Africa can raise some unique concerns for students and staff in our nation's schools. These concerns may be different from those of other immigrant children because to the unenlightened observer the African students often are visually and physically indistinguishable from the Afro-American students who comprise the majority in many of our inner-city schools. Although the presence of newly arrived students from African countries may pose specific challenges for our inner-city schools, their presence also affords the unprecedented opportunity to bring African and Afro-American students together around their shared heritage and to make some strong emotional and lineal connections that were severed long ago by slavery.

In many inner-city school settings where African and Afro-American students regularly interact, however, strained and inimical relations between them unfortunately are becoming the norm. Pervasive and unchallenged myths, misperceptions, and negative stereotypes keep these students relating to each other as undesirable strangers. Some of the more pervasive stereotypes about Africans include images of Tarzan, native savages, and an untamed darkland smothered in wild jungles. Similarly, pervasive stereotypes about Afro-Americans include single welfare mothers with large families, rudeness, and violence-prone dispositions. Africans are told that they can succeed when they get to America because they have a terrific work ethic; they also are told that Afro-Americans do not have a successful work ethic. These stereotypes are sometimes knowingly, but most often unwittingly and subconsciously promoted in many outlets including schools, home, and through the media.

As a theory that incorporates community, relationship, and a sense of well-being, Afrocentricity can be an effective tool to build positive relationships among these two groups of young people. Activities derived from an Afrocentric perspective can help students to develop a shared understanding of their common heritage and values. By providing positive images of Africa and Africans and giving the students the opportunity to develop a new understanding of their shared history, both groups can benefit and their relations may thus be improved. Some of the benefits the students can derive from this approach include a re-energized zeal for learning, respect for self and others of African descent, new friendships, a new interest in Africa, and the courage to learn more about Africa, Africans, and Afro-Americans than has been included in their educational experience previously.

Throughout this book, we will explore various ways to harmonize the seemingly divergent needs of the African students with those of their American teachers and Afro-American peers. To their complete surprise, the African students find themselves in a situation in which they are judged by the color of their skin and/or their accents and by unexpected prejudice from Afro-Americans. This comes as a shock to them because of the preconceptions about America that are fostered in their home countries, but also because, following the end of the colonial era, external judgments based on the color of a person's skin are less prominent in most of the countries on the African continent.

Prejudice can take many subtle and varied forms, and it conflicts with the images still prevalent in much of Africa that America is the land of opportunity, the home of the free. For instance, when asked to describe his experience an African student used one word—*violence*—to describe his initial encounter with American schools. He elaborated that "someone hit me the first day here and that set the tone. I felt embarrassed and sad. I wanted to strike back but I didn't. Students call the Africans 'gay' or 'faggot.'" Another student explained that "when I came to school they was like teasing me, mocking me, telling me I'm a faggot." When asked what they would like Americans to know about Africans, some students answered that "I'd like them to know that I am not from the jungle. Africa is civilized. We don't live in trees. Africa is a beautiful continent."

This chapter begins by exploring the myriad ways in which African students are misunderstood and underappreciated by their Afro-American counterparts. In addition to the obvious distinction of having similar skin color, those African students who manage to imitate the accent of their American peers may be able to "pass" for being Afro-American. Although these students should be easily assimilated with the Afro-American student population, this does not often seem to occur. In perhaps more understandable contrast, those African students who speak English with an accent or speak only a foreign language are categorized as "African," which carries with it the visually-loaded images of a deep, dark jungle where natives swing on vines like Tarzan. No matter how well they may have mastered the English language, however, or how many other languages they may speak fluently, from their first encounters with American peers having a noticeable accent puts the African students in a "less-than" category, a position of inferiority and suspicious difference.

It is not uncommon for some Americans (or even already settled Africans who have been in the U.S. for a period) to advise newly-arrived Africans to retain their accents in order to distinguish them from being categorized as Afro-American, which clearly would be an accommodation merely to attempt to evade any American-held prejudice against Afro-Americans.[3] This can create an untenable contradiction, an emotional Catch-22 where newly arrived individuals must choose to assume a pseudo-identity that negates at least some of their hopeful reasons for emigrating to the United States—to develop a new life, to fit in with all Americans—or to tacitly subscribe to an unfelt discrimination against Afro-Americans that would violate their natural inclination to affiliate with persons they believe share in their African heritage (Miller, 2003; Waters, 1999).

Moreover, in many situations African students are forced to endure the brunt of insidious stereotypes that Americans maintain about Africa and Africans, stereotypes that have been passed from generation to generation through the media and our educational system. At the same time, the images of Afro-Americans provided to the African students are also negative and do not inspire them to investigate the lives of Afro-Americans for themselves. The pernicious stereotypes about Afro-Americans produced through the American media are disseminated throughout the world. The most prominent image of the gang member, a Black male youth with gun in hand, is shown on television and in movie theaters in Africa. It is disturbing that even with global communication systems and satellite television, generally it is only the demeaning stereotypes that continue to dominate the common perceptions.

African students have been exposed to very little accurate information about America before they arrive here. While in their home countries, some had seen American television and movies; some had been exposed to outdated information about America. Some African students have had access to a VCR in their homes and were furnished American films by family members living in the United States. For most African students, however, America is still seen as the "Land of Opportunity" and the myth of the American Dream lives on in the aspirations of many Africans. As with many other people from developing nations, the Africans continue to look to America to provide them with a better future for themselves.

> Musa: America is the land of opportunity. It is free. Everybody is kind. They say it's the land of freedom. But if you come to America you should just mind your own business. My brother advised me that I should mind my own business. I should not go around. I should be in bed by 10:00 and not hang out with friends

Several African students commented that although America was the land of opportunity there were restrictions or limitations to that opportunity.

> Interviewer ("Inter."): What did you think that you would find here in America?
> Amadou: Lots of opportunity. Yep. Lots of opportunity.
> Inter.: Do you think that's true?
> Amadou: Yeah, it is.
> Inter.: In everything?
> Amadou: Not everything, besides the opportunity, there's a lot of ignorance and a lot of bad things that you don't want to know, but there are opportunities.

According to the tenets of Afrocentrism, to know one's self truly an individual must begin with the historical and cultural history of one's people (Akbar, 1998b, 2003; Asante, 1991; Dei, 1994; Hilliard, 1998). Unfortunately, for many Afro-American students the opportunity to know their historical and cultural history has not been readily available. Nothing in their environment, not the presence of Africans in the school, nor the material presented in their African American studies class, appeared sufficient to bring about a positive relationship between the students from Africa and the Afro-American students that embodied the Afrocentric values of mutual interest and respect. For many Afro-American students in contemporary society, their African ancestry had not previously been a major topic of discussion in their homes. The media images of Africa have not motivated the students even to want to learn more about Africa, except perhaps concerning the exotic animals to be found there, in particular lions, the one species most often mentioned by the students who participated in this research, but an animal found in the wild almost nowhere in settled parts of Africa today. Given the existing information about Africa and Africans, no material facts made the coming together of African and Afro-American students seem inviting and yet, when given the chance, these students did come together and they began to learn how to break down the stereotypes and to discover things about each other that they didn't know they didn't know.

An atavistic adage from the Nile Valley Civilization has served as the foundation for Akbar's (1998b) call for an education for people of African descent that is self-directed, in contrast to the standard perceptions of "reactors or participants in the vision and worldview of people who see us as fixtures in their world rather than as co-builders of a world that places our priorities and perspective at the top of the human agenda" (p. 69). Carter G. Woodson in the 1930s asserted that no "systematic effort toward change has been possible, for, taught the same economics, history, literature, and religion which have established the present code of morals, the Negro's mind has been brought under the control of his oppressor" (1990/1933, p. xii-xiii). Akbar (1998b) argues that if the world had heeded the call of Dr. Woodson when he first issued it, then people of African descent "would not have spent most of this century 'chasing ideas that were not our own'" (p. 67). Asante (1988) admonishes "know your history and you will always be wise" (p. 51).[4]

An Afrocentric view of history supports people of African descent in developing a positive self-perception. Therefore, Afrocentricity has been proposed as a tool for improving the self-perception and self-understanding of Afro-Americans. Norman Harris (1998) argues that freedom and literacy for people of African descent must be based in an Afrocentric epistemology and a communal ontology captured in the phrase "we are, therefore I exist" (p. 18). One of the characteristics of this epistemology is the "transcendent order in the world" which combines history, intuition, and immersion and that recognizes the spiritual in the material (p. 21). The presence of recently arrived African students provides an ideal opportunity to develop Afrocentricity as a tool to bring African and Afro-Americans students together because an Afrocentric orientation places "the interests and needs of African people at the center of any discussion" (p. 15).

Stereotypes perpetuated by the media, the curriculum at school, and often reproduced at home, combined to make coming together and sharing a communal history and culture nearly impossible for the students we interviewed. The misinformation about both Africans and Afro-Americans is the proverbial White

Elephant in the middle of their classrooms. Everyone is affected by it, but no one seems to acknowledge it and address it. Despite the efforts of people in the local School District and the staff in individual schools, the system has failed to provide students with critical knowledge of their history and their culture.

The School Environment—Myths, Misperceptions, and Stereotypes

Many students report that nothing at their school was designed to bring the African and Afro-American students together around their shared heritage. Some of the factors that contributed to their misunderstanding each other included the ways that they were segregated by space and interests, the language barriers, the different ways that they are perceived by teachers, and the general myths, misperceptions and stereotypes presented in the curriculum. Despite having already taken the African American Studies class, one Afro-American female admitted that she knew little about Africa. Even though she had participated in the class every day and was one of the better students (which was both a self description and the characterization ascribed by her teacher), she admitted that what she knew was more along the lines of stereotypes than real knowledge. Sitting next to an African student in class did not appear to her to be any kind of opportunity.

> Jasmine: I know a few people. I might not know them by name, but I know them. From what I see there's not much interaction between the students unless they have to be in classrooms together. There's not much interaction.
> Inter.: What do you know about Africa or Africans?
> Jasmine: I don't know too much. You just hear a lot of stereotypes. We the same as them, but we don't know our background as much as they do.

Interactions inside or outside the classrooms did not contribute to the students coming together. They may sit next to each other but they might as well be in different classes. Not even the African American studies class encouraged them to interact. Five of the Afro-American students who were interviewed, and who were currently participating in the African American studies class, complained that memorizing dates and the names of African kings and the countries on the continent of Africa was not motivating them to learn any more about Africa or want to learn more. In another example, one student in the Afro-American studies class said, "I know that Africa is a jungle. I know it." Even though there were Africans in the class who could have dispelled myths like this one, if someone had invited them to share or who would enthusiastically have shared about their life experiences in Africa, they were never invited to speak. Stereotypes about Africa and Africans abound in the classrooms and in the halls and although there are those present who could and would love to dispel those myths, they are not being called upon to contribute.

The African students hear the negative remarks made by some students and yet, most often they remain unchallenged. The lack of interest in information about life as it is lived today in Africa angers the African students who see it as ignorance on the part of their peers and sometimes, their teachers as well. One African student expressed this succinctly:

Inter.: What do Americans know about Africa?
Musa: The village, the animals.
Inter.: What kind of questions do they ask you about Africa?
Musa: They ask me about traditions; they ask me about diseases.

When asked about the relationship between African and Afro-American students, Valeisha, who had become friends with an African student at another school, described the behavior of some of her Afro-American peers:

They say negative things. Yeah, like if we walk into a certain room or something, you'd smell, the first thing a student would say is "them Africans, they stink!" And you can't say that because it could be anybody in the room. I mean they don't think about people's feelings and how they feel about things before they say what they say.

This student did not condone the behavior of her peers but she acknowledged the power of peer pressure. She could not do anything about the behavior of her peers, even if she didn't agree with it. This disparaging remark about Africans having a bad odor was heard over and over again. This complaint about African students was not actually related to odor, but had more to do with the jungle stereotype than a real problem of body odor. It was a way of putting them down just for being African.

At no point during the school day were students encouraged to talk about these experiences. Teachers, Non-Teaching Assistants (NTAs) and School Police had observed these interactions and ignored them or responded by issuing detention or in-school suspensions when students complained. Thus, generalizations such as "Afro-Americans are ignorant" or "Africans smell" became indelibly etched in the daily experiences of students at Jackson High. Resentment would mount when students perceived that nothing was done about these negative comments. Often, the student who complained was the one given detention. This led to disillusionment on the part of the African and Afro-American students with the teachers and the administration and a silencing of the students who were experiencing difficulty or an even greater level of aggression, which then led to suspensions and in some cases to dropping out. Those students both African and Afro-American who wanted to avoid conflicts were learning to avoid each other. Confrontations often occurred when they heard someone say something negative or something perceived as negative or when they bumped into each other. The words "gay" or "stink" or "savage" or "rude" were enough to have members of the two groups go at each other with words, then fists, and that could escalate into serious violence. At least one interaction erupted when an Afro-American female merely called an African "Black" and soon there were fists flying. The School Police were called and the African girl was suspended. Two of the NTAs could be overheard saying that "those Africans are dangerous." For those students who wanted to avoid conflict they would have to ignore things that were said. Fanta explained:

> Because a lot of people try to get into trouble sometimes, they keep on you, sometimes they even say some mean things like when they pass by you, but I don't get into that, because if you get into that, you get into a lot of trouble.

When faced with negative remarks or other provocations, Fanta relied on a Liberian proverb to guide her behavior.

> Sometimes people tell you things; sometimes they say things like "Do you all wear leaves as clothes or do you walk with lions on the streets? You know, they ask all kinds of weird questions. They come up to me asking, "How come you came out so light? A lot of people from Africa are black. We don't see no light people. How come you came out so light? Probably your mom had a white man, husband, or whatever." And I'm like, "yeah okay." You know that Liberian proverb, I say to myself, you know, "A fool is a big disgrace."

a.   Space

One way that the school environment keeps African and Afro-Americans apart is by having African students spend much of their day in the English for Speakers of Other Languages (ESOL) corridor. This one wing of one floor of the building houses many of the African students who attend classes with other foreign students from Asia and Latin America, though the majority of ESOL students at Jackson are from countries on the continent of Africa. This separation is not unusual at Jackson as the school is divided into Small Learning Communities and ESOL is arranged in the same manner as a Small Learning Community with a core group of teachers. The goal of a learning community is to provide students with a smaller, more personalized experience within the larger school environment by establishing a community to which they can belong and in which they can be supported

> When I came here [to Jackson] it didn't seem difficult because you know all the Liberians were walking the hallway and you ask someone, "Can you show me where this is?" And they were like, "Yeah" and they go and show you what you need to know.

However, no matter how many classes they may have apart, they all have classes that take place in other parts of the building and they have lunch together by grade and advisory period. Even though they may have lunch at the same time as their African or Afro-American peers, the cafeteria is an obviously segregated space. Africans, as the minority, sit in one or more sections of the cafeteria and Afro-Americans as the dominant group fill the rest of the space with an occasional Asian or White American either joining the Afro-Americans or the Africans.

There was one table that had both Africans and Afro-Americans sitting together. Although there were Africans and Asians sitting together at other tables, this was the only table with Africans and Afro-Americans. They knew very little about each other, but they were comfortable with each other. It was not enough of an impetus to have them ask each other questions about their lives, but they could at least sit together and make small talk, although the conversations were still largely between the members of each group. They could sit at the same table and not share much except space, but even this was exceptional. When asked how the African students are treated, Valeisha explained:

> I know a lot of the average black students at Jackson treat the African students different. Some of them are ignorant towards them. You can tell the segregation between everybody, because you see a lot more Africans hanging together than you do with the average black students. You could tell the segregation between the city, the inner city kids and the kids from other countries, foreign countries.

Although one student described the environment during the prior year as an all-out war between the Africans and the Afro-Americans, it could not be characterized in precisely that way more recently, although there still were fights between members of the two groups, as well as fights between members of the same group. What could be said about more recent times is that there are fewer outbreaks of violence, but there continued to be incidents of verbal taunting and some fisticuffs between Africans and Afro-Americans. Although this may have represented a general melioration due to routinization of the presence of African students at Jackson, or their presence no longer was seen as being out of the ordinary, one African male characterized his first year at Jackson simply enough:

> Amadou: It was rough the first year. After that, I got friends. People used to mess with me a lot because I didn't speak English and they would talk about my country, and Africa in general, talk about it a lot, curse at me. I couldn't understand. They called me names and I fight, so, that's what was rough, the main rough thing.

This may not appear drastically different from the experience of many youngsters during their initial period in a new school environment; after a period of transition, as the newness diminishes, and as the student's regular personality emerges, at least some classmates will become less intimidating and group affiliations will hopefully emerge. However, for the Africans and their Afro-American peers, even after this time of transition there remained an added factor that induced perpetuation of the tension between the two groups. This tension was unarticulated perhaps because the students themselves could not describe it, but it was acted out with regularity at Jackson in the manner in which these students interacted when they actually did interact. Although Amadou eventually "got friends," his friends all were fellow African students. He had not made friends with any Afro-Americans. His strategy was to stay as far away as he could from the Afro-American students. In general, the African students expressed a need to stick with their own kind, both for familiarity but also for safety. Later in the study, Amadou became friendly with an Afro-American male who also joined our project. But in the final interview Amadou explained that although they had started to get to know each other it would take more time for them to become friends; friendship takes time to develop according to him and you don't make friends that fast.

With 2,000 students in close environs there were bound to be incidents, but the situation was exacerbated by the way the Africans were viewed by many as troublemakers, different, foreign, stuck up, and the way that the Africans viewed the Afro-Americans as rude and violent. In general, many Africans viewed the Afro-Americans as having problems; they saw them as rude, disrespectful, ignorant. Often, the African students were advised to stay away from the Afro-Americans because they were a bad influence. Some of the Africans chose to continue to fight, but many had parental pressure to disengage, walk away, and avoid confrontations at all costs, no matter what happened to them.

> Inter.: And what happened when you fought?
> Amadou: Actually nothing happened. They just took me to the principal and the principal talked to my dad. I don't know what she said, but I know she talked to my dad.
> Inter.: And what did your dad say?
> Amadou: My dad asked me not to fight in school and to forget about ignorance and stuff like that. And so I stopped.

Obviously, not every student was so influenced by a parent, but in many cases African students face severe repercussions if they get into trouble at school and thus tried to avoid confrontations. Even so, bumping into another student in the hall happens easily in the congested hallways with little time between classes and confrontations were not easily avoided. Actual fights erupted between African and Afro-Americans students, both males and females and many near altercations were observed that fortunately did not escalate into outright fights. Students involved in altercations were given detention, in-school or out-of-school suspension, or, in a few instances, the police were called. At no time did the students have the chance to discuss their differences or the underlying reasons for their fighting. Space at the school both contributed to keeping them apart, but also to bringing them together in ways that they were more likely to be in conflict.

b. Language

"In the beginning when I came in I wasn't speaking that good of English. The students were laughing at me and I'd been in a lot of fights" (Amadou). Language is a potent marker in American society. This particular student points to language and how speakers of languages other than English are often viewed as deficient. The characteristic label ascribed to non-native English speakers, at Jackson today as in many other U.S. schools and official institutions, is Limited English Proficiency, which clearly connotes a deficit orientation. However, the fact that the African students are for the most part multi-lingual could certainly be seen as an asset rather than a deficiency. In general, most African students at Jackson speak at least two languages, and many speak three or more fluently.

It is not only their use of language but also their accent that distinguishes the African students. If they spoke English before coming, even if English is the language of their educational system in their home country, they speak English with an accent and thus when they speak they are perceived as different. In general, in this country, accents are considered exotic by some, but a handicap by many. The Afro-American students all mentioned accents as something that keeps the Africans apart. "Afro-Americans make fun of the accents," admitted Tony, an Afro-American student. One student originally from Barbados, who came here when she was younger, talked about this experience when she first arrived.

> Inter.: Did people think anything about you when you first came because you were from Barbados?
> Sylviane: Yeah. They talked about my accent. They talked about how, like the Gilligan's Island show, we ate animals. We went after them and cut them down to kill them by our hands and eat them. I was like, "oh please." They talked about the way I talked. Some people liked the way I talked, but I think most people were like "Something's wrong with her because she talking different than we're talking."

Although Sylviane was born in Barbados, she elected to identify herself as an Afro-American.[5] By identifying herself, and successfully passing, as Afro-American, Sylviane avoided the negative stereotyping of being someone who kills animals with their bare hands and other "barbarisms" and the mistreatment that accompanies it.[6] Later, she said she wanted to learn more about Barbados and still later she included Africa. Sylviane admitted that she can talk like the other students or she can talk like people from back home and that ability to switch accents has helped her to fit in at Jackson.

As Sylviane's experiences suggest, there is pressure on the students to both lose and maintain their accents. Several Liberian and Sierra Leonian male students were trying to pass as Jamaicans. At Jackson, the Jamaicans had a higher status. The school community had a hierarchical order of Afro-American, Caribbean American, and then African. The English-speaking West African boys wanted to move up this social ladder and were trying to convince fellow students that they were Jamaican, not African. When asked how they get along with Afro-Americans, three African students had different responses about the important role of their accent. Fanta said, "Some people think I am Afro-American, until they hear me speak." Physically, she explained, she is closer to the features of her Afro-American peers. Her skin color is lighter but when she opens her mouth her accent gives her away. Bangalee said, "I don't associate with them. Not much. Some of them think I am Jamaican, some of them think I am African." Bangalee would prefer to be considered Jamaican and indeed practices the Jamaican accent. Miriam who has been able to pass for Afro-American said, "People don't necessarily know I am African. I can talk like an Afro-American. When I talk with Africans I can talk with an African accent but some people don't even know I am African." To be African is to be rejected by their Afro-American peers.

Language and accent play a major role in identity development and social status at Jackson. One Afro-American girl explained to an African girl that embarrassment might be preventing an Afro-American male student from asking her out. Valeisha explained:

> He's probably scared of what people would think. I think the thing that scares most Afro-Americans about Africans is just the accent. As soon as they all hear your accent they are ready to run away. They could see you as a regular person walking down the hallway and will speak to you everyday but as soon as you come up to them and start talking to them and you have an accent the first thing they say, "Oh, you're from Africa." You could look like a regular, average, Black Afro-American student and then you start talking and like they're scared and just run away.

As Valeisha points out, other students "could see you as a regular person" but if you happen to have an accent then you are not perceived as a regular person. You are an anomaly. Having an accent is reason enough for Afro-American students at Jackson to walk away from the African students. All of the Afro-American students in this study saw having an accent as a problem. On the other hand, the African students get told by white Americans not to lose their accent or they could be confused with an Afro-American and end up dead or in jail like so many Black males in America.

c. Name

Another way in which the African students are different is their relationship to their names and their names themselves. Although there are some Afro-American students at Jackson who also have African names, the significance of their African name does not impact their relationship with others in quite the same way. For the African students, not having others know them by their names is another way that they feel disconnected from their environment. For the African students, not knowing someone's name is another way to make them invisible. Traditional naming ceremonies in African societies are significant events because the naming of an individual derives from a meaningful identification of a particular relationship, characteristic, or predestination for the development of one's personality.

One remarkably simple illustration of the significance "their" names have for the African students occurred during Dr. Molefi Asante's discussion session with the students[7] when he randomly asked three students their names. They gave him their names but Dr. Asante looked confused for a moment. We realized what Dr. Asante was trying to illustrate for the group so we pointed to three different students. When he asked these students their names, he got what he had been looking for—their African names. The first three students he had called on were Afro-Americans; he thought they were Africans. His temporary confusion resulted from their response with non-African names. He then made an important point. He asked, "How many of you can tell the difference between Africans and Afro-Americans?" He continued, "When I look out in this audience, I cannot tell the difference." Next, he called on four African students and asked them their names. Dr. Asante said, in a very loud voice, "Now that you are in America your names will be changed to Smith, Johnson, Williams, Jefferson." The four African students immediately reacted with negative expressions on their faces and said, "We're not going to change our names." Dr. Asante used this response to demonstrate what had been done to people of African descent when brought to America as slaves many years ago. The Africans who had been forced to leave Africa as enslaved people had been renamed because this was one of the ways their disconnect with Africa could be ensured by the white enslavers. Following Dr. Asante's presentation, many of the Afro-Americans students wondered what their names might have been had their ancestors not been renamed. For the first time, the African names seemed interesting and important; they had meaning.

d. Sports

Because it is such a potent American symbolic enterprise, one might assume that a mutual interest in sports activities might be a place where the students could come together on common ground. At Jackson, however, even sports are segregated and sometimes this creates additional conflict among students. One of the male participants in this study, a member of the soccer team, noted that there are only Africans or Caribbean-born students on the soccer team. Soccer, which the Africans refer to as "football," is the most important sport on the continent of Africa. An African female soccer player, Haja commented on the Afro-American students who tried out for the soccer team.

> My experience is that they're trying to fit in so much that they kind of forget where they come from. I learned that last year on the soccer team, they were so into arguing. How bad do they want other people to see them that they didn't come to practice once a week or so? The coach, he got upset and he dropped them, so, I don't know.

To many on the continent of Africa, soccer is revered much like football in America. Haja sees the American girls as being too concerned about themselves and not enough into the game. African sports players would be respectful of their coach and come on time. To Haja, the Afro-American girls do not seem serious about the game and part of her explanation is that they don't know where they come from. Her reasoning is that if the girls knew where they were from, i.e., Africa, they would take soccer much more seriously. The girls' soccer team did not continue at Jackson, but the boys' team did very well. The members of the boys' team were all from countries on the continent of Africa. There were no Afro-American boys on the soccer team. The gulf between the males was further elucidated when the gym teacher reported that he had to separate the two groups of males by their sports—soccer at one end of the court and basketball at the other end and if the ball crossed the courts there were different reactions on both sides. If the soccer ball reached the basketball end the students would heave it back, sometimes hitting someone with the ball. If the basketball reached the soccer end the students would carefully and gently send it back to the other end. The coach said, "I had to work on socialization skills more than anything else as there was animosity between these two groups." Some of the animosity was a result of the division by sport. There were some African students who would have liked to have played basketball but they were never permitted to join the Afro-Americans and for those African students who did not enjoy soccer there was no place for them in that gym. As for the girls, even physical education was a site of conflict. A requirement to complete the PE class for the girls was to create a dance. The Afro-American girls maintained control of the music that was to be used to create the dance. The African girls complained that they didn't know the music played by the Afro-American females. Two African girls were going to fail gym because they could not create a dance to hip-hop music. As a last resort they asked the teacher if they could design a dance using African music. She agreed and they were successful in meeting the requirements for passing the gym class. But this situation pointed to another way that the African and Afro-American students could not come together. The Afro-American girls mocked the African girls when they did their dance and the teacher said nothing. Thus, despite the hope that at least one common ground was already established between the students, at least one activity where they had established some form of cooperative attitude, it was clear that even in their choice of sports interests that these students remained "worlds" apart.

It would be natural to assume that school would be a site for positive interactions between these two groups of students given the time the students spend in school with the purpose of cognitive learning and social development yet, this was not the case at Jackson. School was a site of conflict, name-calling, teasing, and reinforcement of stereotypes and misperceptions. Even athletics was not a site of their coming together in positive ways. Nowhere at Jackson did the students have the chance to discuss what was keeping them apart. Neither the curriculum nor the extracurricular activities addressed the common background of the African and Afro-American students. Nothing in their school environment seemed likely to bring them together. Rather, many factors including the size of the school, thus the anonymity of the students to each other, and the daily schedule, which did not support interaction, contributed to keeping these two groups of students apart. Although the advisory period afforded students the opportunity to be in a room together for twenty minutes with students they did not normally have classes with and in many cases included an African or two, this was not designed to facilitate interaction. The purpose of the advisory seemed to be to take roll. Given the relationship between the two groups, the advisory period seemed a perfect opportunity for some purposeful interaction that could facilitate the breaking down of stereotypes and could lead in time to cooperation and understanding based on their shared heritage, common values and worldview. In the students' experiences, the school's influence negatively affected their relationship with each other. The next natural place to look for an opportunity to develop a connection to Africa and to one another was the home.

Home Influence

If the school environment was not providing the students with any opportunities to learn about their connection to Africa and to each other, then it might be hoped that they would be getting that connection made for them at home. This, however, proved not to be the case with the students who participated in this study. On the one hand, for the Afro-Americans home was not a source of connection to Africa or their African heritage. On the other, for the Africans their homes were not a source of understanding the experiences of Afro-Americans. Indeed, the Africans were advised to avoid the Afro-Americans because of the standard negative stereotypes about Afro-Americans that prevailed in the homes of the African students. Africa, African ancestry, African culture, or history seemed not to be discussed in either the Afro-American or the African homes in a way that they could access this connection to Africa and to one another. Thus, the home influence was a contributing factor to sustaining poor relations between the two groups. Surprisingly, although one of the Afro-American male students who participated in this research has an African mother, this was not reason enough for him to learn more about Africa. Patrick explained that he believed that the

> people living in Africa walk around without shoes. They hang on trees. They don't have concrete. They have dirt roads. I've heard dumb stuff like that, though I don't really consider them different. You know I'm kinda' ashamed that we're not interested. My mom is from Nigeria and she knows that we're not interested in hearing about where she's from. If we ask, she'll tell us, but we don't ask. You only listen when you care about it, and we don't care about it.

Patrick and his brothers didn't seem to care to learn more about Africa and his mother was reluctant to force on her children a better understanding of her heritage. She got the message loud and clear that they were not interested. Sadly, school didn't encourage their interest. The media didn't support them in being interested, and in fact contributed to the stereotyped images described by Patrick. Nothing supported them in being interested in where their mother is from because she is from Africa. Who would be interested in people with no shoes, people who hang on trees? The negative images of Africa and Africans make it impossible for this son to be interested in where his mother is from. The negative images block the possibility of his being interested in Nigeria, his mother's birthplace. It would seem natural that Patrick (and other similarly situated students) would like to be proud of his mother's birthplace, his mother's homeland but how can he when the images are so degrading? In the midst of his participation in this study, Patrick went home and talked to his mom about what he was learning about Africa. He had a new enthusiasm for learning about his mother's home country, an enthusiasm that had been stifled because of such demeaning stereotypes of the continent.

One Afro-American male student who at first did not agree to participate in the study said, "My mother said I should only be interested in where I came from and I came from here [the United States]." The connection between the

"African" in Afro-American is missing for many people. When informed by an African student that they (that is, the Afro-American students) came from Africa too, the answer by the Afro-Americans frequently was a resounding "No," not from all students, but from many of them.

When asked what their parents had told them about Afro-Americans the resounding answer from the African students was, "Nothing." One student went on to explain, "We don't talk about them." Miriam, an African female who has been here for fourteen of her sixteen years at first said nothing but later added something about stereotypes that she had heard.

> Inter.: What have you heard at home about Afro-Americans?
> Miriam: Nothing. Nothing really. All my dad said was, oh when you come here the Afro-Americans are going to change you. They're rude and stuff like that. But really some are rude and some are not. You just have to look at them and see how their behavior is.

All of the students participating in this study seemed reluctant to speak badly about anyone. For the Africans, to speak badly is to be disrespectful. None of the students were proud of the negative stereotypes and images that they knew existed. Once we started discussing the negative images and demeaning stereotypes they became eager to speak more positively about each other. What we found most interesting was how many students had talked about this project with someone at home, many with their parents. They did not see their parents as sharing the demeaning stereotypes of the other group, or at least they saw them as open to hearing about the coming together approach we were taking to encourage the students to interact in more positive ways. Every student had told someone else about the project; most informed their parents and had gotten positive responses. It became evident that there was increased interest in a shared heritage when it is discussed.

> Inter.: Did you tell anyone about this project?
> Marcus: Yeh, told my pops. He said it was decent. He told me don't stop learning.
> Damon: I told my mom and pop and they said it was good
> Inter.: Why do you think they thought it was good?
> Damon: Because I am learning more stuff about Africa.
> Inter.: Does everybody think that learning about Africa is good?
> Several: No. Some people don't care.

Damon, who had told his parents about the project, talked about a book report that he had done when younger. This book was among the resources we brought for the students to peruse. Damon had picked it up and said, "I have this book at home," so we were intrigued to discover what else he might have at home and how much interest in Africa there was in his home.

> Inter.: You had the book *Africa is not a country* at home?
> Damon: Yeah!
> Inter.: Had you read it?

Damon: Yeah! I did a report on it in 6th grade.
Inter.: Did you have any other books at home about Africa?
Damon: Yeah, a couple of them but I don't know the names of any of them.

Not that knowing the names of any books is necessarily useful but at this critical time in the development of their identity these students at Jackson, both African and Afro-American, had little access to information about their common heritage. Knowing one's history and therefore one's self is the key to healthy personhood (Akbar, 1998b, 2003).

Lamentably, people of African descent have long been denied the chance to learn their history in school. Both the colonial masters and the slave masters set up the educational systems to meet their needs not the needs of the colonized or enslaved. After seeing the film, one of the African students said, "We need our parents to be teaching this. We can't just depend on the school." The students at Jackson could not depend on the school to teach them their connection to Africa and to one another, but they hadn't found it at home either. Neither school nor home had provided the students with the opportunity to learn about their history and their culture and make a connection to Africa and to one another.

The Media

What is most noticeable when the students talk about what they know and how they know it is the role of the media. When asked to describe the images they have of Africans from the media, one Afro-American student responded, "That they're savages. That they don't know anything. That they're not schooled. That's the image that they put out there in America on TV shows and movies." Only three movies were mentioned by the students, "Amistad," "Roots," and "Shaka Zulu." These three films have provided the bulk of the images and information that the students have about Africa and Africans. Both "Roots" and "Amistad", although major contributions to understanding Afro-American history, also helped to create the image of the Africans as "those who sold us (the Afro-Americans) into slavery." The Afro-American studies teacher informed us that he does not spend much time on Africa in his class (perhaps the only class in which it would be presumed that the students would learn at least something about Africa) because "the Africans sold us into slavery." On television, NBC did a salute to the 25th anniversary of the original showing of "Roots" on rival network ABC and it is worth noting that for many people, both black and white, "Roots" marked the first time on a major television station or for some, the first time ever, they learned about the story of the Middle Passage and the cruelty of the slave trade. In addition to films, television shows, and the evening news broadcasts have contributed to the negative images by focusing on the villages.

Inter.: Where do the stereotypes about Africans come from?
Fanta: From here.
Inter.: Where do you think the Americans get their ideas about Africa from?
Fanta: I think it's from the news because sometimes I notice with Africa or other

places, they always go to places, which are remote like the villages. I mean, I know they should do that, but I know you should say the real things about it somewhere.

The only other sources of information that the students noted were the commercials for the "Save the Children" and "Christian Children's Fund" and other groups raising money for starving children in Africa. National Geographic and the Discovery Channel provide the bulk of the image of Africa and they focus almost entirely on the animals or the terrain. Both the commercials and National Geographic and the Discovery Channel contribute to the stereotypes of Africa—jungle, desert and living among the animals. Christine, an Afro-American female, currently participating in the Afro-American studies class provided some information about her exposure to Africa.

Inter.: Where have you gotten your information about Africa?
Chris: Well, not much from TV, but movies.
Inter.: Uh huh, and what sort of movies?
Chris: Like, an example is "Amistad." I seen that movie, I think, in 8th grade. It leaves a very strong and positive message that they were sending out about what happened during slavery.
Inter.: Anything else about that film, what you thought about it or felt about it, or what you thought the message was?
Chris: Well, I guess they were sending out the message about how things were in slavery and how the Africans back then changed it, by trying to speak up.

It is interesting to note that this student called those who fought against slavery, Africans. She had not been left with the perception that Africans sold them but rather the slaves were Africans. But this brings up the reasonable question, does she see the slaves as her ancestors? And if she saw the slaves as her ancestors, how could she not see Africa as her ancestral home? The reason the Afro-American students could not see Africa as their ancestral homeland, we contend, is that they have been presented a distorted view of Africa in their schools, their homes and the media. The jungle and savages are the pervasive images of Africa. What adolescent would embrace a heritage of savages? What does it benefit someone to be of African descent if the image is one of monkeys swinging from trees? When asked where the Africans think the Afro-Americans get their ideas, the students said the media. Haja explained:

I think they get their ideas from movies. Because when I came from Africa people would ask me "Do you live in trees? Do you have a pet lion?" and I was like "What? What are you talking about?" And when I saw the movies on TV about where I come from I was like, "Nah, I don't live in trees. I have a house. I have a dog. I don't have any lions." They say, "Why don't you go back to Africa!" I have to come here and get my education and then I could go back.

A typical response from an Afro-American student to any form of complaint from an African student was "go back to Africa. If you don't like it here then go back to where you came from."[8] This may be a common remark, heard by many immigrants as invective, but it is particularly iniquitous when the image of the home they are directed to is so derogatory and especially for those immigrants who want to go back home but cannot because of war.

Currently, the focus of many news media broadcasts is on AIDS in Africa. Brandy wanted to know how the African people contend with dying; and then almost in the same breath, she asked about how they do school.

> Brandy: The television show said there's a lot of people dying from AIDS over there. Like anybody can get it instead of having sexual relations and like that. I'd like to know how they like dying, some of them dying, you know what I mean, but like, do they get angry at that? I want to know how they did that? How do they like, when they have babies, who would deliver them and stuff like that? How do they do school over there?
> Inter.: Where have you gotten your information from?
> Brandy: Commercials. I seen a lot of these. I don't know what it's called though. I always watch it. Sometimes it's sad. Like little babies be hungry and stuff, like the commercials.

This same student was going to do her senior project on Blacks and AIDS but later decided that there was too little information about it available. Although there is a wealth of information on AIDS in Africa from a multitude of websites to books and films, there is too little information available to these students. They rely on their school, their home and their media for their information. There is too little information available to them to combat the images of Africa as jungle, of Africans as living with the animals and as carriers of the AIDS virus.

> Inter.: Where have you gotten your information about Africa and Africans?
> Jasmine: It's just what I hear and read and the news. It's just a place, a land full of desert and hungry people.

Jasmine was the only student in the group who had taken the Afro-American Studies class and she had completed it prior to engaging in this project. It's jolting how little this experience helped her to have up-to-date, accurate information about Africa and images that are more appropriate. The images of Africa and Africans presented in their lived experiences are so negative that they do not inspire the students to inquire further.

As the African students we studied were recent arrivals to this country, it is important to examine their previous education experiences, the role of education in Africa, and the influence of colonialism on their education. We sought to understand the experiences of students from Africa in schools in America but were dismayed to discover that there were only a few extant studies done on the experiences of African immigrant students, and these were conducted in Canadian schools (Yon, 2000). Although the experiences of African-born students in Canadian schools, are remarkably similar in some ways to those of their counterparts in America, they also experience vastly different difficulties than those faced by the students at Jackson High. The dynamics in Canadian schools are different because the schools in the extant studies comprised a majority of white students, and exogenous racism played a major role in a way that was more muted at Jackson where the majority of students were Afro-American, with very few Caucasian students enrolled.

Various scholars have proposed ways to improve the quality of the education administered to and experienced by Black children in our country, from culturally relevant curriculum and teaching, to critical pedagogy, to African-centered education. Although the dynamics of race are experienced differently in a predominantly Black school than they would in a predominantly white school, it is important to examine race and racialization in every context where Africans encounter American stereotypes about race. Students of color, whether Afro-American or African, are affected by race in America. Ogbu's theory helps to explain the impact of the history of Afro-Americans on their interest in and ability to succeed in schools that they see as seats of white dominance. Nigrescence helps inform the selection of high school students and the importance of Black identity development at this stage of their lives. Afrocentricity, as developed by Akbar, Asante, Dei, Harris, Hilliard, and Myers paved the way for this study. This project was in response to the challenge put forth by Akbar (1998a) "to execute the next step in the progression of this paradigm shift" (p. 248). Akbar explains that "we have a new grasp of the concept that Africans view the world differently, thanks to the work of Asante, Karenga, Carruthers, Jeffries and others. We now need a new implementation, both in social construction and in technology" (p. 248). We will explore the myriad ways in which each of these theories helps to illuminate the educational experiences of students of color but also has significant limitations when evaluating the educational experiences of African students in America.

Chapter Summary

In this chapter, we have described some of the factors that were contributing to the strained relationships between two groups that share a common ancestry, Africans and Afro-Americans. Neither school, nor the students' homes, nor the media had contributed to their developing positive relationships with one another based on a shared history and culture. Myths, misperceptions and stereotypes abound. Tarzan, wild jungle, and native savages continue to predominate as the images of Africa and Africans most Americans can identify. Afro-Americans are depicted as living off welfare, being rude and antagonistic, and prone to violence. Although the students spent many hours at school, they did not have the chance to come together to learn from and about one another. Segregated space contributed to keeping them apart. Even physical education and sports were not sites of positive relations. Language kept them apart as did their names. Nothing had encouraged the students to come together, to learn from and about each other. Negative media images contributed to keeping the students apart. The image of an African slitting the throat of a chicken made them look like savages rather than utilitarians. The images of AIDS victims dying in various countries in Africa merely highlight the genuine anomie attached to anything that involves Africa or Africans; rather than incite compassion for the unconscionable toleration of the demise of whole populations by this disease, a blaming the victim mentality engendered by the media's response to this plague has inured most Americans to the point where they no longer recognize that these are human beings dying without surcease. That the Afro-Americans had come from Africa many years ago and that slavery had been designed to destroy their connection to Africa was not previously made clear to the students. The "African" component for the Afro-American students retained an abundance of negative connotations and the behavior of the Afro-Americans towards the Africans was so negative that it made a coming together of these two groups unlikely.

And yet, although stereotypes filled the space between them, many of the students still were willing to explore their common history. They were eager to learn more once the truth of their connection was made real by the film. This study was not about gathering information. It was more about a connection that was severed many years ago. The results affirm a story about students who discovered a connection that is real but that previously had been unavailable to them because of a wall of stereotypes, myths, and misperceptions that divided them. When the students made the connection between them they wanted to know more, and then more. When the wall that had separated them came down they wanted to explore their new-found connections. For Valeisha, living in a village in truth was preferable to living in myths and misperceptions. She articulated the desire that she shared with her Afro-American peers to learn the truth about her ancestry, her heritage, her culture, her homeland, Africa. As Valeisha eloquently said "I want to know the truth. I'd rather give up all the benefits of technology and live in a village in truth."

In the next chapter we compare pre-American and post-American school entry from the point of view of several highly motivated, intelligent, and resourceful African students who were overwhelmed at the difference in educational quality between that of their home county and the U.S., and how the lowered expectations in American schools were thwarting their efforts to accomplish all they had aspired to for many years while attending school in Africa. We will explore the African students' frustration with the student and teacher attitudes towards Africa and Africans, the negative reactions to their having an accent or having difficulty with English, and their desire to work together with their peers on common activities, to help each other. We also describe the students' experiences with segregated spaces at school for ESOL and their inability to be accepted by their Afro-American peers. The students convey vividly their perceptions of the prevalent stereotypes about Africans by Afro-Americans, and about Afro-Americans by African students. Moreover, the students report on how they relate to each other and begin to take the stereotypes apart, to see through them and their underlying mistaken premises about the other group. We will explore the various ways in which the students feel disconnected at school, both intellectually and emotionally, and the ways in which they attempt to cope with this disconnect between their aspirations and reality. We will present some detailed descriptions of the effects of negative stereotypes about Africa that interfere with an authentic experience by Afro-American students of the cultural heritage they should share with the African student, as well as the misconceptions about Afro-Americans that confound the authentic experience that the African students have relating with their Afro-American peers.

CHAPTER 2

African Student Profiles –
Previous and Current School Experiences

This chapter provides a brief description of the educational experiences of several highly motivated, intelligent, and resourceful African students. Some of these students were overwhelmed at the difference they experienced between what had been expected of them in their African schools and the quality and lowered expectations they encountered at Jackson. The students expressed dismay that the perceived lower expectations were thwarting their efforts to accomplish all they had aspired to while attending school in Africa. Despite what the various governments in Africa may promote or want for their young people, how did the students themselves see their educational experiences while in Africa? When they resumed their education in the U.S., did their perceptions about the expectations change? How do they see the American educational system, their particular school, their peers, and their teachers? These are some of the questions to be explored here.

This chapter also investigates the African students' experiences of frustration with the student and teacher attitudes towards Africa and Africans, the negative reactions to their having an accent or having difficulty with English, their desire to work together with their peers on common activities and to help each other to succeed. We also will explore the students' experiences with transitioning to daily events at Jackson and their struggles to be accepted by their Afro-American peers. The voices of the students convey frankly their perceptions of the prevalent stereotypes about Africans by Afro-Americans, and about Afro-Americans by African students. Moreover, the students report on how they relate to each other and begin to take the stereotypes apart, to see through their false veneer and their underlying mistaken premises about the other group of young people.

It is essential that an Afrocentric perspective guide the research of Africa and Africans and persons of African descent. Had this been the predominant view of earlier generations, the Europeans might have been exposed to a spiritual connection to all things and an interdependence and commitment to community, cooperation and harmony with all things that could have changed the course of history. Researchers studying people of African descent must be aware of the bias of a Eurocentric focus and approach. An Afrocentric method and framework both in the collection and the analysis of data provide a more promising approach because this model uses "codes, paradigms, symbols, motifs, myths, and circles of discussion that reinforce the centrality of African ideals and values as a valid frame of reference for acquiring and examining data" (Asante, 1990, p. 6). According to Asante, the Afrocentric "ontology seeks to use rhythm to harmonize with those forces that appear external to the individual" (p. 20). Rhythm can be discerned when one is in concert with the rest of the universe, a part of the whole, in harmony with the visible and the invisible, and rhythm "dictates the beat of your life" (p. 49). Therefore, no study of people of African descent could be comprehensive if it did not let their voices be heard and then follow the beat of their worldview. As Asante admonishes, however, an "African birth does not make one Afrocentric; Afrocentricity is a matter of intellectual discipline and must be learned and practiced" (p. 115).

The "crucial role of education perceived by the students themselves, accounts for the remarkably high level of their academic aspirations and expectations" (Clignet & Foster, 1966, p. 143) and provides a "plausible reason for believing that secondary school attendance has a homogenizing effect on the attitudes of students, tending to attenuate differences in social-economic and cultural background" (p. 144). Without the active and creative engagement from the students in the activities used in our study and their description of the process, we might only have been purveying another form of colonialism. Nobles (1991) argues that social science may be "guilty of scientific colonialism"—exporting data for processing from foreign shores, retaining the right to all access, while declaiming and maintaining itself as the center of knowledge about the "other" (p. 296). There are endless stories recounted in both the professional literature and the anecdotal world of research traditions about the inadvertent damage done to people of the "Third World" in the name of research and development. As objects of study many of these people have in the past been deemed savages, uncivilized, and in need of salvation; this was the pattern pursued by the early settlers on the North American continent (MacDougall, 2004). The colonizers of the African continent were incapable of seeing with African eyes, and Akbar (1991) denounces the damage done by Eurocentric models to persons from the African continent. The paradigm of Eurocentric research is based on the notion that the "human being is assumed to be at his best when *he* is *white*, *materially* accomplished, achieved through *competitive, independent* assertiveness. *She* who is *black, poor* and *submissive* is by definition inferior, abnormal, and/or unintelligent according to this model" (p. 723). Just as the colonialists saw only through their own lenses, traditional research about Africa and Africans has been distorted by adhering to a paradigm that is European, white, and male-centered.

The Promise of an American Education

The African students reported that overall they felt that the expectations academically at Jackson were more relaxed than they had been in their African schools, but also that respect for the purpose of education seemed to be missing here. One myth about African education is that it is of low quality. Many of the African students attending Jackson felt that they were viewed by their peers as being "stupid" just because they are African. Some of the common experiences that students reported were similar to the following comments, which are illustrative of the disparities remarked by the students between their American and African educational experiences:

It's easier here. We had a lot more work over there.

Teachers are respected in my country. Between the teachers and the students
here the respect is missing.

I want to become someone good who will help to teach my people. I want to do
good. I want to go to school and become somebody good, like a teacher.
School at home is better, a little bit harder.

Abram told us that he had a more difficult time mastering the educational
requirements in Africa because of the need to learn several languages. Abram
had been to a French school, an English school, an Amharic school and a Somali
school too. He was facile with adapting to many changes and learning languages. His favorite subject was Math. He also said that "school is cool, but a
little bit hard" and later in the interview he said "all I want is to be an educated
person."

Although the prior life experiences of the African students at Jackson may
have been vastly different, these students were unanimous in their desire to get
an education. Their prior experiences were a myriad collection of the kinds of
disparate backgrounds that could be expected from the third largest continent in
the world. For example, the students from Liberia and Sierra Leone had experienced the horrors of civil wars in their countries, while the students from Senegal came from somewhat prominent families and had gone to relatively prestigious schools. Although the students from Liberia and Sierra Leone were forced
to leave their lands as refugees of war, their hearts and extended families were
for the most part still in their home countries. The students from Sudan also had
been forced to emigrate from Sudan and had done so very sadly. Although they
were from the Northern part of Sudan, not yet affected by war, there were political difficulties which had forced their parents to leave their beloved Sudan.
Every African student expressed a deep desire to return to their country one day
after having achieved an education that would help them contribute to the development of their country or enable them to help their families. The Ethiopian
students had come with their family to join relatives already here. They too had
high hopes that getting an education in the U.S. would enable them to go back
and be successful in their country.

Despite their avowals about wanting to get a good education, the students'
behavior was not always consonant with that goal. This is similar in the way
that Mickelson (1990) described the concrete and abstract inconsistencies found
in her research study with Afro-American students. School does not necessarily
support their participation in ways that would help them succeed. When they
are teased, harassed, belittled or ignored, some of the African students under-
standably found it difficult to cope with the disparaging remarks and they might
have fought back, which made them seem violent by comparison. These struggles were an added burden on their already difficult transition to American high
school mores. One Liberian student who had only been in the U.S. for 6 months
already had a reputation at Jackson and was regarded as aggressive and "crazy."

He did not see himself this way, however; he understood himself just to be try-ing to fit in. What we observed was a young man who was very confused by the reaction of the teachers and students at Jackson. Yes, he had been aggressive but so was everybody else in his experience of the hostility exhibited by the other students toward him and other Africans. He felt attacked from the moment he arrived, and he felt on the defensive all the time. He was called derogatory labels, from faggot to dirty to foreigner, and he thought he should fight back to maintain his own sense of self-worth.

Others had decided to disengage from school since it was perceived as a hostile environment and unchallenging academically. For still others, the only way to succeed was to become invisible, blend in, or to stay as reticent as possi-ble, simply complete the work as expected, turn everything in when due, and meanwhile try to find a teacher or a friend to help them when they did not un-derstand something in class. It would not be an easy undertaking for any student to fit into a new environment. Graduation rates at Jackson during the 2001 academic year were very low, even by the country's inner-city school stan-dards (Orfield & Lee, 2004). Of the 400 young people who would start their freshman year at Jackson, fewer than half would graduate four years later.

Descriptions of the Students

One significant factor that contributed to the adjustment that the African students were able to make to life at Jackson was whether they were with their families; family support helped some students stay focused despite the difficul-ties at school. Another factor was whether the students were able to return to their home countries and consequently could anticipate that their time in the U.S. might be limited. They could tolerate more of the difficulties, or accept more of their frustrations about their situation, while focusing on their goals for their future and their return home. Those students who felt or knew that they could not go back to Africa, or at least did not believe that they retained this as an option any longer, experienced a more challenging adjustment to the difficul-ties they faced. This comports with the categorizations described by Ogbu (2003) relating to the capacity for immigrants to adapt to a new culture in situa-tions where they might have the option to return to their home country.

Peter was a 17 year old Liberian refugee who was oppositional in almost every stance he took. He had only been at Jackson a short time but already had earned a very negative reputation. He talked about his mom being ill; his "mom" actually was his aunt with whom he was staying, but it was culturally appropriate to call his mother's sister "mom" because she was the person who was caring for him.

> She wants to go back to Africa to do some traditional medicine. She goes to the hospital and she's gonna stay a couple of weeks after that she comes back. I think to myself I can't say "Mom I need some advice." She's been telling me some things, but I need someone else who can tell me things like, don't do this, don't do this. To me, you see your friend doing it and you want to do it too. But

it might not be right. But you think it's right because you see someone doing it. The person you see doing it he never be in trouble, but you do it and you always get in trouble. That's why we say "Sheep luck and goat luck are not the same."

We first encountered Peter, who appeared to be everyone's favorite target for scapegoating, as he was cursing in the hallway and about to be suspended, again. He complained about how he was being mistreated. He said that the other students were always trying to provoke him, calling him names, taunting or challenging him. It was rumored around Jackson that Peter had been a rebel in Liberia and with his disposition he appeared ready to assume an offensive stance; he was ready to pounce at every turn. He saw injustice everywhere and he was not going to tolerate it any more. Peter needed much more support than anyone at Jackson could provide. His every move got him into trouble, it seemed. Peter is like many children of war who have been so traumatized that they can no longer navigate emotionally on an even course without an intervention and some competent counseling; but Jackson could provide no counselor for him due to recent reductions in such resources by the school system. Peter hoped that he would be able to find a job and work and live a peaceful life in America, but it seemed to him that someone was always picking a fight with him. America was not the place he had hoped it would be; he could not find the peace that he was seeking when he left his war-torn homeland.

Although many students who emigrated from Liberia and Sierra Leone had experienced horrific wars, only a few were as obviously traumatized as Peter. Some were managing to focus on school and maintained a relatively normal outward appearance although they manifested some noticeable adverse effects from their experience of war to those perceptive enough to observe and to listen to them. Kalilu, was a 19 year old refugee from Sierra Leone. His mother died in the war in Sierra Leone, and he had been in the U.S. for 2 years. He was savvy and wise-mouthed, which irritated so many of the teachers because he had a retort for everything. He had a strong personality and abundant energy, and if he had channeled these positively he could have been a true leader. As it was, he was leading many of his fellow students astray and into the world of drugs and violence. He, too, like Peter, was a product of a devastating war that not only took lives, destroyed families, and kept children from school but also imprinted in the minds of too many youth the horrors of mutilation and random killings that scarred them emotionally and spiritually.

Hamed was born in Liberia and escaped from the war by migrating to neighboring Guinea. He had family there and spent nine years living in Guinea with his grandmother while his father tried to get settled in the U.S. When his father finally had managed to achieve some level of financial stability, he brought Hamed and his brother to join him. However, when Hamed arrived, he discovered that his father had developed cancer; his father died the following year, leaving his wife to care for the children. Because of his experience of the war in Liberia, Hamed now considers Guinea to be his home. He is in a different situation than the other Liberians because he had another place to call home. Hamed exhibited the strongest sense of self and an ability to focus on his schoolwork despite the teasing and the challenges faced by every African student at Jackson. Hamed founded and was elected the first president of the African Students Association ("ASA"). His brother Sidiq was also at Jackson and just a year behind him. Hamed was looking after younger brothers and cousins as well. While his mother worked two jobs, he also worked to help with his family's circumstances. Hamed was determined to succeed; he stood out above the rest of his peers and it was only natural that he should be elected president of the ASA. He worked tirelessly to organize his peers and to generate activities to promote a positive image of Africa and Africans. During the year that we worked together, Hamed composed more than a dozen poems, 2 dramas, and several articles for the ASA Newsletter. His brother Sidiq, on the other hand, was "too" quiet for the teachers and did not do his work as seriously as did Hamed. Although he was younger than Hamed they both were in the same grade at Jackson.

Hamed had attended a local school while he lived in Guinea and the language of instruction was French. He can be understood easily by most Americans and in fact, has developed quite an American accent. He respects himself and is proud to be an African. Hamed used his creativity to express his disappointment in his writings, but also to share his dreams and to promote a more positive image of Africa and Africans. He knows that he has African roots and he is proud of who he is. What most disappointed him with America was how hard his mother had to work and still found it hard to provide for the family. She was an in-home caretaker and worked 7 days a week. He was also annoyed that the stereotypes about Africa were so negative and degrading. He commented that Afro-Americans know so little about Africa.

> Their parents don't tell them their history. They don't know. They go to school to learn how their great, great grandparents came here and they can't listen to teachers. So how would they know? So when people tell them they are from Africa they don't believe it. They say I am African American. But the African name there, though, is the first. They don't realize how it is so.

Although some of the students retained very little of their original accents and could easily be understood by most Americans, Hamed pointed out that just because someone has an accent, or is just learning English, does not mean they are ignorant:

> Some students they are very shy to speak in the class. It's not because they don't know the answer to question. They do know, but they are shy because when they say any word the other American students make fun of them because of their accent and it's not like we don't know the answer. We do know the answer, but our English is not the same.

According to Haja, a 16 year old girl from Guinea, what most helped the African students survive the daily challenges at Jackson was the existence of the ASA. The ASA "worked to show Jackson students a different image of Africa by organizing African cultural fairs, African feast days, plays about life in Africa, and fashion shows featuring the clothes and music of students' home countries" (Socolar, 2002, p. 20). Haja and her sister arrived in the U.S. with a friend of the family from Guinea. She was a large girl with quiet determination. She became a leader in the ASA because of her willingness to show up, do the work, and be responsible. She was a great student who did her work fastidiously. She was eager to learn and paid attention better than most students so she stood out in that way. Haja had high aspirations of helping people as a career, but she was frustrated and bewildered by the ignorance about Africa expressed by her American peers.

> I don't really like the way they make fun of us and stuff, like they never been there so they don't know. They say like, every time they get into an argument, they say, "well why don't you go back to Africa." I'd be glad to go, but I came to get an education. I don't know, they think that we're not happy or we're poor or we don't have any homes, we live in the forest or whatever. I got sort of tired of it. I say that I'm gonna bring you a picture of where I live, so I brought them in a picture of my house and I have a backyard and stuff like that. And I would like to go back today if I could, but I can't. I have to come here and get my education, then I could go back. I'd like to go to college first, then go back to Africa and help them. I would like to go back and help fix some stuff. Maybe I'll go to government and give them some ideas that I have.

Miriam, also a Liberian, was only a few months old when her family came here from Liberia. She had no accent when she spoke and this allowed her to pass for Afro-American; she admitted that she also could speak with a Liberian accent when she wanted or when it was appropriate. She had not identified herself at school as a Liberian. Some time after the ASA was instituted, she realized the camaraderie that she could find in the ASA and with her Liberian peers. She was very vocal and added a special perspective to this group. She talked about how sad it was that she had lost her Liberian identity for all these years but was happy to have found it again. This served as a lesson for the students who had more recently arrived. Losing one's sense of identity, heritage, culture, self can seem like the thing to do to fit in but it has consequences. Miriam was proud to call herself Liberian once more.

Bintu, from Senegal, lived with her father and siblings. Her mother, a physician, had remained in Senegal. Her father managed a hair-braiding business here, where she and her sister both worked. Bintu came from a family of higher social class than many of the other African students. She had gone to a school in Senegal with a science specialization. Just as her mother and father could go back and forth to Senegal, Bintu also expected that she would go back and forth to Senegal after completing her American education. She saw Jackson as a means to an end. Even if the education was inferior, the diploma from the U.S. would still be meaningful back home. She was disappointed that Americans didn't seem the least bit interested in Africa, and she considered her education at Jackson to be inferior to the one she was getting back home. Although Bintu was from a French-speaking country, her ability to learn languages was excellent and she was soon speaking English like her peers, though her French accent remained prominent. Bintu knew how to learn a language not just by imitation but also by studying the vocabulary and grammar and modeling her language on the teachers not the students. What disappointed her the most was that there were students who wanted to disrupt the learning process. She was very serious about wanting to learn and was not happy with the level of disrespect she saw exhibited by the American students in her classes at Jackson.

> The Americans are disrespectful. In addition they don't like to work. Even if you want to work, they will not give you the chance to do your work. Because you see in an environment like this, you are in class, for example, if you are in a class with only foreign students there isn't much chatter. If you go "upstairs," there are the students who want to learn but the majority don't want to learn. You come in to class to learn but they are there talking, insulting the teacher and that makes it difficult for the rest of us to learn, to concentrate, to do your best. And the teacher what can he/she do with students who are talking, disrupting class. Nothing. The teacher puts us all in the same category. They can't distinguish between who wants to learn and who is disrupting. This student is here to learn; this one is not.

Most remarkable to us was Bintu's comment, "En Afrique, tu n'as pas le problème de racisme."[1]

Among the African students at Jackson, we met three brothers from Sudan, who rarely were apart. They seemed to be together all the time. The eldest was obviously caring for his younger brothers; and they all were good students, with good grades, good behavior, and many teachers who agreed that they enjoyed having them in their classes. The main disappointment expressed by all three was that no one even seemed to know where Sudan was located – or that it even was a country—or know or care about knowing anything about Sudan. These three had a lot of family support and did not need much from the staff or their peers at Jackson. They just wished that both students and teachers were a bit more knowledgeable and interested in them, their countries, and their lives.

Camara came here by himself because his family was being persecuted back home. He was supposed to have joined an uncle but his uncle didn't want to be responsible for him so Camara had to work to get by; consequently, school was secondary to him. He was 19 years old and could not manage higher than mid-high school level work; he could not find anyway to learn and survive on his own; the classes were beyond him intellectually and he needed to earn money to live. Sometimes he slept on friends' floors; other times in a car. With the help of a social worker, he finally got into an apartment and started to be able to take care of himself. Camara took the book written in French by Camara Laye to read. Although he really wanted to get an education, his survival came first; he had to pay rent and purchase food and he had no one to depend on to provide these for him so he learned to be self-sufficient without the education that was available.

> There are some groups who come here and say that they want to help the Liberians in particular. All of us are suffering. All of us from Africa need some help.

We haven't all had the same education. We are all different. We are very, very different. There are meetings that concern the Liberians or the Sierra Leonians. That's not the problem but the problem is that we have to come together and understand each other. It's not a question of jealousy. In one way we could share each other's ideas.

After her mother died, Fatou's grandmother raised her and they lived in Sierra Leone; Fatou had only seen her father occasionally over the years because he had emigrated to the U.S. When she finally had the opportunity to come to the U.S. to be re-united with her father, it was a very difficult situation because he had a new wife, and their children comprised an entirely new family. Her father's new wife did not accept Fatou. In fact, it was almost a Cinderella story with Fatou doing most of the housework, sometimes not being fed if the stepmother got angry at her and her father ignoring much of what was going on. Fatou tried very hard in school, but she did not have the necessary skills or support to succeed. She retained in her memory horrifying images of the war in Sierra Leone. She told the story of one of her friends who was told by the rebels to kill her baby. When this young mother refused, the rebels cut off part of her ear and made her eat it; then they killed her baby. This image was a striking reminder that no matter how difficult her transition to the U.S. would be, it was definitely superior to the circumstances of war. Fatou worked so hard to make it in America. She tried to do her homework though she hardly understood what the teachers meant exactly. She wrote for the ASA newsletter and participated in the association though she was always looking for a job and way to be able to take care of herself so that she could escape her family situation. Her stepbrothers were mean to her at times and the stepsister moved in with her boyfriend and ultimately became pregnant, so she was pre-occupied and had little attention on Fatou's circumstances. Even she could not wait to get out of the house. Fatou had thought that coming to America would bring her some peace but she found no peace in her life in America. One morning, on her way to Jackson, she saw two bloody bodies on the street. When she related this episode to us later, Fatou reflected that "in my country, it was war, what is it here?"

Aliya is tall and beautiful, and many people first reacted to her by telling her that she could be a model. She couldn't be bothered with school since modeling could easily give her a better lifestyle than an education or at least that's what she thought. She tried to earn the money for the photos to send to a modeling agency. She did have a boyfriend who could take care of her basic needs so she basically moved out of her family's home to try to make it. Although she is tall and beautiful, modeling is an elusive dream of many and a reality for so few. Aliya could not handle school. She was older than the other students and there was nothing of interest at school, nothing except the socializing. Aliya had imagined that she would become white when she walked off the plane because everyone in America was white.

Wata was a very shy and reserved, light-skinned Liberian girl. She got by with her sweet smile; she rarely spoke and never disrupted class. She had a lot to say and many emotions to express especially about the loss of her sister. Her poetry is touching; reading it, you are moved by her love for her sister. She wanted to read and write and participate in the world. Until the ASA Newsletter was created, Wata could find no other outlet for her creative and emotive expressions. She could have gone through Jackson and never really connected to anyone or anything but the association brought her into a world that valued her and asked her to contribute.

Aisha, also from Liberia, was small and overlooked by almost everyone because she appeared to be so young. She could maneuver her way through the school because there was nothing threatening about her. She would walk with her eyes down, not making eye contact. She was small and could almost make herself disappear. In the group discussions she became very lively; it was as if it was all bottled up and had to be brought out when given the chance. Her comments were typical:

> Americans are rude. Sometimes I come inside they knocking my head, talking, cursing at me. I don't think they should act like that. Probably because we were born in Africa and we came here and we wasn't born here, so they just think they are not Africans - but they are Africans. So we are all Africans. We all have roots. We have to be together. We don't have to picking at one another and doing that kind of stuff. I don't like that.

Abram and his sister were the only Ethiopians at Jackson, and they stayed together for the most part; Abram was very protective of his sister. She was very pretty and many of the boys asked about her. Both Abram and his sister were quiet students who presented themselves humbly to their teachers. They were considered "good" students—they were quiet, did their work, and were obviously interested in learning. They listened in class most of the time and actively participated, asking for help sometimes before or after class. In his earnest commitment to his education, Abram even declined a position of leadership in the ASA because he was concerned that it might affect his studies. Abram and his sister moved away from the area with their family prior to the conclusion our this study, so their contributions were meaningful, but limited.

Fanta was disappointed with what she found in America. She was one of the first to complain that this wasn't the America she thought she'd find because she had believed that all the students would be white. She was surprised to find herself in a school with black students and they didn't act like she thought they should. She was proud of being an African and definitely saw her values as better than the ones she was seeing around her at Jackson and in the neighborhood. According to Fanta, her Afro-American peers were

> kind of ignorant. When I came I found it difficult, like people are mean to me. Because, in Liberia, when Americans go there we don't treat them mean, we treat them nice. But here, when you come here, they watch TV and see other things about Africa, they think everything is true, but its not. They treat us different, like we're vicious. They even ask me questions "do you all walk with lions" or "do you do this with lions," all kinds of silly things. Sometimes they used to ask me, "How come you're so light, everyone from Africa is so black?" You know eve-

ryone from Africa is so black and they treat me different because they be talking about eye and stuff and they always wanted things from me like pins, paper, but whenever I ask for anything they're not gonna give you that. I was so nice, and when I gave them those stuff, one minute they gonna joke with me, the next thing they start laughing at me. I try all the time.

I was one of the lighter ones we have people saying that you white so, and everyone teasing me about my eye and was talking about me and all that African stuff. We had to form a black, African community or some kind of organization so we can say what we think.

Identity Development

The African students experienced a form of identity crisis in the sense that they did not know where to draw the line between their own culture and that of the new society in which they lived (Waters, 1999; Yon, 2000). Due to this conflict between their heritage and the expectation that they conform to a new culture, they attempted to create the impression that they already had been Americanized. But was this for the better? Most of them had become Americanized for the worst reasons. For instance, they would try to speak Americanized English when some of them could not read basic English or understand the American accent well. Their behavior tended to portray that they had assimilated into American culture so they would appear to be a regular part of this society. All eleven students reported that they felt that school was "easier" here, easier as in much less rigorous, not necessarily easy because of the obstacles of language and culture.

Amadou: In my school in Africa, we had 12 subjects to study each term. There they give you a lot of things that you have to put in your head like a lot of languages. Here you have only one language. There you take French, English, Arabic and other languages. It's much more difficult. Americans don't respect other languages, only English.

A common phenomenon is to find that the students who speak the same language congregate together or if they can speak the same language and are from neighboring countries they form a sub-group together. But at the same time, when they become the majority of the group there tends to be a split again because they want to speak the language of their country, of their homeland. Then the other people are left out. From looking at their faces you can see that they are lost. One minute they were a team. The next meeting they were split by language grouping—it seems like cultural loyalty predominates.

Another major issue with the African students is the difference between social time and learning time. They want to have their social life and the education conjointly, so they can learn and affiliate at the same time. This predilection for group learning affects their focus on education, which is a key issue. As with many other typical teenagers, the boys want to impress the girls and vice versa. There is a lot of attention and energy expended on selecting the proper dress and hair and way of talking, even dancing, but little time seems to go to any actual classroom learning. Acting cool is what is most important. The students are more focused on what they will do to impress each other, they give more attention to socializing than to learning. Their manner of dressing is the accepted mode they derive from television or is media-approved because television is their principal guide to life in America. They need new, more realistic guides to typical life in America than television provides. All of the students were trying to put some time into learning so that they would learn more English—they have a legitimate goal. The students appeared to put a lot more effort into their time in school and with their learning.

> Hamed: The way they see you: that's how they are going to treat you. If you behave well and you respect other people; if you're not telling anybody no, if you're not telling anybody anything bad then they won't say anything bad to you. They will leave you alone because you are not the same; you don't have the same behavior. If you come and start to behave like they do and you start playing with them and if you play with somebody it's forced that the person play back with you. If the play is not going in the same direction then it becomes two different things. One can't travel without their behavior. You can't leave your behavior behind regardless of who you are. Regardless of what kind of condition you are in, good behavior will never hide; it will reflect in all that you do.

One student admitted that

> what we do out here is not what our parents taught us. We don't know how to cope with this society. We imitate and it's a bad reflection on us. And those we imitate are laughing at us. Some don't seem to back off. We have to step back ourselves and reflect that this is not working for us. Our imitation isn't working and we're losing who we are in the process.

Another student pointed out that most of the African students go to work right after school. So, with the little they are able to accumulate in earnings they buy themselves all the commodities of those whom they are imitating, just so they can fit in without being identified as different. But they are identified by their accent, which they too often cannot disguise. They are laughed at and belittled, and they feel ashamed and betrayed. Those that are laughing at them are also people of African descent but that doesn't seem to provide any connection for them. One African remarked that

> the Afro-American students don't even know that their ancestors came from Africa. Why are they called Afro-American if they weren't African first. How come they don't know? Haven't their parents told them where they came from? If only their parents could teach them about where they came from then they would be able to accept them and learn from them and work with them and compromise in certain areas. It would be mutually beneficial.

To their surprise, their accent is a major deterrent to their fitting in at Jackson. There is a certain cultural background that they are missing. Even if they imitate the American ways they can't fit in. The students felt that if they could organize themselves as Africans then they could support each other in this adjustment process so as to not lose the values that they have while they try to fit in.

One of the students commented that it would be hard for the Africans and Afro-Americans to come together because of the jealousy that exists among them. When they reflect on their schooling experience in Africa, many conclude that it was in some ways better than it is here. They were acquiring a lot of knowledge there, but much less is happening here or expected from them in terms of academics. Yet, there are so many more obstacles here, the discipline problems, what it takes to survive each day, the unruliness of some of their fellow students, the lack of understanding from some teachers, the problem of being a foreigner and having unfulfilled expectations of what it would be like coming to America. Many students believed that everything would be easier, and things would be simpler. These expectations compounded the problem for most of the African students because the reality so drastically differed. Many of these African students had not harbored the same expectations about their education while in Africa; they arose each day, went to school, did homework, and respected their parents and teachers. Thus, in many ways it was much simpler for them in Africa. When asked what advice they might give to fellow Africans thinking about coming to America, some of the students remarked sincerely that those back home would be wise to investigate for themselves and not simply accept some of the hyperbole or publicity about how America welcomes others to its shores.

Hamed: Africans back home they can't understand or believe anything you tell them. If you tell them that America is hard, they can't believe it. We try to tell them but they don't believe us. The person who comes will say "Oh, is this how it is here?" Only then will they see what we were trying to tell them. America is not all that. It's only after they come that they understand. They are back in Africa saying "send this to me, send that to me." They think that the minute you get down from the plane they start paying you right away. We heard that you can pick money from the trees. It's not that way. If you're back there you have everything and you can go to a good school and you can do what you want to do. If you get vacation to come here okay but this is not the place to come unless you are going back. Stay there and get your education. Don't come here. You can get a better education back there. If you're on the welfare program here, if you've come to America as a refugee, then you have no choice of school because of the area that you live in. Sometimes the children don't even get to school. Their parents don't know what to do.

Fanta: In America and in school, peer pressure, people are being mean to me, people doing wrong, people stereotyping other people and all that, that's why I can't say things. But, I tell my mom, I tell them that America's not great. America is different than I expected. People go homeless and I didn't know that before I came here. People are being so violent, killing people. I know every country has this, kids have problems but . . . I was surprised. They have some ghettoes and they got some places that look really bad. I wasn't expecting that, because all they said was America is the most beautiful place. It's clean, and I know it is, but they got some bad places. So people shouldn't be saying things that are not true. Some of the row homes are not that clean. You don't see everywhere to be perfect, but here the media make it look so negative.

Many African students reported that they learned more in their own country, regardless of their country of origin and regardless of the ostensible quality of the schools. Even those who attended refugee schools, many of whom had only a blackboard as classroom resource, felt that they were learning more there than here. Why should this be the experience reported by the African students when the opposite would appear to be the assumption of many Americans? The African students would answer that there is respect for the teachers, and the students take learning seriously. Interrupting when the teacher speaks could get the student thrown out of school. All of the African students lamented the lack of respect they observed or experienced at Jackson; they described the students in their schools in Africa as generally more respectful.

> Teachers are respected in my country. Between the teachers and the students here the respect is missing. You come to class to learn but the students here are talking, insulting the teacher and that makes it difficult for the rest of us to learn, to concentrate, and to do our best. And the teacher, what can she do with students who are talking, disrupting class? Nothing. (Bintu)

> When you're in class with American kids, there is someone over there talking, singing, you know, making noise. I mean the teacher; he or she doesn't seem to care. If you want to pay attention, you can just go ahead and pay attention. Sometimes, if they've been rude or bad when the teacher is teaching, maybe someone is talking or saying bad words to the teacher, she can't teach anymore. She can't continue, you know, and that's not good. (Aliya)

In addition to the lack of respect in the school between teachers and students, African students report a lack of respect for them as Africans on the part of the Americans, both the students and teachers. The African students also complained about the use of profane language on the part of the American students. Fatou complained: "I don't know why these students curse all the time. They can't say anything without a curse word in the sentence." She had just barely gotten these words out of her mouth when a student just in front of us on the stairs said loudly some of the very profanity she found objectionable.

It surprised the African students how little anyone at Jackson (or in the communities in which the African students reside) seems to know about Africa. They get asked the strangest questions like "Do you have houses?" "Do you have cars?" As one student remarked,

> that's the thing that I don't understand. I think that's crazy, because I think Africa is better than here. Most of the houses here are small compared to what we have back in Africa. If you say you have an eight-bedroom house there, they can't believe that. When I was in Africa I was very happy. The first thing they gonna ask you is where did you live in Africa? When you tell them you lived in a big house and when you tell them that I got everything in my country, they

couldn't believe it.

When asked what they would want Americans to know about them, the most frequent answer was: "We are civilized. We respect ourselves and others. We respect our parents and our teachers. We help each other."

> The first thing I want them to know is that Africa is not a jungle. Second, that people who live in Africa are not animals and third that Africa is a beautiful continent.... I am very proud to be African and I want to let them know that I will defend Africa until the day I die. I will stand up for the rights of all Africans.

Several students commented that they "want Americans to know that Africans are hard-working," "Africans are family." Another pointed out that he has commented to Afro-Americans about how they have all come from Africa, but to his surprise the Afro-American students disagreed with this. Not only did they not agree, it seemed to the African that they were insulted by his comment. He found this difficult to understand but he did not venture another comment like that again.

> Everybody knows that all black people, you know, in earth, come from Africa. That's the first thing. But then black people in this country don't know that they come from Africa. When we told them that they come from Africa, they gonna say "No!"

A common refrain we heard repeated by one African student after another was "I want all Americans to know that African people do not stink." Another African student wrote, "I like my country better than the U.S. My country has many things that are beautiful. Africa is the greatest continent in the world and has many civilizations."

One of the major difficulties for the African students is what they previously were told about America and what they have read or seen in movies or on television.

> When I was back home, my dream was, first of all, to come to America and make a lot of money. Yeh, that was my first thing. But when you are still back home and you hear about America, you think there is everything in America. You think you are going to come here and make easy money, something like that. It's a kind of easy life. Once you arrive you see a lot of things. You're gonna be surprised. You ask yourself if you are really in America. (Michelle)

The remarks about America being the land of plenty, with the streets paved in gold, was not so surprising to us as the naïve expectations shared by one student who related that she had been warned by others that

> The first thing they said is that when you get down off the plane, as soon as you get out into the breeze, the air, you gonna change skin color. Yeah! I was like, what? They said, they don't have a lot of black people in America. They have a lot of white. Yeah, they said the breeze is gonna make your skin change color; you gonna be white. Yeah, that's what they said. When I came here, when I got

off the plane, I was just walking indoor. (She's referring to the fact that getting off the plane is not outside. One is inside one of those moveable connectors to the interior of the airport.) When we were coming out of the airport I said, "Dad, why people lie?" He said, "why?" I said "they told me that when I come here my skin is gonna change." Then he just laughed at me. He said, "Those people invented a lot of stuff. It's not true."

When asked "Why don't some people tell the truth about life in America?" the students explained:

The Africans back home can't understand or believe anything you tell them. If you tell them that America is hard, they can't believe it. They can't believe it because they say "You are here." So anyone who says that he or she wants to come here we have to say, "May God give you a visa." We try to tell them but they don't believe us. (Hamed)

I called my friends after I had been here for three months. They were like, "how you doing?" I said, "you gotta come here. I can't say anything to you guys. You gotta come here and see for yourselves. It's just like a 'secret society.' (In a secret society in Africa one swears never to disclose anything about the society.) You gotta come and see for yourselves because all the people were coming and telling people that not all the way they think about America is how we think. They tell us it's a lie. My father was telling us it was a lie. He was telling us he had to struggle to work hard to get money to pay our school fees. All of us were thinking "why he can't get money?'" Now we know it was a lie. I feel so sorry for my dad. He works so hard. He goes to school and he works so hard. I didn't know that before. (Fatou)

When I sit and think about some of the conditions that they are in here, I ask myself, why is it that some Africans have to leave their country and come and live in some of these conditions. Why do they leave Africa and put themselves in this kind of hardship when they have everything back home. They live in the worst neighborhoods and many people live in the same house, people sleeping all over the house, the living room, every room, sometimes 10 – 15 people in one apartment. There's a whole lot that I see that makes me want to cry. (Michelle)

African American history is actually a misnomer if it is meant to suggest that it is history that is significant only *for* Afro-Americans. While it is *about* Afro-American experiences in America it most definitely is *for* all Americans because it informs an integral part of our common history. African American history was developed to counteract the story told in American schools that is a distortion of American history much like the story of the Native Americans. Native Americans have worked long and hard to change the story told about them. It is still not an accurate representation of their history but those of us who have had the chance to read beyond the classroom have been able to read a more accurate history of Native Americans told from their perspective. It's true of the history of people of African descent. Those of us who have been able to read widely and travel widely have had the chance to see the story of people of African descent from multiple perspectives including continental Africans, descendants of slaves, African immigrants to this country and others. America needs Afro-American history. America needs to know more about Africa. People of African descent need the chance to be connected to all others in the world of African descent. As one African college student said, "Don't let any African tell you that because you were not born on the continent, you are not African. You are African."

Having experienced the reality of life in the U.S., their expectations are not met and this leads to disillusionment. New students in the U.S. need to have some sort of orientation or transitional exposure to the vicissitudes of life and the system of schooling in America as well as what to expect by way of diversity training. They also need to have parental involvement in their education. In Liberia, the PTAs play a major role in education, and most parents are involved in one of these groups. The PTAs actually function as liaisons between the school and the parents and assist the school in disciplining students. Hamed remarked that

> We know where we are from and we know our parents. They don't play with us. They do play but everything that would be a problem that would affect us we in Africa even we are tall and big they tell us what to do. In America it is the same thing for us and I like that too. Parents should tell me what to do. Because I'm too young. I don't know what is good for me. I don't know what is bad. So it's good to have somebody give you advice and tell you what to do. I don't think other kids think that.

New students also need to be able to study their home country, their history, and their continent and be able to focus on their culture, to share this with their American peers. They need a support group to look back at where they have come from, what their goals are and strategies on how to achieve their goals. There needs to be some education about how Americans see them and how they can best maneuver the system. They need to reflect on where they are from and where they are going. To just put them in the system is definitely not working for them. They say violence is in the school. Teachers think that they are bringing the violence with them. Many of the African students have complained about the disrespect of the American students and their use of bad language and yet some of the Africans are mimicking that behavior now. Their parents did not grow up here so they cannot advise them. They don't know what is going on. They think that education in America is the best. They do not know what their children are going through day in and day out.

Perhaps because of some embarrassment, or as a function of some misguided attempt at self-aggrandizement, in their communications regarding the quality of their life in the U.S. some Liberians distort the versions they report to members of their community who have remained in Africa. To impress others, they exaggerate the conditions of their occupations, their housing, and their life here. To remain special to outsiders, America still must appear as the land of the gold-paved roads where everyone's life is a paradise. But being at Jackson and living in the neighboring areas is not the paradise that these Africans imagined they were coming to when their excitement to fulfill their dreams led to the

U.S. If this truly is the American dream then some of them would rather be back home, but because of the war they cannot return. This is what seems to be making the Liberians and Sierra Leonians the most miserable. Other students from Guinea or Senegal talk about going back home. They are here to get their degree but they don't have to stay, in fact they say that they are looking forward to going back. Getting a degree in the U.S. can be prestigious back in their country. It can help them get a good job so they are only here temporarily. Treating their American education in strictly utilitarian terms, they will endure any complications in their life while at Jackson because this is simply a means to a higher end.

A vibrant social life was the norm in most African countries. Everything about community norms was social. Family and friends gathered often. There was time set aside for social gatherings regularly. In this respect, their lives are dramatically altered by many American norms of life in the inner cities. They are afraid to go out. The children are forced to come home straight from school and stay inside. There is no social life as such as it once existed for them so naturally in their home countries.

Liberians and Sierra Leonians have lived with rebel intrusions for more than 10 years, and these became a way of life. Some of the students have retained the rebel behavior. They will not tolerate any injustice no matter how small. They feel the need to speak up. They feel a need to fight back. There is no system of checks and balance now through the parental support network such as there was in the local PTA. The parents are not involved enough. Their survival is still too much at stake to be taking the time to pay attention to what is going on in school or their assumption is that everything is okay.

The students from the war-torn areas do not want to admit their tribe. They know that people were killed because of their tribes so they still do not want to let others know. The tribal conflicts seem to be a problem for them even here. They are reluctant to admit who they are and where they are from. This is definitely an identity problem.

Some of these students felt humiliated and abused by the new culture, the new environment. They also tend to put a lot of blame on the Afro-Americans for the humiliation because they don't know who they are. During conversations, the African students tend to express regret over their expectations of the United States. It definitely isn't what they expected. They said they got most of their expectations of the U.S. from the movies and from their relatives here who didn't give them the true picture of America.

Some students expressed dissatisfaction over the teacher-student relationships at Jackson.[2] They viewed these relationships as biased, preferential, and favoring some students over others. Moreover, there are discipline problems aplenty at Jackson, and the students see the teachers as contributing to these in the way that the teachers mete out discipline. As one student said, if you are playing with the children, they play with you too. And why should you punish them when the students believe that you are the one who started the playing. It is unfair to the students for teachers to be provoking them and then holding them to different standards.

Some of the African students chose not to participate in class because they are afraid of being laughed at by the other students. They feared raising their hands and being called on because they believe they will be ridiculed by their peers if they do. They see themselves as good students who are not given the chance to participate and to show what they can do. Some of the students feel that they are not treated fairly. The students feel that no one will look at what they have studied or what they do know. They are being judged as illiterate because their English level is low. They declare "I've done Physics and Chemistry and yet I am treated as if I am stupid because my English is not yet as developed even though my French is good and I can understand the basic concepts even if I struggle with the language. It's all about English. Nothing much else seems to matter in my education."

In general, the students were very protective of their parents. What they were trying to protect is the key to the problem. The solution lies somewhere in the great unspoken silence that separates those who transition successfully to their new American lives, and those who continue to struggle. If they are unable or unwilling to confront the differences, to break the cycle of attempts to adapt and frustration at the resistance they encounter from Americans, they are going to continuously blame society, the environment, the Afro-Americans for most of their failures of acceptance in this society. The real problem is that the parents cannot support the students. They don't know what they are going through. Their parents are just trying to survive themselves. They come home from work tired and worn out from trying to accomplish their own transitions. They may not be aware of how their children are really doing in school. They can't necessarily help them even if they had the time to help them.

How can these children cope with this education system when it appears disinterested or obstructive to their success? Moreover, it appears to operate as a system designed to prepare these students for the lowest jobs in society simply because their circumstances have landed them in a poor, inner city environment. The students blame the teachers because their parents blame them too. They expect them to teach them all that they need to know. The question is, all that they need to know to do what?

Teachers in Guinea would call the parents or go visit them if there were any problems with their son or daughter. They would be punished if they ever disrespected a teacher or didn't do their homework. The Africans don't understand some of the inherent prejudice of American society, which is based on racial inequality, racial exploitation, and racial humiliation. To most of the people around the rest of the world, the word America means "white" (Howard, 1999). The environment in which they live makes them look at their brothers as the problem. They are in the poor areas and live with their Afro-American brothers and sisters and see them as the ones keeping them down. Africans don't necessarily know anything about Afro-Americans. There are divisions in the groups and there are divisions in the Africans too. One drop of black blood and you are "Black." The children don't know that. They really don't know what to make of American society. All they know is black and white.

Chapter Summary

This chapter provided a description of several highly motivated, intelligent, and resourceful African students who were overwhelmed at the difference in educational quality between the schools they had attended while in their home country and the expectations to be met at Jackson. The lowered academic and behavioral expectations they encountered at Jackson were thwarting their efforts to accomplish all they had aspired to for many years while attending school in Africa. This chapter also investigated the African students' experiences of frustration with the student and teacher attitudes towards Africa and Africans, the negative reactions to their having an accent or having difficulty with English, their desire to work together with their peers on common activities, to help each other as method for facilitating learning. We also explored the students' experiences and the challenges they faced in their efforts to be accepted by their Afro-American peers. The voices of the students articulate their perceptions of the stereotypes many Americans hold about Africans, as well as similar stereotypes the African students harbor regarding Afro-Americans and America in general. The students related how they interacted with their American peers and began to identify ways to rise above the stereotypes and to begin to appreciate their underlying mistaken premises about the Afro-American students.

Similar to the approach presented in this chapter, in Chapter 5 we will profile the select group of Afro-American students who participated in our study. There, the students will describe some of their reasons for electing to discuss their experiences, concerns, and prior interactions with the African students at Jackson, as well as describing the sources for the information they had already about Africa and Africans.

In the next chapter we explicate some of the more common circumstances in which African students first encounter America. This discussion will include an exploration of the circumstances in which they arrive in the U.S., as well as a description of the backgrounds from which they originate. In the next chapter we also describe some of the pernicious, but intractable stereotypes about Africa and Africans that seem to permeate the interactions at Jackson.

CHAPTER 3

Myths and Misperceptions About Africa, or
"I Don't Live in the Jungle"

A person who knows not
And knows not that they know not is foolish - disregard them
A person who knows not
And knows that they know not is simple - teach them
A person who knows not
And believes that they know is dangerous - avoid them
A person who knows
And knows not that they know is asleep - awaken them
A person who knows
And knows that they know is wise - follow them
All of these persons reside in you --
Know Thy Self And To Maat Be True.[1]

As a nation, we remain woefully ignorant about Africa.[2] According to Asante (2003), "[d]espite the fact that a great many African-Americans know next to nothing about African life, Africa is the most prevailing symbol in African-American mythology. Our writers and poets have frequently invoked the sacred name of the continent as a symbol of all our aspirations and strivings" (p. 84). The story of Africa is not yet fully told. The growing presence of students from the continent of Africa at Jackson High proved to be a salutary opportunity for a select group of Afro-American students to discover and renew their connection to Africa, a connection that had been severed long ago, and to affiliate with African students who had previously seemed mysterious and different. For a select group of African students, having the opportunity to interact in some shared positive exchanges with their Afro-American peers created an exciting connection with them across the vast void created by longstanding misperceptions and stereotyping. This connection had not yet been made at school. It required a direct intervention predicated on the theory that the African ideals of community, connection, and respect for others were at the foundation of an inchoate relationship inherent in the African heritage shared by both groups of students. It required the knowledge of the historical connection that existed and a commitment to presenting that connection to the students in a way that touched them in the heart, at an emotional and visceral level, in order to override the prevailing prejudices and misconceptions that had resulted in very strained relations between them previously.

In this chapter we describe some of the enduring misconceptions about Africa that continue to be perpetuated by the American media, in many of our history books, and throughout much of the subject matter taught in our schools. Our discussion will include a brief description of the backgrounds from which the African students originate, paying special attention to their experiences of the education they had before emigrating to this country. Ultimately, here and in later chapters we will attempt to describe the various ways in which both the African and Afro-American students have encountered information about their counterparts in their prior educational experiences, what preconceptions they hold about each other, and how the lack of shared information has contributed to their attitudes. We will explore in Chapter 4 how their refugee or immigrant status may contribute to the ways in which African students experience life in America (Ogbu, 1974). The influence of colonization remains a major influence on the African nations today. As we will discuss in more detail later, the language of origin is an important factor in how these students were educated while in their home countries, as well as how they interact with their Afro-American peers at Jackson.

Although Africa is a continent with more than 50 individual countries, each having its own idiosyncratic governance, social structure, and cultural customs, with more than 1,000 languages and dialects spoken throughout, and with more than 800 million people,[3] Africans share a common worldview that transcends language, ethnicity, and country of origin. Despite the continent's rich and varied heritage, its people have endured a protracted struggle to counteract the overwhelming dominance of Eurocentric ideas, which form the theoretical underpinnings for life in America. Long before the Europeans had discovered its riches, Africa was a continent of many empires with proud and varied histories. However, when the Europeans wrote the story of Africa they told it from their own perspective. In their reporting on the history of the continent, the European colonizers introduced a distorted version of the African worldview.[4] The Europeans saw the Africans as lacking the capacity to develop this glorious continent themselves, and this view better served the Europeans' mercantile, conquering aspirations. There was great economic benefit to labeling the Africans as savages. In fact, what these early Europeans missed, and subsequent Eurocentric histories have overlooked, was that prior to the influx of Europeans into their continent, Africans were living in harmony with their environment (Asante, 1980; Bernal, 1987; Bynum, 1999).

An African worldview is rooted in the ancestors and committed to co-existing in harmony with the earth, the environment, and with every other living creature. In contrast with the European view that the material and the spiritual can be separated, the African sees no distinction between these realms. A pattern of co-existence predominates in the Afrocentric worldview. The colonial view that the world had to be conquered, dominated, controlled is antithetic to an African worldview. For the African, it is the responsibility of the entire community to respect nature and work together for the common good, not individual gain. From this perspective, education is seen as a tool for community development not just personal enrichment. In Cameroon, for instance, as in many countries in Africa, education is characterized as a "potent weapon" in the "battle against hunger, malnutrition, poverty, ignorance and disease" (Luma, 1983, p. xi).

Despite limitations in resources that may be even scarcer in most regions of Africa than in the poorest districts in the United States, most Africans share a thirst for knowledge that brings students to school even when their circumstances are extremely difficult. Students in Africa often overcome great obstacles—long distances walking, inclement weather, sickness, hunger, and much more—and still get to school prepared to dedicate their energies to learning.[5]

The African Educational Systems – Stereotypes and Realities

The educational systems in much of the world were either established by Europeans or modeled on the European system. Education in Africa has been greatly influenced by the colonial powers. Datta (1984) as well as Bray, Clarke, and Stephens (1986) describe the pre-colonial and postcolonial history of education in Africa. Pre-colonial education was the responsibility of the community and did not occur within the confines of a formal schoolroom. Young men and women were trained in the skills necessary to be contributing members of their community. Oral history was passed on from generation to generation. Colonial education, on the other hand, was designed to train low-level workers for the colonial government. It demanded the acquisition of the colonial language and forbade the use of local languages.

Although the commitment to getting an education is strong in Africa, as a group Africans haven't had a culturally appropriate modern education. Boahen (1987) argues that it was "colonial miseducation rather than education" (p. 106). Most Africans have been subjected to a colonial education by the British, French, Portuguese, or Belgians. Furthermore, "[u]niversity education was totally ignored in all the colonies until the 1940s" (ibid.). Their education systems were not designed to empower or educate in the liberatory sense (Freire, 1985, 1997, 1998a, 1998b). The majority of those who attended school were being trained to take low-level jobs (Burns, 1965; Busia, 1968; Woolman, 2001). Those who were educated overseas in the colonial countries were considered for higher-level positions. Not only was an education abroad considered more valuable, but also many Africans with a degree from the United States have been able to move up to more prestigious positions, in some instances in the recent past this would include Ministers or even Heads of State. The education acquired abroad, though, has traditionally come attendant with some serious consequences because those selected were forced to deny everything African and adopt the colonial language, culture, and dress; everything that was African was banned. According to Boahen (1987), the

> most serious negative impact of colonialism has been psychological. This is seen, first, in the creation of a colonial mentality among educated Africans in particular. . . . The final and worst psychological impact has been the generation of a deep feeling of inferiority as well as the loss of a sense of human dignity among Africans. Both complexes were surely the outcome not only of the wholesale condemnation of everything African already referred to but, above all, of the practice of racial discrimination and the constant humiliation and oppression to which Africans were subjected throughout the colonial period. (p. 107)

The situation may have improved significantly since colonialism ended, but remnants of colonialism continue to hold substantial power and influence, particularly in the political structures in most African countries (Boahen, 1987, p. 108; Williams, 1994). Colonialism had a devastating impact on the African continent, although much has been done to restore a sense of pride in African history and culture (Boahen, 1987, p. 111). According to Akbar (1998b), the system of education in most African countries effectively enculturates the population with European history and values in order to ensure the preservation of European culture. Wilson (1993) and Akbar (1998b) have focused attention on the value of coping skills passed from generation to generation, and found that these for the most part are absent from the repertoire of most students of African descent. "In being forced to lose their past, Afrikans are, in effect, forced to lose the priceless wisdom and invaluable coping skills painstakingly accumulated over aeons of trial and error by their ancestors" (Akbar, 1998b, p. 123).

However, despite the recurring attempts through colonialism, slavery, and the Eurocentric educational system to distort or perhaps even eviscerate African history, values, and culture, the African worldview has survived and been passed on both in Africa and the Diaspora (Wright, 2004).[6] Nonetheless, the bitter residue of colonialism and its strains of white supremacy predominate even today in the common image of Africans as savages. Yet, on closer inspection, Africans have much to teach the world, if only we Americans will take the time to listen and learn. They are survivors. Some Africans possess great wisdom; some elders possess great truths. They are connected to the earth and to one another. They have not lost their connection to the essentials in life, to their community. Those of us of European descent have made individualism a sacred icon on whose altar we worship. Africans can recall their ancestors and honor them. The circle of life is yet unbroken in some parts of Africa. The Afrocentric worldview is a welcome alternative to the materialistic view of life.[7] Until very recently, there was little emphasis on exploring any other culture in European/American schools except the dominant culture and its historical interpretation of other cultures and countries. Multiculturalism, when it was tolerated, often involved only a holiday here and there, some exotic clothing and foods and a poster of a hero or symbol of another culture here or there. Murrell (2002) declares that "[s]imply being included in the 'faces, facts, and festivals' approach to multicultural education turns out to be a fancier way of marginalizing children of color" (p. 41).

Moreover, in some instances to focus on "other" cultural values in our schools has been considered to be un-American (Buchanan, 2002). The title of Pat Buchanan's *The Death of the West: How Dying Populations and Immigrant Invasions Imperil Our Country and Civilization* makes this staid position very clear. From an Afrocentric point of view, even those populations that appear to be on their way to extinction, indeed, all immigrant communities, may have something significant and valuable to teach us. We have more to learn; we are not a world unto ourselves. As Cicero remarked many centuries ago, "if you do not know where you come from, you will always be a child" (Goldhill, 2004, p. 5).

Schools in the U.S. for the most part are not designed to educate Africans or Afro-Americans about Africa, their historical and cultural heritage. Almost no student who attends public school is learning much more about Africa except relating to its array of wild animals and its place in global geography. For example, E.D. Hirsch's Core Knowledge kindergarten lesson is typical of what is taught about Africa: Nile River, animals, and Jane Goodall (the white contribution to Africa).[8]

Schools in Africa, originally set up by the colonial masters, have not been educating the African students about their heritage either. These systems were designed with the same enculturation focus, to civilize the savages by bringing them European history and culture. For those with an extended family and elders telling stories, more of their heritage has been available to them, even though it was not taught in school. But nowhere in Africa is the story of the Afro-Americans told. That they are descendants of Africans is obvious to the Africans because of their skin color but they have little or no idea what the Afro-Americans have experienced as a people since their coming to America. Slavery and the Middle Passage as well as the long struggle for Civil Rights on the part of so many Afro-Americans were not taught in any of the schools that the students in this study had attended.

African Students Outside African Schools

Little has been written about the effectiveness of education in Africa; even less has been written about African high school students getting an education in the United States. Meanwhile the number of immigrant students in U.S. schools who hail from the continent of Africa continues to expand. Their presence, while currently seen as negative by many students and even some faculty in the inner-city schools, could be turned into an asset and a benefit leading to increased learning opportunities for all. African high school students, whether in Africa or the United States, are an understudied group. Although very little has been written about the educational system of any of the countries in Africa, what has been published has predominantly focused on the system of education in South Africa.[9]

To our knowledge, there have not been any published studies of African students in American schools. However, there exist several relevant studies of African students educated in Canadian schools. One study of African students conducted in a Francophone (French-speaking) high school in Canada addressed the identity development of continental African students in a school environment that was predominantly white. Ibrahim (1998) developed the concept of racialization or "becoming black" to characterize the experience of African students who discover that in Canada they are categorized in a particular way: The Afro-Canadian students are defined first by the color of their skin. They do not bring with them an understanding of what it means to be Black; they discover what it means.

African students discovered that, given their blackness, they were already imagined, constructed, and thereafter treated as "Blacks"—with the historical memory and representation of blackness in North America which is mostly, if not all, negative. (p. 281)

The African students in this study defined themselves based on popular Black cultural images. Their dress, language, and mode of conduct were modeled after hip-hop images. They became what others assumed them to be. Ibrahim (1998) argues that "African youth . . . are allying themselves with blackness, specifically, after understanding that the effects of racism felt in their everyday life has a long historical memory and trauma" (p. 29). The African students' use of language, in particular, was one way of being seen as Black.

Relying on Ogbu's (1974) theory about the impact of voluntary or involuntary arrival in a new country, Ibrahim argued that African students in Canadian schools displayed elements of both voluntary and involuntary immigrants, the elements of involuntary because they were considered Black, and therefore as lesser members of society, and the elements of voluntary because they know they are not Black in the sense of members of the citizenry with skin of color but rather they are African or Ivoirian or Somalian (Ibrahim, 1998, p. 230).[10] Relevant to this study is a discussion between two students about how lucky they were to know where they actually came from; according to Ibrahim, the students discussed the "rupture of the historical continuity that occurred because of slavery and the slave trade" (p. 230). He argued that it's not knowing where one is from that is sufficient but "more importantly, what kind of historical memories are available that help one to read his or her present social conditions" (p. 230). Ibrahim's study describes how continental African students struggle with identity development in a society that has already defined them based on the color of their skin.

Dei, Mazzucca, McIsaac, and Zine (1997) conducted a study of 150 Black Canadian high school students in a predominantly white school district. According to Dei et al., "Black" included students born in Africa and the Diaspora (p. 28). The students in this study described the various ways in which they felt "pushed out" by the system. "Schools were described by students as hostile places full of interracial tension" (p. 87). One of the suggestions by Black parents to counteract the failure of the public schools was to set up Black-focused schools, which could provide

a more culturally congruent environment, free from racial hostility, stereotypes, and low expectations. In addition, the centrality of African and African-Canadian history, culture and experience focuses intellectual attention on the lived realities of Black students, rather than situating them on the margins of Euro-Canadian history and discourse. (Dei, Mazzucca, McIsaac, & Zine, 1997, p. 187)

Avoiding racism was the prevailing theme. Dis-identifying with being Black is one way that students cope. "The process of 'disidentifying' with the Black community involves adopting the attitudes, behaviors, and characteristics of the dominant society" (p. 244). One student said, "I didn't want to be associated with Black people, with anything that has to do with Africa because . . .

what I hear is all negative things" (p. 244). Another way of coping with racism in school was to resist by engaging in oppositional behaviors such as "truancy, arguing with teachers, and ultimately dropping out as their response to being Black in a predominantly White school system" (p. 238).

A third study, a critical case study of a multi-ethnic suburban school, focuses on the ways in which the various races/ethnicities are represented at school. Ryan (1999) examined the ways in which discourse favors some students and penalizes others. He points to the role of the media and curriculum in perpetuating stereotypes and negative images of people of African descent, in particular. He found that students from the continent of Africa and Native people received the poorest treatment in curriculum resources (p. 126). Not only are students of African descent poorly treated in the curriculum, but Ryan found that the teachers had negative ideas about them as well (p. 103). Almost all of the teachers at this school were of European descent and had not been provided with alternative discourses to the prevailing demeaning images of people of African descent that fill the textbooks and the media. Ryan's challenge to educators is to critique the media and curriculum discourse and "replace oppressive racialized discourses with ones that work in the interests of those not always served well by schools" (p. 22).

Yon (2000) studied a culturally mixed group of students in an inner city high school in Toronto. In contrasting the "melting pot" idealization of the multicultural environments of many American cities (Glazer & Moynihan, 1970; Jacoby, 2004; Nahshon, 2005; Zangwill, 1908), Yon provides a critical exploration of Canada's "cultural mosaic" approach to understanding its complex network of cultures by studying the ways in which culture is perceived as a shifting concept manifested in "the tensions, contradictions, and surprises in the ways youths make culture and identities" (Yon, 2000, p. 21). Identity (personal as well as cultural) is not stable and bounded, as superficial presentation would lead one to suspect, but rather in most contexts it appears "slippery and shifting" and in perpetual evolution (p. 5). In this way of perceiving cultural and ethnic differences, race is seen as a malleable concept that "divides those who belong [within a particular group] from those who are made other" by not being members of the same group (p. 12).

It would be expected that the dynamics of racial categorization for African students would be different in predominantly white than in predominantly black school environments, if only because what was "in" at one school and who became signified as "other" would be determined by the critical mass of a particular group of students. Jackson, the site of our research project, had a predominantly Afro-American student population and manifested all of the issues and challenges that an inner-city school with this composition could expect, such as overcrowding, lack of adequate resources, and environmental stressors not prevalent in schools in more affluent communities.

Said (1993) cautioned us to attend to our interdependence as a world community and he reminded us that we no longer are able to solve the problems of the world without including the world. In Said's terms, we now live in one global environment with a huge number of ecological, economic, social and political pressures tearing at its only dimly perceived, basically uninterpreted and uncomprehended fabric. Anyone with even a vague consciousness of this whole is alarmed at how such remorselessly selfish and narrow interests—patriotism, chauvinism, ethnic, religious, and racial hatreds—can in fact lead to mass destructiveness. The world simply cannot afford this many more times. (Said, 1993, p. 20)

Earlier, Frantz Fanon had provided multiple examples of the damage to the African mindset imposed by colonialism. In *Black skin, white masks*, Fanon describes the black man as self-divided.

The black man has two dimensions. One with his fellows, the other with the white man. A Negro behaves differently with a white man and with another Negro. That this self-division is a direct result of colonialism subjugation is beyond question. . . . No one would dream of doubting that its major artery is fed from the heart of those various theories that have tried to prove that the Negro is a stage in the slow evolution of monkey into man. (Fanon, 1967/1952, p. 17)

Fanon explained that "not only must the black man be black; he must be black in relation to the white man" (p. 110). This experience of duality is related to the "double consciousness" identified initially by DuBois (1986/1903). Fanon forces the reader to face the inhumanity of White supremacy. Blackness has been associated with all that is dark and bad, "evil." Fanon (1967/1952) writes that for many of the so-called civilized people, "Negroes are savages, brutes, illiterates. But in my own mind I knew that these statements were false" (p. 117). One cannot read Fanon without feeling the anguish of the oppression wrought by colonialism as a malicious wrong grievously committed against a large part of humanity.

Asante published his pioneering work *Afrocentricity* in 1980. There he gave a resounding voice to what people of African descent knew intuitively—that there was an incongruence for them between the Eurocentric mindset they were being instructed to adopt and the rich African culture with which they were surrounded. The European colonizers had missed the mark with their descriptions of the Africans. The Africans welcomed strangers, as was their custom; they valued living in harmony with one another and with their environment. They thought the European visitors were honest traders who wanted to strike up a friendship with them. As a theoretical framework and methodology, Afrocentricity is crucial to understanding persons of African descent because it is through the Afrocentric lens that the ideas, values and experiences of people of African descent can best be understood. Asante (1990) reminds us that for most of modern history, Africa and Africans have been defined and presented through a Eurocentric lens. "Africa was seen as marginal, uncivilized and on the periphery of historical consciousness" (p. 119). Europeans justified colonialism on the basis that the Africans were savages who had not learned to conquer their environment. Wilson (1993) used the term "amnesia" to explain what has happened to Black identity as a consequence of colonialism.

White supremacy is to a large extent founded on the social amnesia of subordinate Blacks. The ruling White supremacist needs to deprive a massive Afrikan
population of a common cultural platform from whence to mount a collective
counterattack against its domination and requires that it negates their common
Afrikan identity, cultural, historical memories and related practices. . . . The subordinate Afrikan can only be what he needs to be for dominant Whites if he has
no true knowledge of who he is and how he came to be who he is. This requires
that he not remember who he truly was. . . . The reclamation of their true history,
cultural continuity and unalloyed identity by Afrikans would precipitate the ruin-
ous collapse of White hegemony. (pp. 121-122)

Asante (1998a) has argued that any analysis of people of African descent
must focus on people as subjects and not objects. He writes: "Afrocentricity
offers hope for actualizing the masses of Americans around the idea of African
peoples as subjects rather than as objects" (p. 43). Afrocentricity is "placing
African ideals at the center of any analysis of African culture and behavior" (p.
2). We discuss Afrocentricity in more detail in Chapters 6 and 7, but for now its
influence on the evolving educational systems in Africa, and even in some
American schools, will be the focus of the remainder of the present chapter.

Jarrett (1996), Keto (1994), Serequeberhan (2000), wa Thiong'o (1986),
and, most tellingly, Achebe in *Things fall apart* and Soyinka in *Death and the
king's horseman*, all have described the pernicious effects of colonialism. Keto
(1994) argues, for example, that "Africans are not and cannot be peripheral
dwellers in somebody else's unfolding historical panorama" (p. 12), and "the
Africa centered perspective provides the type of history for people of African
descent that makes sense of what they, rather than somebody else, went through
first" (p. 121). According to Harris (1998), the concepts of freedom and literacy
are central to African and Afro-American life in a way that differs significantly
from the Eurocentric characterizations of these terms. Harris defines freedom as
the "ability to conceptualize the world in ways continuous with one's history"
and literacy means "the application of historical knowledge" (p. 16). For the
African and the Afro-American, the difficulty with expressing or living this way
of perceiving freedom and literacy lies in general denial of their history by
Eurocentric scholarship. Even though many are beginning to recognize the importance of Africa, African philosophy and African history, "the fundamental
antagonism of Whites toward Africans, be they on the continent or in the diaspora, has not altered over time" (p. 17). Harris argues that one can only be free
in the Afrocentric context when one is knowledgeable about who one is and
from where one has come. It is doubtful that mainstream media today is the best
history teacher of an Afrocentric perspective; nor, indeed, are our schools.

The goal of redefining freedom is to provide "a basis for the African-
American consciousness to merge with the best traditions in African and Afro-
American culture in order to more fully contribute to the forward flow of human
history" (p. 17). Harris follows Asante's guidelines for Afrocentricity in which
harmony is the ultimate goal and a "mighty victorious consciousness" is key.
As Asante (1988) postulates: "Know your history and you will always be wise"

(p. 51). Freedom and literacy for people of African descent must be based in an Afrocentric epistemology and a communal ontology. One characteristic of the Afrocentric epistemology is "transcendent order in the world" (p. 21) which combines history, intuition and immersion and which recognizes the spiritual in the worldly. For true freedom to exist, people of African descent cannot rely on the interpretation of freedom, such as the right to vote, etc., but must focus on the inner change. In order for there to be true freedom for people of African descent they must free themselves from a Eurocentric perspective and construct their identity based in African philosophical thought.

In Africa, young men and women were trained in the skills necessary to be contributing members of their community. Oral history was passed on from generation to generation. Colonial education, on the other hand, was designed to train low-level workers for the colonial government. It demanded the acquisition of the colonial language and forbade the use of local languages. The first formal schools in Africa were set up by the missionaries with the very specific objective to bring people to God, to convert the heathens to Christianity and colonial culture. Post-colonial education was largely an attempt to recuperate from the colonial system and find ways to preserve the cultural heritage just about destroyed from the colonial attempt to extirpate it.

African Students in American Schools

In many respects, the African students at Jackson were seen by the Afro-American students as being very different from them. Although similar in color of their skin, the African students talked different, dressed different, and behaved different. But this difference was not constructed as neutral or benign. Rather, it arose from negative stereotypes. As a stereotype, the jungle image seems intractable and inescapable, a distorted perception that abides in the minds of many Americans. Sadly, the images of the jungle and the savages who are believed to live there are alive and well at Jackson. Saturday mornings you can still find Tarzan in a cartoon on television swinging from tree to tree in the African jungle. Because the term most often identified by the students in connection to Africa was "jungle," and assorted words such as "trees," "forest," "animals," and "savages," the jungle stereotype was a salient reminder of the gulf that separated the African and Afro-American students. In the initial interviews in this study, the African students were asked to describe how they are seen by Afro-Americans. One African male expressed his anger at the way Americans talked about Africa.

> Inter.: And what were some of the things they said about Africa?
> Musa: I don't think I can remember but I don't know, like certain things such as, "in Africa you don't wear shoes," "you spend the night with animals," stuff like that. There were worse things probably, but I don't remember.

Demeaning stereotypes are never easy to overcome. LB's voice was agitated when he talked about the inane questions he had been asked and the underlying assumptions that people were making about Africa. Again and again the African students would say, "We are not from the jungle. We do not live in trees." One African female student explained it this way:

> Inter.: How would you describe the relationship between Africans and Afro-Americans at Jackson?
> Aminata: It's not working well with me. Because, it's like, when you come and tell them that you are from Africa, they actually ask you if you were living in trees, or you're living in a jungle, but it's not true. Whatever they do here, we do that back home.
> Inter.: Anything else?
> Aminata: We live a better life at home, it's just the war. That's why people come here. If it's not for war, I would like to stay back home.

That an African would prefer to live in Africa was inconceivable to the Afro-American students. The negative images promote the idea that the Africans should be grateful to be here. But many are not. BS would like the Afro-American students to understand that she had a good life back in Africa and if it wasn't for the war she would still be there. She was happy and had everything that she needed. "Whatever they do here" is what she could do back home before the war. Only the war caused her to come here. Except for the war she would never have left especially now that she has experienced America with her own eyes. Many hope to return.

When they were asked to describe how the African students interacted with the Afro-American students, one Afro-American male student commented directly:

> Antoine: Some of them, they want to kill em.
> Inter.: Do you know why?
> Antoine: Because we ignorant and rude sometimes. Children can be ignorant and rude, that's the only way I put it. I mean, I've seen a couple of Africans try to stab a couple of American boys and stuff in the lunch room, try to stab them with a fork and everything. It's like, like they have no mercy, they try to kill you the quickest. I mean this boy was trying to kill this kid because he said something smart to him. I was like, damn, no reason to be killing anybody, but that's the way they think, I guess. I don't know. A lot of people, a lot of them be saying, if you mess with them, they kill you. That's why nobody mess with an African boy. Most of them are big, big men. They come in all different shapes and sizes but they all stick together, that's what they do. They go straight to the big one and they bring in the big one, and you gotta' either fight that boy or you gonna' get pounded straight down to the ground real bad. Just like, when it comes to Africa, it's like they put on different fight than we are, because we Americans and they Africans.

The stereotypes of the jungle and uncorralled, wild animals make the African students look like inveterate killers to the Afro-Americans. Under this distorted perception, a fork can appear to be a serious weapon when the false image behind that fork is someone who slits chickens' throats and humans' throats with ease on a daily basis to survive. It is a small step from these negative stereotyped images to the place where verbal insults can escalate more easily thanks to these images of the Africans as savages.

In addition to the jungle stereotype, there are other misperceptions about African and Afro-American behavior and attitude that contribute to their relating poorly to one another. Some of the images of Afro-Americans as expressed by the Africans included welfare, crime, lack of knowledge of their roots and jealousy. Fanta, an African female, described the images she had of America and Afro-Americans before coming here and then what she discovered upon her arrival.

> When I was in Liberia, all I ever heard about America was like this is a beautiful country. I love this place, but I mean, I see people lying on the streets when I came here. I knew a lot of crime and violence scenes were going on here too. I see some people and people, yeah, it just was, they're not serious because like, some people depend on welfare to do everything for them; they don't want to get a job or anything.

The Afro-Americans talked about their belief that the African students behave like they think they are better than others. The stereotyping and misperceptions were from both sides.

Another factor that keeps the students apart is how the students are treated by the teachers and the administration. Several Afro-American students noted that the teachers seem to prefer the African students while some African students complained that the non-teaching assistants ("NTAs"), some teachers and the School Police seem to favor the Afro-Americans. Several teachers commented that they enjoy, some used the word "prefer" having the foreign students in the classes because they say the immigrant students seem to want to learn. One teacher admitted that she favors the African students because they are so polite and greet her with a smile every morning. A Teaching Assistant said that the Afro-Americans, in general, do not act like they care about getting an education, whereas the foreign students seem to want to get an education and are willing to do the work. In several classes that I observed only the foreign students had done the homework. Fanta, an African female, says that the Afro-American students are jealous of the Africans. Everyone mentioned that the Afro-Americans do not know who they are and therefore are jealous of the Africans because they know who they are. This was mentioned by the principal, some of the teachers and also, by some of the Afro-American students as well.

Fanta points out that she thinks that the other students say mean things because they are jealous and yet, that cultural and historical knowledge brings with it some mandates such as respect. She explained that one major difference between the African and Americans was the age of adulthood. Turning 18 does not hold the same privilege in Africa as it does in America and an African child no matter how old may never be disrespectful to a teacher, parent or elder. This difference sets them apart and sets up a precarious comparison that makes the Africans look "good" and the Afro-Americans look "bad," in particular with the teachers. Teachers hold a place of respect in most African societies. No matter one's age, no one has the right to be disrespectful to an elder.

Inter.: What has been your experience with the Afro-American students?

Fanta: I think that they're just jealous because, you know, we don't look like them, we don't act like them, we act like Liberians, or other Africans here. Most of us, we like, we different, so sometimes they be jealous and they say mean things.

Inter.: How are you different?

Fanta: I'm different cause I don't act like them. I try to speak like them, but not actually and I'm really different. I believe in myself and I'm setting one goal to achieve that and I'm trying to stick to that. But most people here, they don't do that. When we are 18 and stuff, we know we older but we don't take our self, at 18, you know, as someone being very big. Parents be talking to them, and they be like, "Oh get out of my face." Excuse me for that expression, but they are 18 and they can do whatever they want. And they say all that stuff, so, that's how I am not like them. My mom says do something and I do it and I'm 18, but I don't want to be rude and doing stuff like going out all the time and all that stuff.

In general, students from the continent are seen as more respectful by themselves and by the teachers. Knowing where you are from is the explanation given by one of the students for why the African students are seen as better behaved.

There were many instances when students talked about who might be jealous and why. It's obvious to the students that some teachers prefer the African students. They are preferred because, in general, they do their homework, hand in their assignments, participate in class, ask for extra help, stay after school or come during the advisory period for help, ask questions, and are obviously struggling. Several of the teachers described their respect and appreciation for the African students in their classes.

There are, however, some major exceptions to the student behaviors that met with approbation by teachers. For most African students, an American education still seems like a valuable undertaking, but not for all of them. Some of the African students have given up. Their frustration with the school, their peers, their teachers, the class work, the mistreatment they must endure, the lack of connection between what transpires at school and the rest of their lives has become so untenable that they are either resisting and getting suspended, or quitting school altogether.

There is a growing population of recently arrived African adolescents who are dropping out of school. Teenage girls are becoming pregnant; both males and females are turning to selling and using drugs; others are getting low-paying jobs and trying to make a living. Some of the African students who had started at Jackson are now in jail, on drugs, prostituting themselves on the street or falling into a whole host of other street activities found in our major urban areas. With these lamentable outcomes, it is not the mythos of the high quality of American education that has predominated in the lives of these unfortunate African students but rather the insidious influence of the American dream gone sour.

Chapter Summary

In this chapter we described some of the circumstances in which African students first encounter America. This included a brief explanation of when, where, and how they arrived in this country, and a delineation of the educational backgrounds that they brought with them from their home countries.

In the next chapter we delineate some of the salient misconceptions about America that many African students initially develop through the media representations in their home country. America as the "Land of the Free and the Home of the Brave" and the "Land of Opportunity" were perhaps once relevant slogans to encourage immigrants to venture to our shores, but these no longer apply for a significant proportion of the immigrant population. Unmet expectations lead to disappointment and consternation for those who embark on their pilgrimage to America hoping for a better future for themselves and their children, which becomes especially frustrating when the stark reality is so different for many immigrants of color.

CHAPTER 4

Expectations and Disappointments: Immigrant Life in America – Better Education, Better Life, and "The Streets Are Paved with Gold!"

We now explore some of the typical conditions of American life that African students first encounter on their arrival in this country. In this chapter we delineate some of the salient misconceptions about America that many African students initially develop while in their home country through the media representations that epitomize the American way of life. Images and stories extolling the attractions of America as the "Land of the Free and the Home of the Brave" and the "Land of Opportunity" perhaps once induced optimistic and progressive emigration to this country, but these aphoristic phrases no longer convey the reality experienced by a substantial proportion of our immigrant population.

Immigrants historically have encountered varying degrees of opposition to their transition from their home of origin to the U.S. (Gerstle, 2001; Jacobson, 1998; King, 2000). The American "melting pot" approach embodies inherently racist features by advocating assimilation and acculturation into American mores in an effort to yield a more homogeneous society. Under this mantle of purchasing harmony at the expense of reality, those who adamantly insist on assimilation inadvertently, or even sometimes directly, demean, exclude, or discount valuable contributions that might be made by those perceived to be different or strange.

Educating the young has always been perceived as the most efficient method for promoting and extending the values and norms of a given culture. This rationale has applied to public education in the U.S. almost from the founding of our nation, although originally reserved for children of the landed gentry (Best, 1962; Franklin, 1987, pp. 323-344). In the mid-seventeenth century, the commonwealth of Massachusetts became "the first jurisdiction in history to require universal primary education. . . . But the purpose of education was to train orthodox ministers and indoctrinate law people" (McDougall, 2004, p. 60). The American system of public education was greatly expanded in the latter part of the 19th and early part of the 20th century specifically to accommodate and to ensure assimilation into the American way of life for the latest wave of immigrants from Europe, and in response to the demands by newly freed slaves (Katz, 1995; Tyack, 2003, 1974). According to DuBois (1972/1935), the "first great mass movement for public education at the expense of the state, in the South, came from Negroes" (p. 638). Moreover, DuBois has shown that the "public school systems, in most Southern states, began with the enfranchisement of the Negro" (p. 648-649).

Yet, over the course of our history not all those who have arrived in America have arrived as willing newcomers. For instance, some were forced to come here originally as slaves, and racism against newcomers and those unlike the

Americans already in this country has been a perennial obstacle to the full participation of various ethnic groups, including the indigenous populations (Ogbu, 2003). Although legislation and various court decisions, such as *Brown vs. Board of Education* and its progeny,[1] have attempted to mandate an equal education for all, race remains a key factor in determining the allocation of resources that exists today in our urban centers and their schools[2] (Williams, 2003). To be African in America today is to be Black, and to be Black still means, for most persons of color, to have access to fewer resources, especially in our inner-city schools (Perry, Steele, & Hilliard, 2003). To be Black means that the story told in our public schools makes you, by dint of the color of skin alone, an outsider.

American textbooks are silent or, what is far more debilitating in its impact, derogatory about both Africa and Afro-Americans and their history and culture. As discussed in the previous chapter, for many Africans, to be an educated person is the most important thing in life. Belief in the inherent value of education is commonly held by most African students and they must confront almost immediately an apparent contradictory feeling about the purposes of education that is rampant in many American inner city schools.

The "American Dream" and the Expectations of Africans

Despite some recent sobering events, the myth of America as the land of the free remains very much alive in many parts of the globe.[3] One characteristic that historically has induced a positive image of America as the land of democracy is the belief that in America we enjoy universal suffrage, or we at least espouse this as the ideal. American exceptionalism is predicated on a number of the democratic principles that make immigrating here so appealing to people who do not enjoy some of the privileges and freedoms most Americans take for granted. However, even Americans may have come to realize that universal suffrage is a chimera, and our adherence to democratic principles waxes and wanes with the times and we share our space with more or fewer others depending upon how secure we feel about our own access to the privileged life we have become accustomed to possessing or expecting to happen for us.

In their homeland, the African students learned very little about the realities of American life. Some had learned all they knew from imported American television and movies; some knew only that their families believed coming to America for their education was the best opportunity for them. Three of the African students interviewed for this study could play video tapes at home and they had family members here in the U.S. who sent them American films. In almost every case, America was still seen as the paragon of freedom and economic achievement and the myth of the American Dream lives on in the imaginations of all of the African students. They are looking for a better future, and they hope that America will prove worthy of its invitation on the Statue of Liberty. One student declared that "America is the land of opportunity. It is free. Everybody is kind. They say it's the land of freedom." Several African students commented that although America was the land of opportunity there were restrictions or limitations to the opportunities they might find here. When asked how he had learned about America, Amadou explained that his ideas about America came first from American movies.

> I used to watch movies. I got a lot of ideas about America from my family and from the movies. I could tell from the movies that there was a lot of ignorance. I've learned things since I came here.

High expectations about improving the quality of their existence by moving to America can lead to disillusionment and disappointment for many immigrants when reality replaces anticipation and diverges dramatically. Many African students thought America was going to be perfect but instead discovered drastic discrepancies from the picture perfect postcard images that they had in their minds or the projected promised land they heard described by their friends.

> Inter.: What was in your mind before coming here?
> Fanta: I thought it was gonna be a good and happy life.
> Inter.: Is everything okay, the way you expected it?
> Fanta: Not really. I can't seem to find the America I thought I was going to find. It's hard here.

How can America, the land of opportunity, the land of satellite communication, be promoting such antiquated images of Africa and Africans?[4] Today, children can watch Tarzan on cartoon and laugh at the struggles he faces in the jungle. Even one of the "Survivor" television programs, so-called "reality TV," showed only the barren land of their selected site in East Africa, the dangerous animals threatening them at night, the hospital with the AIDS patients and the exchange of the goat for French fries. This show did nothing to combat the stereotypes; it strongly reinforced them. The media continue to play a major role in the development of the negative images of Africa, Africans, and Afro-Americans. Demeaning stereotypes are perpetuated by all avenues of the media, and these get carried over into our schools (Entman & Rojecki, 2000; Harris, 2003; Holtzman, 2001; Kellstedt, 2003; Lasch-Quinn, 2001; McGowan, 2001; Pollock, 2004). Nowhere could the students find positive images of one another or the story of their shared history and culture.

At the same time, the images of Afro-Americans to which the African students are exposed before they arrive in the U.S. are overwhelmingly negative and do not inspire them initially to affiliate with their Afro-American peers. The demeaning stereotypes about Afro-Americans disseminated by the American media are widespread, and unwittingly believed, throughout the world. The images of gang members with tattoos and sneers, the Black male youth with a discharged weapon in hand are shown on television and in movie theatres as far away as the continent of Africa.

The prevailing image of the black youth is the hoodlum, the gang member, the stereotype of the inner city black males most common in America. To many Americans, all black youths are dangerous thugs ready to pounce and shoot and ask questions later (Cashin, 2004). These negative stereotypes are prevalent not only in the culture at large, where their impact is mainly deleterious to the stereotyped group, but they also influence the perceptions the African students have about the Afro-American students. Such negative stereotypes keep the students from seeing one another in any positive way. African students could be overheard regularly complaining about the Afro-Americans. These complaints included comments about their American counterparts being rude, ignorant and violent, or as illustrated in the terse summation by Valeisha, "they're nothing."

> I've noticed that there is still a lot of negativity going on cause I was walking in the hallway and I just happened to be walking by two African students and one was saying, "The Americans are nothing. We're better than Americans." And you know I can understand why she thinks that way because you know a lot of students in this school don't appreciate the Africans. But you can't walk around in the hallways talking like there's nobody around because you know not everybody feels that way. And I felt some type of way because she was stereotyping me with the people that she associates with or the people that do things to her. And that was right before I came to this meeting. So I just looked at her whatever and I just kept on walking. I was like you can't change everybody's mind. So I just left it at that and I just kept going on my merry way.

Several times, African students were overheard saying that the Afro-American students "don't know who they are or where they are from." The students had no outlet, no context for these hurtful remarks when they occurred. The negative images and remarks only served to keep the two groups apart.

African students who act out in school are considered by other Africans to be "trying to be American" and are looked down upon by their peers. Disparaging remarks could be heard almost daily about several African male and female students who according to their peers were disrespectful and not serious about school. Teachers could also be overheard complaining about them and saying many of the same things such as "He's just acting Black" of "He's getting too Americanized." Haja, an African female, talks about her little sister who has been here since she was much younger and has not had as many years back in Africa. "My younger sister is really Americanized. She's loud and obnoxious. The influence of her friends is rubbing off on her and she acts more American." No one is jealous of those who act out. They are scorned by the Africans and laughed at by the Afro-Americans. The misperceptions serve as barriers and prevent the African and Afro-American students from coming together.

Reality and Disappointment for the African Students

The majority of the African students were not as well prepared for what they found as compared to what they anticipated finding. Aliya said she honestly was shocked to see Americans whose skin color was similar to her own. She had believed that all Americans were white and seriously worried that she would turn white when she stepped out of the plane in New York City. For many of the African students, life in America was very different than they had imagined it would be.

As Fanta explained in Chapter 3, she was surprised to find in America so many people who are homeless, a fact which points to an obvious anomaly in how America is presented in the media as "perfect." She did not expect to see homelessness or "ghettoes" in America. Two oppressive facts about life in contemporary America are the growing poverty of our urban centers and the "massive educational failure of the inner-city schools" (Labov, 1982, p. 148). Basically, urban schools function at the lowest rung of the publicly funded educational programs provided in the U.S. (Kozol, 1991). Many Africans who arrive in America end up in the inner-city, where they join the ranks of the Black underclass.[5] Tragically, our public schools generally are failing Black children whether they are African, Afro-American, Caribbean American, or other children of African descent. There is a great deal of research documenting the "Black-White Achievement Gap" (Hale, 2001; Thernstrom & Thernstrom, 1997, 2003). According to Reid (2001), "the 'achievement gap' has bedeviled the nation's schools for decades" (p. 13). Indeed, it seems almost daily that experts present new strategies to combat the achievement gap that exists for minority students who lag significantly behind their white classmates in almost all academic areas.[6] There are increasing data on the ways in which public schools fail to teach Black children effectively because teachers and school administrators do not understand the unique needs and learning styles of children of African descent, have low expectations of students of color, and fail to connect schooling to their home experiences. Consequently, public schools are unable to provide these children with culturally appropriate teachers, methods, curriculum, and materials, despite significant data confirming the major difference these ingredients make in the lives and education of these youngsters (Delpit, 1995; Gay, 2000; Hale, 1994, 2001; Hale-Benson, 1982, 1986; Irvine, 1990; Ladson-Billings, 1994). Former U.S. Secretary of Education Roderick R. Paige once declared that there is urgency involved in making our classrooms safer, in equipping each child with reading and math skills, and in closing the inexcusable achievement gap that exists among students attending public schools across this country, particularly among minority students and economically disadvantaged students. (Roach, 2001, p. 24)

Rothstein (1994) painted a very grim picture of the educational environment of inner city schools, one that regrettably remains quite contemporary for many immigrant students:

> The overly corrective education of the poor, the constant efforts at moral suasion and thought control, the most insistent demands that students remain immobile and quiet—these are all part of the transformation purposes of state schools. The children of the immigrant and poor find failure a constant companion. (p. 169)

Many immigrants in the U.S. must enroll their children at the public schools in the poorest neighborhoods. Some immigrants arrive in this country financially more secure or with family connections and consequently they may be able to move into better neighborhoods. For those who come to this country as refugees of war or without significant financial support, the poorer, inner-city neighborhoods may be their only option. They can only afford housing in the poorest neighborhoods. In the case of the neighborhoods surrounding Jackson High, of the two dominant groups of immigrants most of the Asian population in the neighborhood has moved or is planning to move to the suburbs, while, for a variety of socioeconomic reasons, the Africans find such mobility very difficult (Cashin, 2004). Moreover, due to the inescapable identifications resulting from the color of their skin, African immigrants find some forms of American racism their constant nemesis. It is certain that the options they have available to them in housing and employment are limited by entrenched racism.[7] Many of the African men living in poor neighborhoods, when they are lucky enough to find jobs, work in parking garages while the fortunate African women work in fast food preparation or as nursing home aides. These may be the best jobs open to the African adults, even though frequently they already possess a college education accomplished in their home country.[8]

Tactics for Engaging African Students

Gay (2000) argues for culturally responsive teaching based on five premises for improving the school performance of students of color: a) culture counts—education is a socio-cultural process and demands an understanding and appreciation of culture; b) conventional reform is inadequate—to date, education reform have attempted to address issues of student achievement by "divorcing it from other factors that affect achievement," such as ethnicity, culture, environment, and experience; c) intention, no matter how beneficent, without action is insufficient—being "color blind" is not the same as being culturally responsive; d) the strength and vitality of cultural diversity should be seen as positive factors; and, for the most part, e) test scores and grades are symptoms, not causes of achievement problems—in other words, blaming minority students, without searching for additional contributing factors in addition to individual effort, does not contribute to improving student achievement in the least (p. 12). Gay argues that "both immigrant and native-born students of color may also encounter prejudices, stereotyping, and racism that have negative impacts on their self-esteem, mental health, and academic achievement" (p. 18).

Akbar (1998b) builds on the work of Carter G. Woodson's *MisEducation of the Negro* to show how miseducation is still occurring in schools and in society today and how its foundation is the cultivation of an "alien" identity (p. 5). Akbar writes profoundly of the role of education as a vehicle for transmission of self-knowledge, a legacy of competence, acquired immunities to the negative vicissitudes of life, and a shared positive vision of cultural heritage. He argues convincingly that the dominant culture has set up a system that meets its primary needs of continued dominance by using the values of education instilled in the white community and their purposes for education. Akbar points out that the same system cannot meet the needs of the people of African descent because it has omitted, and much worse negated, their productive history. The liberation of people of African descent requires an education designed to teach the African ontological and cosmological understandings of the universe—inclusive, responsive and interconnected—and to teach the shared history and ways in which the African cultures have been preserved and maintained despite oppression and suppression. The presence of African students in a school could support the learning of this history that has been ignored, the history of the continent of Africa and its peoples.

For years, many African families may have struggled against great hardships in the hope of allowing their children to be educated in the United States. Some have paved the way by emigrating first in an effort to establish a stable home for their children in this country. One African father we interviewed, the father of six, related how much he had sacrificed financially and emotionally to bring his children here to get an education. After arriving in this country alone, he worked nights for many years at a parking garage and took courses during the day to complete his college degree. He did this with the sole objective of eventually bringing his children to America for a better education. After long delay, his children having finally arrived, he ultimately was deeply disappointed about what was happening to them while they were in their "good" American school. He was concerned that his children were rapidly losing their African values and acquiring many that he found unacceptable. His children now showed disrespect for their elders, which would have been unthinkable back home in Africa. Worse yet, his children showed no evidence that they were learning anything worthwhile in school.

This proud and self-sacrificing father had come to feel that his children were wasting their time in school and that they had nothing valuable at this point to show for all of the effort he had expended to provide an American education for them. Nevertheless, he still clung tenaciously to the belief that an American education is worth so much more to his children's future than the education they would have had in his country. He staunchly believes this without any actual experience of what is happening in his children's classrooms. His children attend urban public schools with all the challenges that are endemic to many urban schools. While in school, moreover, his children are mocked, teased, and experience almost daily humiliations. This father is chagrined because this cannot be the high quality education he had anticipated for his children, when even the school social climate robs them of their peace of mind.

African students have been relegated to the lowest status group at the school and are at best ignored and, at worst, attacked by their peers. These youngsters either become more and more invisible, or more and more aggressive in reacting to this mistreatment; their reactive aggression can result in their getting disciplined. Should this occur, they risk getting further disciplined at home by their parents or guardians for having been disrespectful in school. This is because in African societies, teachers, as with all elders, are to be treated with respect.

Moreover, as discussed in Chapter 2, a vital sense of a vibrant community is endemic in most African countries, but this same spirit of community has not fared well in its transfer to inner-city school environments of the U.S. One of the African students described her discomfort in disheartening detail.

Inter.: How did you feel when you came here?

Aliya: As far as that, I feel bad, I was like Oh my God, this is America. I don't like it here. I want to go back. Then sometimes I was just like this, I want to see my mom. I cried every day but now I'm getting used to it. I still want to go back though.

Inter.: What made it difficult when you first came?

Aliya: I was just home by myself. Then I would go to school at the Newcomer Center. It's okay there but when we would go upstairs for lunch, the students they'd be like laughing at us when we were talking. They said if you have an accent they gonna laugh at you. They said bad things about us. They made us feel so bad.

All of the African students we encountered expressed a strong desire to return home to be with their family and friends they left behind in Africa. Here in the U.S. they are separated from their community by doors, streets, and highways, a fear of crime and the other inescapable day-to-day realities of poverty. Living in poverty brings the pressure on many immigrant parents to work long hours to make ends meet. The African parents spend most of their energies working at parking garages on night duty or at nursing homes for 12-hour shifts. There is little time left to spend with their children. It takes an enormous effort just to survive and they are bereft of the community support that they had back home. In most African societies, even those entrenched in seemingly perpetual war, there is an extended family that provides support. For those Africans, especially those who are refugees in America, the extended family support no longer exists. The reality of poverty in America can lead to disappointment and disillusionment for many Africans. For those Africans living in poverty, the high expectations of achieving the American dream go unfulfilled.

Ogbu's Cultural-Ecological Theory of School Performance

John Ogbu (1974) has studied the differences in school performance between dominant group students and minority students. Over the course of several decades of research, Ogbu developed a system of classification of minority groups as "involuntary" or "voluntary." Voluntary immigrants are expected to experience less difficulty assimilating into their new culture because they have chosen to come to the U.S., and they are willing to adapt to the anticipated difficulties transitioning into this new culture. Because they voluntarily emigrate, and because they have the option of returning to their place of origin, they often are able to adjust to their new environs without feeling compelled to relinquish their cultural roots (Waters, 1999).

In contrast, Ogbu has characterized the involuntary minority groups as "castelike" (Ogbu, 1974). Those who were forced to come to the U.S. experience much greater difficulty assimilating. For descendents of the slaves who were forced here, it is even more complicated because of the tortured history of oppression wrought by slavery (Ogbu, 2003). For some involuntary minority students, school is seen as an institution that reproduces the dominant, white culture, and education therefore represents a recapitulation of one means of continuing with oppression.

Ogbu has argued that until inner-city Afro-American students see viable economic alternatives that result from having an education they will continue to resist the educational process. Although some of the African students would fit into the voluntary immigrant category, and others in a separate category that Ogbu calls "refugee," their ability to assimilate is restricted by the color of their skin. Their ability to assimilate is also restricted by their accent. They can't be white; they don't want to be Black with all its negative connotations and oppressive stereotyping.

In a series of articles and books, Ogbu (1991, 1992, 1994a, 1994b, 1998, 2003) has explained that there several factors that may impact on the school performance of Afro-Americans and other non-immigrant students. These factors include: (a) their frame of reference; (b) the surrounding community's folk theory about how one advances in society and the role education plays in the paths to advancement; (c) relationship with the system; and (d) issues of collective identity, cultural and language differences, and alternative frames of reference. Each of these factors can dramatically impact a youngster's relationship with American education, and they exist independent of any additional effect from how the individual student is treated by the school or by the wider society. According to Ogbu and Simons (1998), the two main components necessary to effectively redress the problem of minority schooling are remediating the deficiencies presently in the system and bringing the system into alignment with positive community forces (p. 156). Ogbu and Simons have asserted that "race has its own unique influence on the school experiences and outcomes of black children and similar minorities which is not explained by reference to socioeconomic factors or class struggle" (p. 164).

Which classification applies to a specific minority is determined more by the history of that group's presence in America. "Involuntary (nonimmigrant) minorities are people who have been conquered, colonized, or enslaved" (Ogbu & Simons, 1998, p. 165). In Ogbu's schema, both Africans and Afro-Americans fit in the involuntary category of the colonized and yet they do not have access to any shared experiences about the colonization or its aftermath. The students for the most part only identify with what separates or distinguishes them. When they began to dialogue as part of the present study they started to see each other in a new light. This light is a connection based upon their shared heritage and this puts them on common ground.

Fordham (1987, 1996) describes the enormous price that Black students often must pay to succeed in school. According to Fordham (1987), immigrant students of color "who minimize their connection to the indigenous culture and assimilate into the school culture improve their chances of succeeding in school" (p. 57). Racelessness or becoming un-black is hallmark of this strategy and the students who adopt this approach in an effort to fit in often get accused of "acting white" and then are ostracized by their peers (Fordham & Ogbu, 1986). School is seen as a site of oppression; those who play the game successfully are perceived to be selling out as "student-halfies" (Fordham, 1996, p. 327). Fordham points out that many schools make no effort to help their minority students of color to "reclaim and reconfigure their African humanness" (ibid.). She accuses the administration and teaching staff at a predominantly black school in our nation's capital of deliberately steering "clear of any perspective that might help matriculating students understand how and why their African ancestors' humanness was appropriated, mutilated, and reconstructed" (ibid.). Without their humanness, where can these students go for rejuvenation and affective relationships? The coming together of African and Afro-American students around their shared history could support members of both groups in seeing their success in education as a critical part of the continued mutual struggle for equality.

O'Connor (1997) interviewed six high achieving Afro-American female students who were neither resisting nor "acting white." They were succeeding in school as a form of struggle against the "institutionalized racism that Afro-Americans confront" (p. 611). Their success was a part of a greater struggle. They did not minimize the racism nor consider it insurmountable. Mickelson (1990) initially found Afro-American students to be positive about school, but ultimately found that although the students would talk about positive expectations of schooling in the abstract, their ordinary conversations or concrete experiences did not support those abstract views.

Adolescence is a time of major identity development and African and Afro-American students in an urban high school face multiple pressures (Blair, Judd, Sadler, & Jenkins, 2002). What activities, experiences, situations can contribute to their developing a more positive understanding of themselves and one another? African students who emigrate to the U.S. bring with them a rich heritage, a longstanding commitment to getting an education, a cultural value of respect for elders including teachers, prior experiences with schooling in their home country, and many other experiences that could enrich classroom interchanges. They are not empty vessels to be filled; rather they have knowledge and experiences that when explored could help Americans better understand Africa and Africans. The presence of Africans in an urban school provides the opportunity to address issues of racism, oppression, culturally relevant curriculum, critical pedagogy, and Afrocentricity. From this type of explanatory scheme, miracles can happen.

Cognitive Dissonance: Disconnect Between Expectations and World View[9]

Respect is a term used by the African students to describe the difference they see as existing between students in Africa and students in the U.S. Respect was used repeatedly to describe the relationship that should exist between the teacher and the students. It was experienced as lacking in the interactions between students and teachers here. It was lacking between students and other students. The African students noted that they were not respected because they have an accent. They were not respected because they do not speak English well. They were not respected because of their skin color. They were not respected because they are different.

Furthermore, the African students noted that many of the Afro-Americans students do not seem to respect themselves. In a similar vein, some Liberians and Sierra Leonians did not behave as if they respected themselves either. To their dismay, this lack of respect conflicts with their heritage as Africans. All of the African students acknowledged the importance of respect for teachers and peers, and identified the apparent lack of the expected respect as beguiling to them. The African students were alarmed at the manifest disrespect they observed regularly at Jackson, in student behavior, for instance, that the African students considered to be rude, obnoxious, or counterproductive to the learning experience. However, they also were quick to try to explain why they felt that they were justified in not respecting some of the teachers at Jackson. They wanted to respect all of their teachers, they believed strongly that they should, but the behavior of some of the teachers toward all of the students really was making them angry. Some of the teachers did not seem to take their teaching seriously and they exhibited difficulties in maintaining order in the classrooms. The lack of discipline, the fact that students can and do disrupt the teacher's teaching makes it difficult for them to learn. They want to learn. They want to listen. But as they said, if there are things flying around the room and students shouting and walking around talking to their friends how can they learn in that environment.

They also would like to respect their fellow students, but the behavior of some students was making them angry as well. American students would call the African students names, laugh at them when they responded in class, pick fights with them, tease them, and in general make them feel humiliated and afraid to open their mouths. They are angry because they say that they are not getting a better education. The African students were certain that they actually had had a better education in their country, and yet they continued to want to believe the claims that the American education was to be envied, and would be worth all the effort to get here to get an education because this would secure their future endeavors were successful. Despite the mounting evidence to the contrary, they still hoped that their American education would mean something if they go back to their home countries. They know that if they get a college education here and go back to Africa they can generally get a good position just because they have a degree from the U.S., but they already are learning that this outcome will not mean that they will have learned anything more or better in the U.S. than would have been the case had they remained in the educational system in their homeland. They find it hard to explain this because they are afraid of being heard as complaining. They have already heard the response to complaining which is "Then just go back to where you came from. We don't need or want you here."

The African students believe that respect is not as important in the American society as it is in the African society. They also think that respect is not part of the upbringing of children in America. Language use is a clear example of that. For example, "can I" is always used when it should be "may I." To the Africans, it seems that politeness is not part of American culture, and yet some people seem to expect to be treated by others that way when they aren't reciprocating. They hear the American students say terrible things to each other and to their teachers but when they follow suit they get in trouble.

Most African students are afraid to engage in discussion with the American students because they might use an expression that could disturb their American peers. The Liberians who confront the American students seem constantly to be fighting and getting in trouble. They can't ignore them or they get accused of being stuck up. They can't be like them or they get laughed at or they get in trouble. They can't seem to do anything except try to look like they are accepting of the disrespectful behavior while trying to separate themselves from it. The African students attribute the arrogance of the American students to a lack of paying attention or listening to the opinions of others, and on the supposed supremacy of their culture. It is incomprehensible to the Africans that American students do not respect their teachers. To an African, a teacher is deserving of respect because they are the holders of knowledge and knowledge is to be respected. In Africa, teachers, regardless of their chronological age, are deemed to be elders and are respected as highly as are parents. Knowledge is a blessing, being taught is a blessing and a teacher who passes on knowledge is deserving of respect. The African students do not want to be disrespectful but the students in their classes are disrespectful and they just want to fit in. It seems as incongruent to them to disrespect knowledge as it would be to disrespect those who hold the knowledge.

In Africa, people live in an extended family system. Teachers are part of that family system. Any African adult male would be called uncle and the females, auntie. Respect is inculcated early on. Children learn to respect all elders. This is in remarkable contrast to American society, but here the African students no longer form part of the kind of extended family system that they cherish from their home culture. What was important to them in Africa, respect, their elders, knowledge and wisdom, their interconnectedness, no longer were perceived as priorities because what had been most important to them previously is not highly valued by others in America. The ones who are most successful in adapting to American mores talk about being invisible, minding their business, staying away from the Americans and the other Africans, and being careful about who you associate with. Although this feels to them like anti-African attitude, it is the only way that they see to survive and fit in. It has become all too obvious to them that you can get a diploma without necessarily learning anything. Furthermore, they are quickly discovering that no matter how well a person of color does academically there will remain obstacles to success that will prohibit them from reaching the highest echelons of American society. They see already that they will never be an important person here. One African student sadly revealed that she could not get away from America soon enough.

> For many of those who can return safely to Africa, their life in America means only biding their time. They will get their diploma and go back to their home countries. For those who are trapped here because of war and other crises, they seem to harbor no great hope anymore about what they can expect to achieve while in America. Many of the students believed strongly that they were learning more about life in the classes they had in Africa. They have little tolerance because nothing seems to happen of much significance in their classes here. They start skipping the classes where they felt they were learning nothing from being in class. They are angry about wasting their time. Schooling was a privilege in

their country, and they took it seriously. Teachers had control. Here, some teachers have no control. Students disrupt the class continuously and no teaching, no learning occurs. They learn not to respect those teachers who have no control. To them, both the students and the teachers are to blame for this lack of respect, as is the larger society that allows this to occur. America is not all that it was cracked up to be, and they feel deceived.

The students expect fair treatment from their teachers because this is America. They have experienced preferential treatment based on bribing and family connections but they think that in America fairness rules. During an ESOL English class one day, a student, a refugee from Sierra Leone, was engaged in an assignment to write about an early experience. The student was initially not making any attempt to write, but she remained seated at her desk motionless. When asked why she wasn't writing, she said that she couldn't write about an early experience because all she knew was war and she didn't want to think or write about her early experiences. She offered to write about when she was older, after the war had ended and her family could eat again without worries, and she recalled one particularly happy occasion when they had food and they all ate together as a family. She asked the teacher if she could write about her later experiences when she was happy again and the teacher replied, "No. I don't care if there was war. I'm sure you can find something to write about that's an early experience." Having been misunderstood, and denied her request to write about some actually pleasurable experience of her youth, this student elected not to write anything. A short time later, this young woman stopped coming to school, another casualty of our educational system's inability to adapt to the needs of our young people.

There were a few teachers at Jackson who were going out of their way to help the African students. They saw them as hard working and eager to learn as compared to their Afro-American peers. In this way they received preferential treatment. The teachers expressed a keen interest in some of the African students who demonstrated such a thirst for learning, not often found in the environment at Jackson which suffered from the many ills of schools in poverty neighborhoods beset with violence and a sense of "nihilism" (West, 1993). There were already at Jackson, however, many Afro-American students who also were anxious to learn and they too had to struggle in the face of these many obstacles to learning.

Prior to their arrival here, the African students were unaware that the American educational system carried with it a culture that in many respects promotes values that are contrary to African values. They thought that America, as the land of the free and the home of the brave, the melting pot where all cultures could live in peace together, was a place of freedom of cultural expression. They thought that the Western form of education would be focused on improving one's life and providing young people with the tools to be successful adults.

The definition of success itself is a cultural value that is not universal in its meaning. Many immigrants think that getting an American education is the key to a better life, but many Africans who have been through the system now see what it took away. They have paid a significant emotional price for this education. For the African students, the Afro-American students do not appreciate the real value of the American educational system. Amadou, an African male, explained the way he sees the difference between himself and his Afro-American peers.

> Inter.: Why do you think the African students think education is so important?
> Amadou: Because we know what we left behind. Maybe because we didn't have a lot of opportunity and if we come to America, it's because they have a lot of opportunity. We try to take all that we can. You know, we care about an education. Americans don't think that way; they abuse it. They got everything right now, so they don't have to worry about the future because they already have it.

When Amadou talks about what he left behind he is not alone. All of the African students talked about their previous schooling experiences with pride. Even though Amadou's schooling experience had been a relatively positive one for him, the idea of an American education held a great deal of stature in his country and many others on the continent. The reaction on the part of every African student was that the American students at Jackson did not appreciate what they had at their disposal and how much they were apparently rejecting without appreciating its true value. The Afro-American students appeared to take their educational opportunities for granted. For the African students, doing homework, taking tests seriously, participating in class, volunteering for projects, asking questions, and attending every class every day was an integral part of their school tradition in their home country. Although Liberia and Sierra Leone had experienced tragic wars, even for those countries' young people getting an education was considered of utmost importance. As one remarkable, but disconcerting, illustration of the level of commitment to education maintained by many African youth, a 10 year-old boy holding a rather large weapon once accosted a vehicle traveling through the perimeter of a demilitarized zone in Liberia. During a halting conversation with the passengers while he searched their car, this young person explained that when he grew up he wanted to be a "teacher." He offered this admission in complete seriousness, and without any sense of irony given the precarious circumstances attending his declaration.

Working in the Liberian and Sierra Leonian refugee education programs in Guinea and the Ivory Coast was a lesson in the commitment and dedication of many teachers and students who made schooling their priority. Despite having no supplies, the students and teachers came every day and did the best they could despite enormous obstacles. Children brought their own logs to sit on; teachers used black paint on wood to make blackboards, and they all came even when hungry, frustrated, or tired. For the African students, getting an education was a major goal and one that required specific behaviors on their part including respecting their teachers and doing the work. Thus, their observations of their American peers, who were primarily Afro-Americans, indicated to them that they did not share the same values regarding education. Later, during some of their interactions with their Afro-American peers as part of this study, the African students discovered that their initial assumptions were incorrect, and many of the Afro-American students did value getting an education as one of the top priorities and took schooling very seriously. It was only in their face-to-face sharing what is important to them, however, that both groups of students could come together and find their common values. In coming together around their values, the students could see each other differently than the stereotypes that had been keeping them apart.

Chapter Summary

In this chapter, we explored some of the typical conditions of American life that African (as well as many other immigrant youngsters) encounter on their arrival in the U.S. We delineated the salient misconceptions about America that many African students have brought with them and explained how the American Dream looks from inside of a racial and ethnic hierarchy that allocates resources and approbation determined by the color of one's skin and the size of one's wallet.

In the next chapter we profile the select group of Afro-American students who participated in a study about perceptions of the differences between educational experience in Africa and America. The students describe their reasons for electing to discuss these issues, their concerns and their sources of information about Africa and Africans and their previous exposure to students from the continent.

CHAPTER 5

Afro-American Student Profiles

This chapter describes some of the Afro-American students who shared with us their perceptions about Africa, how they came by them, and what they already knew about the African students at Jackson. They describe the differences as well as the similarities they recognized between themselves and their African peers. The voices of these students communicate their recognition of some of the prevalent stereotypes about Africans held by Afro-Americans, and about Afro-Americans that they feel are projected by the African students. Moreover, the students report on how they began to relate to the African students when they came to recognize that much of the time their interactions with them were being influenced by unacknowledged prejudice based on deficient or inaccurate information. When the students began to see how their presumptions interfered with their capacity to relate realistically to the African students as equals, they began to see past these mistaken premises and discovered new ways to relate to the Africans that could have an enlivening and enlightening effect on their efforts to understand and gain a greater appreciation for their own history.

Like the African students we introduced in Chapter 2, the Afro-Americans were self-selected from the African American studies class at Jackson. There were four Afro-American females and four males we got to know fairly well through regular contact and through their contributions to the activities used in this study. We later learned that one of the participants was the child of a Nigerian mother and a Jamaican father; however, this young man identified himself as Afro-American. We also learned that one of the female participants was born in Barbados, and came to the U.S. when she was much younger; she also identified herself as Afro-American. We already explored in an earlier chapter some of the motivating reasons for young people to elect to identify with a particular social or ethnic group when other options are available to them.

We purposefully chose some students from grades 9 and 10 so that not all of the participants would graduate from Jackson and leave at the end of this study. We hoped that some of the students would be motivated to continue with their interest, share some of the enthusiasm they manifested while engaged in this study, and perhaps infuse some positive energy into future classroom discussions related to African American history. We were quite impressed when the students themselves proposed that they share some of what they learned with a wider array of the Jackson students. In this way, they both recognized the value of disseminating useful information about the African heritage and acknowledged that peer pressure represented a significant obstacle to widespread acceptance of what felt like "brand new ideas" about the African students at Jackson.

The Promise of Education

The educational system in the U.S. often has been touted as the envy of the world[1] (Nisbett, 2004; Usdan, 1998). It is useful to remind ourselves that this approbation first was attributed to the American system of higher education, not its investment in public education at the grade and high school levels (Geiger, 2004). At a time when few developing countries have the resources to dedicate to the task of permitting their young people to spend 12 plus years gaining a suitable education—something that would be taken as a luxury in countries where there are not enough adults to produce economic sustenance for the country—that the post-graduate training provided in the U.S. is something much of the rest of the world envies is less remarkable than it first appears. The real test of the quality of an educational system is how well it prepares its children to become adults, not how well it progresses them toward academic prestige and economic advancement.[2] These latter are "luxuries" for a high proportion of the world's population and only over-developed countries are in competition for superiority in this realm. At the more fundamental level of preparing to replace one generation of citizens with the next, the American public school system is falling far short of the mark for our children of color.

The Philadelphia system created the Office of African and African American Studies (OAAAS) which has the following instructional goals: a) destroying myths and stereotypes as they relate to people of African ancestry, b) helping all students gain an appreciation and understanding of the cultural heritage of people of African ancestry; c) helping each student develop a frame of reference and a conceptual basis for understanding and attacking the persistent problems resulting from racism in American society; and d) helping students develop the skill of inquiry to differentiate between factual knowledge and propaganda.[3] Truly noble goals for all of our nation's children. Yet, despite the heroic efforts of so many people before and since the Civil Rights movement of the 1960s, Black History still is not readily accessible to every child in most of our public schools. There are pertinent and enlightening materials to be found on the website of the OAAAS and in their offices; there are textbooks available now at the elementary and secondary levels; there are videos, films, and other educational materials and resources. The problem is that this information is not readily accessible to students, particularly those from the inner cities where many families live in poverty, and, even if this information were readily accessible, information alone does not provide our children with what they really need to transcend a longstanding reliance on inaccurate representations about Africa and Africans.

Memorizing one of Martin Luther King's speeches or the names of the countries on the continent of Africa or the early African kingdoms simply is insufficient to convey the complete story of the significant contributions made to our country by persons of African descent. The story of people of African descent has not become a part of the fabric of life in America. An obvious reminder of this is that Black History Month and Martin Luther King Day remain the symbols most young people recognize as a substitute for a full acknowledgment of the history of persons of color and the nexus between that history and the evolution of the success of the United States. Black History, for most in the mainstream, remains only a superficial recognition, perhaps celebrated during a brief period annually, and certainly not assimilated by most segments of society. Even worse, Black History remains inaccessible to most of the children in our public schools. Many public schools continue to be the site of misinformation that perpetuates a distortion of Black History in which the story of people of African descent is not accurately told, and the African worldview is not available as an alternative to the dominant narratives about the contributions of persons of European descent to the evolution of civilizations. Tarzan swinging from the vines, the beasts in the jungle, and tribal wars remain the core projections in the mind of most Americans regarding the reality of the African continent (Walker & Rasamimanana, 1993).

Because there is such a dearth of fair and comprehensive information about Africa and persons of African descent, the presence of students from Africa at Jackson should have promoted a wonderful opportunity for the Afro-American students to gather a better appreciation for the ties that exist between these two groups of students. Instead, the relationship between African and Afro-American students at Jackson could easily be described in terms of hostility, with racial slurs and personal attacks being heaped by both groups on the other. Keeping these students apart were the myths, misperceptions and stereotypes relating to all things African. Nothing in their environment seemed designed to bring them together not even the one African American studies class that served 100 of the 2,000 students attending Jackson. Sadly, even the self-selected group of Afro-American students who joined this study, all of whom had completed or were then-engaged in the African American studies class at Jackson, evoked many of the same stereotypes when they described what they already knew about the African students. In an almost mirror image of the misperceptions about Afro-Americans that the African students held, which we discussed in Chapter 2, the Afro-American students observed that the Africans were different because of the way they dressed, the way they spoke, and the priorities they held regarding their education and their families. For the most part, the students' impressions were guided by the media's representations about Africa in precisely the same way that the African students predicated their impressions on media portrayals of Afro-Americans.

Casual interactions between students at Jackson had failed to provide any opportunity for them to connect either emotionally or informally. Even interactions in the classrooms were without substance; the two groups may have been sitting next to each other in class but they might as well have been in different parts of the world. Evidently, not even the African American studies class was a suitable environment for engaged communication between the students because several lamented that memorizing historical dates and the names of African kings and the names of the countries on the continent of Africa had not induced them to learn anything more about Africa. For example, during one of these classes, a student remarked vehemently that "Africa is a jungle. I know it is." Although there were several African students in attendance who could have dispelled a myth like this, they were not invited to comment and, because of their wariness about how it would be received, they did not volunteer to correct this student's misimpression. Stereotypes about Africa and Africans abound in our schools and even when there may be African students who could provide more accurate information, they are not sought out nor are they called upon to contribute. The irony is that because Jackson comprises predominantly Afro-American students, in this particular environment there should have been no concern about threatening to replace the Eurocentric versions of history; everyone should have welcomed having more information about Africa, including the teachers.

Spurious generalizations about both groups had become entrenched among the common experiences of students at Jackson. Resentment grew when nothing was done about these negative comments, which, in turn, led to further disillusionment on the part of both groups who looked to the adults at Jackson for assistance and guidance. Furthermore, for those students ensnared in any conflict between African and Afro-American students, silence or unfair reprobation from the adults led to their suppressing their displeasure, or prompted an even greater level of aggression when the students provoked physical fights. The African and Afro-American students who wanted to avoid all conflict simply ignored each other. The epithets "gay" or "stink" or "savage" or "rude" were enough to propel several members of each groups to engage in an altercation, first with words, then fists, and perhaps escalating into more serious violence. Without transcending the prevailing negative stereotypes of all things African and without providing a course of study in African American history that incorporates activities to reconnect students with the African continent at a level of shared history and culture, it is highly improbable that young people will become motivated to learn about a land still considered by most American to be the "Dark Continent."

Descriptions of the Students

Brandy is a 17 year old senior whose impressions about Africa were overwhelmed with images of emaciated, dying children. She really wanted to know how the African people could adapt to so much loss of life as was portrayed in the American media. At first, Brandy was wary about learning anything new because of all the tragic images that she harbored of starving children, AIDS patients, and people being displaced or killed in the ongoing military struggles in several African nations that she had seen on television commercials for charitable organizations and in other media outlets.

> Do they still sleep? The news programs said there's a lot of people dying from AIDS over there. I want to know, because there's a lot of people dying from AIDS. Like anybody can get it instead of having sexual relations and like that.

Brandy had seen "Roots" when she was younger and at that time she had imagined that she wanted to visit Africa one day. But she believed from what she had learned through the media that Africa would be too hot for her to be able to tolerate, and besides there were too many people dying there. She wanted to know how they coped without getting very angry about all the people who were dying. Brandy commented on how the African students at Jackson remained separate, and how she could not understand them so she was not convinced that she and the other Afro-Americans would be able to get to know the Africans better.

> They always stick together. They just have their own language. Some are like I'm not hearing things. I don't know. I have spent school programs with them; like on Wednesday, we go to a meeting together where they speak their minds and stuff like that. Yeah, they just like us. They just do different things. They got each other.

Brandy was reticent at first to engage in activities with the other students and she wasn't sure that any of this mattered. Like many of her American peers, Brandy's curiosity about Africa had been sparked initially by media attention on the plight of several of the African nations, and was unrelated to any potential connection she might have discovered about an ancestry from Africa. In the end, though, she was surprised by how much she had learned that was positive, how fun it had been, and how important it now seemed to her to know more about Africa than the few recurring images of its undernourished children and the woeful destruction wrought by the AIDS epidemic and internecine wars. In fact, she brought her brother once to share the experience. Brandy became extremely engaged and she wanted to know about more pedestrian and immediate things like the weather, the food, and especially about the people behind the images she had seen in the media.

Valeisha, a 16 year old 10th grader, was one of our stars. She is petite, light skinned, and very vivacious, vocal and lively. A few years previously Valeisha had attended a school in a different city where her best friend was originally from Africa. Her best friend from Africa taught her to dance, to drum, to enjoy Nigerian foods, and to appreciate the contributions to world culture by Africans.

> I forget what part of Africa she is from, but I talk to her a lot. My friend I got her to teach me how to play the African drums. And she taught me some of the African dances that they do. I mean, it's a really good experience; it is really fun to do. And I don't know how people can sit there and do that, make fun of another person right in their face, like they don't have any feelings.

During the time that we knew her, Valeisha was so moved by her experiences interacting with the African students that she composed a drama about what it would be like for an Afro-American girl to go to Africa in response to the dying wish of her grandmother. She was the lead in declaring that the students needed to reach the entire school in small groups.

> The Africans stick with each other. I guess it's because the students here don't try to get to know them as a person. They just judge them on where they came from because they have a set picture in their mind of Africans, you know, living out in the jungle and in nature and they just don't think that over in Africa there

are students too. You know, they stereotype things. I know a lot of the average black students at Jackson treat the Africans different. Some are ignorant towards them, and then you can tell the segregation between everybody.

Jasmine, a 17 year old senior, was involved in many social activities at Jackson. She was reserved initially but she had that quality of quiet strength which made her a born leader. She enjoyed the activities in our study and was eager to learn more once the opportunity presented itself. She always had thoughtful things to say when she reflected on the activities later. Although Jasmine had completed the African American studies course she expressed great surprise at what she began to learn during this project. She recognized that she had left the African American studies class still harboring a substantial collection of stereotypes.

> From what I see, there's not really much interaction between the students unless they have to be in classrooms together, there's not much interaction. You just hear a lot of stereotypes.

Tony, a 16 year old 10th grader, was another taciturn participant. He was very quiet and rarely spoke but when he did it usually was to communicate some important message. Tony was critical of the way some of his peers interacted negatively with the African students, but he recognized that a disconnect between the two groups of students was mutually reified and not without its ironic foundations:

> I think the African-Americans, they stay to themselves and Africans, they stay to themselves – like each group stays with each other. I think that probably African-Americans might make fun of them or something because of the way they talk, but, I don't listen to that stuff. Like, if they talk funny and then they were like, "oh what did you say," and then they say it again and they started laughing in their face. I think that's ignorant.

Tony was so pleased when he actually had the opportunity to become friends with an African student. He also surprised himself when he ended up talking about what we were doing with his sister at home. One of the most rewarding moments in our interactions with Tony was when we contacted his father, who thanked us for the program that we were doing. Evidently, Tony had gone home after one of our interactions and asked his father about his background and history. Tony had been the only one of our Afro-American participants who admitted that his father already had tried to teach him about his heritage and about Africa, which was reflected in his father's approbation for our project.

> I think Africa is where life was originated, like everybody came from Africa, that's what I heard. That's where gold came from, and I don't really know that much about Africa, but I would like to learn more about it. I watch the news and if they have like certain things about Africa, it might catch my attention. I watch it.

Patrick, a 17 year old senior, was one of our funniest participants. We learned that his father was Jamaican and his mother Nigerian. He acknowledged that he was aware that his mother was from Nigeria but she never talked about it because she believed that Patrick would be uninterested, and Patrick for his part had never exhibited any curiosity about Nigeria.

> The African Americans they stay to themselves and Africans they stay to themselves. I think that the African Americans might make fun of them or something for the way they talk, but I don't listen to that stuff. Also, the teachers, they don't care. Like, the kids are bad, I mean Philadelphia in general, they have a lot of good kids in Philadelphia, but in my opinion, a majority, like 60-70% are mostly bad. Like in New York, I can say that, because I went to a certain school, not that it was better, but my neighborhood school, I lived in a pretty good neighborhood; but the kids there were better. The teachers, they were good too. From what I've seen, most of the times they are not that good. Like, they might make a comment, things that bother me, they're weak; they make comments. I only heard a couple of comments, but something like that to the Afro-Americans. Most of the time, in my classes, they get along, but what I see in the hall, or I hear people talk about them is bad.

Patrick always had a joking tone and wanted to lighten up every activity. He was a young man who could have appeared to be apathetic but who cared very much about his heritage. He appeared to resist everything initially. He would make comments like "do we have to?" or "why are we doing this?" but after an explanation he always participated enthusiastically. We were delighted to learn that in the middle of this research project Patrick asked his mother about Nigeria; this opened an exciting opportunity for them to share that had never happened previously. Patrick seemed surprised by how much he enjoyed being with his African partner when we engaged in small group activities.

Sylviane, an 18 year old senior, identified herself as Afro-American but we later learned that she was born in Barbados. According to Sylviane,

> the Afro-Americans, they act different. They're separate from the other ones. Like separate from Africans. They think they like two different people, but in reality they are already the same people. Some people think that they live in huts, they live in this jungle, it's not good enough where they live in. They speak different languages and something is probably wrong with them.

Sylviane had never considered that she might have ancestors from Africa. It was only after the group had met with Dr. Asante later in the sequence of activities that Sylviane started to recognize a connection between Barbados and its African heritage. It was a surprise to her that there was any connection between the land where she was born and Africa. It was a like a new found identity for her and she relished it because she knew firsthand what it was like to be looked down upon because of an accent. She had been mistreated the same way as so many of the African students.

I mean they say negative things. That's not me. I try to be nice to everybody. I try to give a positive reflection of what I want people to fall back on. But you know, just one person can't help the whole entire school. I know, there was just one African girl in my gym class, and I stopped for a little while and I talked to her, and then when I see her in the hallway she always stops and she's like, "Hi, how are you doing", and "I like your hair."

Sylviane had experienced the ignorance about Barbados demonstrated by a number of her American peers because of the questions that they asked like "do you know how to use a fork?" Sylviane was somewhat shy in the beginning but as she discovered that she had so much in common with the African students she began to open up and participate more actively. It was a wonderful sight to see Sylviane really share with her African peers about their lives and interests.

Marcus was a 10th grader who had a lot to say; he loved to narrate stories. He told us in great detail about a particular book that he had loved very much when much younger, about how to survive as a black male in America. Marcus was so easy to talk with because he just enjoyed conversation and seemed to have a very positive outlook on life. A major concern of Marcus was

if you go into African American class it's where they always have pictures of people sitting on rocks there, tribes and like that, and basically that's where we came from, but some people don't like to see that. Because they said it makes us look like that's all we're good for. Basically, I don't know nothing about it, the people, haven't been there, but what people think Africa looks like is that people wearing their shirts off and all that other stuff. That's what everybody visualizes, because if you never been there, you picture grass and people sitting around fire and all that stuff, the huts they make because that's basically all they show on TV. That's basically what Africa was like. So you can't be ashamed of that. But why can't we show people coming from school, you know, African people graduating out of school or something like that, or sitting on a rock with and sticks and stuff like that, they was like, "how you gonna show all that?" You haven't been there, how you gonna see what it looks like unless, you know, TV. I know its fake, but its kind of like a vision of what it looks like, so, I would say that's just what it looks like.

Damon was a 17 year old senior who was eager to participate because he wanted to get to know the African students better. He knew that they were present in the school and he had gotten to know at least a few of them a bit. He described the relationship between Africans and Afro-American students at Jackson as

the American-Africans and Africans, they're cold to each other, they don't say nothing for nothing, but the female Africans and African-American females, they get into a lot of fights over each other. I guess with like religion you know, I guess that's why. Someone probably said something smart to somebody, that's probably how. That's how they always start out. They say something about them.

We were surprised by Damon's explanation that religious differences were the source of the antagonism between the two groups and that the fights were more frequent between female students.

Myths, Misperceptions, and Stereotypes

The Afro-American students shared with us some of the impressions they had about the African students. From these, it became evident that standing in the way of the students at Jackson knowing more about Africa, the land from whence their families had originated long ago perhaps, were the prevalent stereotypes either endorsed or tolerated at school, in their homes, and through the media. The stereotypes of the lazy, rude, hostile Afro-American and the savage, jungle boy or girl from Africa have prevented the students from connecting to each other and to comprehend any truth about their connectedness. Marcus, for instance, commented on some of the open hostility exhibited between the two groups:

> Basically, they don't get along for nothing. Nobody gets along. It's like they're more aggressive. I'll put it this way, we play around too much and they be serious about everything most of the time. I'm not trying to stereotype but I'm saying that they be serious and we be playing around here, they don't play around either, and we, like in gym, would just be starting with them and all this kind of stuff and you know they be cursing at them and all this stuff, it's like we playing with them and they'll curse you out, just over playing around. They try to play it off or they go running and tell the teacher or something. All last year a lot of them got beat up real bad, lots. The Africans would fight, everywhere you went and it was all Africans, everywhere you went it was fighting, all over the place. They didn't want anybody to see them fighting. The Africans basically stick together. I noticed that last year. You fight one, you have to fight the whole family and that's one thing I admired about them, because they all stick together for some reason and us, we want to be nuts and just have a little crew with us and just stick with them.

The Afro-Americans believed that the African students harbored their own prejudices against them, and these influenced both the reactions of the African students and the responses they evoked in their interactions with the African students. In addition, the Afro-American students perceived that there was at least the possibility that the African students were better treated by some of the adults at Jackson. One of the difficulties identified by the Afro-American students was the perceived preference on the part of teachers for immigrant children, in general. In some contexts, teachers may believe that immigrant children better appreciate the opportunity to obtain an American education, while American children take it for granted. According to these teachers, immigrant children want to learn, but American children think they already know it all, or expect to be entertained or just don't want to learn.

To develop a positive connection in the midst of all of the negative stereotypes and misconceptions that permeated the interactions between the students, we recognized that a suitable intervention would be successful only if there was a bridge created between the opposing views about each group. Our expectation was that once a connection was made through a sequence of activities the Afro-Americans engaged in with the African students, then the students would generate additional ways to keep building on this connection. To our delight, after only a brief series of activities, all of the students were eager to pursue a relationship built more on mutual respect and appreciation.

Our study builds on the work of Fordham (1988, 1996), Ibrahim (1998), Ogbu (1974, 1998) and Solomon (1992), who have studied groups of Black high school students in various settings. As discussed earlier, the work of Dei (1994), his colleagues (Dei, Mazzucca, McIsaac, & Zine, 1997), and Ibrahim (1998), all reporting on research that was conducted in the Canadian school system, collectively demonstrate some of the many difficulties faced by continental Africans in North America. The key difficulty is their experience of having to contend with racism and being defined by others primarily by the color of their skin. This can be a significant challenge for many young people whose previous encounters have not prepared them for being stereotyped based exclusively on their skin color.

The present study was one attempt to get beyond the difficulties the students routinely encountered to find a way to bridge the gap that exists between the Afro-American and their African peers. In Fordham's study (1996), the Black students who tried to succeed in school were accused of "acting white," which created additional serious peer pressure problems for them. The Black students also expressed an interest in connecting to their African heritage. In Solomon's study (1992), the West Indian students had created their own space in which to dominate. They found sports to be a world that they could occupy and even excel at in comparison to their indigenous peers. In each of these studies, being a Black adolescent student meant having to find a way to define oneself in the face of the racism that still permeates much of North America. Substantial research persuasively argues for the importance of Afrocentricity in educating children of African descent (Akbar, 1998b; Asante, 1991; Dei, 1994; Hilliard, 1998). Afrocentricity provides one positive vehicle for enhancing and celebrating the identity development process for our children of color.

First, the key to students' positive identity development is for them to know who they are and where they are from, what heritage precedes them. By making the connection to their African heritage, the students came to understand that they had more in common than previously suspected by either group. Second, it became clear to us quite early on that no single intervention would be sufficient to produce even nominal change outside of our small cohort of students because of the power of peer pressure. Valeisha had proposed that we invite more of the Jackson student body to engage in some of the same activities we had shared, and she asked the other students who were the initial participants in our study to work with her to accomplish this objective. They agreed that more students needed to be informed in order for them to be able to act on their newfound understanding of one another. While Margaret Mead (1989/1934) tells us that a small band of individuals can make a difference, the students, both the Africans and the Afro-Americans, knew almost intuitively that in their environment reconciling peer pressure is critical to the success of any change in behavior. The students requested that more of their peers would be permitted to become involved in this enterprise, that more students hear from Dr. Asante, that more students see "The Language You Cry In" documentary. The students had similar ideas about sharing their experiences. Valeisha's reasoning about the need to engage others in the process of bridging the antipathy between the African and Afro-American students made perfect sense.

The Influence of the Media: *Roots, Amistad, Shaka Zulu*

It has been relegated to the American media to communicate many of the facts about the rest of the world that then are taken for granted, and our young people arrive at our public schools already saddled with a surfeit of presuppositions about what is really going on beyond the boundaries of their own neighborhoods. It was interesting to note that the African student were in school all day with these Afro-American students but the only ones the Africans generally interacted with were those who lived in the same neighborhoods. One Afro-American students admitted to knowing several of the African students but couldn't remember any of their names. When asked "How did you get to know them?," he responded,

> It just happened. When we got into groups, they sit all of us in groups and they just tell us, we tell each other our names. Usually if your class is with them all the time, that's when you start talking to them, hanging with them. (Damon)

Only one of our participants knew the name of a person from the other group.

> In class, I sit next to a girl, she's from Africa and she's pretty, she's a polite person. We do a lot of group work together. She says, when we do group work and we gotta answer a lot of questions about history and how the world, and how it evolved and how things have changed, she has a lot of great answers. Yeah, she knows a lot of stuff. (Valeisha)

"What do you know about Africa and Africans?" For many of the students at Jackson, this question seemed not even to have been asked, let alone considered with any attention. That the Afro-Americans may have come originally from Africa was not acknowledged in any concerted manner in any context, within or outside of Jackson. Damon explained,

> Africa is where we're all from. I know about them. I don't know much about them though. It wouldn't bother me if I knew a little bit more about them.

The standard symbols recognized by the Afro-American students convincingly demonstrated that the knowledge base from which they drew was seriously outdated and unsympathetic. Such knowledge as they could share with us illustrated that there were ultimately significant areas of misinformation, which detracted from any appeal Africa might have had for a young person searching for an identity by foraging in the history of ancestors.

Jungle.   Some people they talk with an accent, the accent, they might make fun of their accent or the way they talk. Like they walk around without shoes and something like that? Or they hang on trees or something, stuff like that? Yeah, that's what I hear. (Damon)

They're savages. They don't know anything. They're not schooled. That's the image that they put out there in America on TV shows and movies. (Valeisha)

I saw *Roots* at the movies. I saw *Amistad*, too. I only consider them different like from here, I know sometimes I make a couple of jokes, not jokes of them, but jokes, because I have Indian friends and they talk about Africa, you know my friend he says he thinks I'm an Indian, you know kind of like we have dirt roads, like they don't have no TV or whatever, stuff like that. You only listen when you care about it. I think if people know more about it, they wouldn't make the comments they make. (Patrick).

Roots and the commercials about the starving babies. Commercials, I've seen a lot of these. I don't know what it's called though. I always watch it; sometimes it's sad. Like little babies be hungry and stuff, like the commercials. Africa, it's just what I hear and read and the news, it's just a place, land full of desert and hungry people. (Brandy).

News and if they have certain things about Africa, I get it. It might catch my attention, I watch it. And from school of course.   I want to visit Africa. I just thought about how all my people came form Africa. I want to see how they lived and everything.   I want to learn about history, like if I was related to Harriet Tubman or something. (Tony)

In history class. And in movies like *Amistad*. I seen that movie I think in 8th grade. It leaves a very strong and positive message that they were sending out. About what happened during slavery. I guess they were sending out the message about how things were in slavery and how the Africans back then changed it, by trying to speak up. If people know more, you have more respect. (Sylviane)

Afro-Americans' Expectations of Education

Sylviane had many similar experiences with the African students about her accent and how different life was here from Barbados. Only after the presentation by Dr. Asante did she see her African connection and then she was determined to find out a lot more. Sylviane commented that

People can do certain stuff when they want to. Like cultures, race and everything. Like, um, Indians, yeah, Indians. But black people, they don't, they can't do anything they want.   They always like, object to. They supposed to be no people. But I think, black people, they're okay. I would like to know how the Africans feel emotionally about, you know, like attending Jackson school and how they feel about the separation between them and the other students. And, how they think, I mean, I want to know more about Africa itself, Africa the continent, the cities, the language and their religion.

Earlier in this chapter, we mentioned that Marcus had told us about his fondness for a book he'd been given by a beloved relative. It turns out that a few years earlier, Marcus had been accosted by some other youths who stole Marcus's backpack, which contained this particular book which he cherished. The only thing that he missed from his backpack, he told us, was this book that his grandmother had given him. He recalled that the book was about how to be a Black man in today's society. It had inspired him and he never got tired of reading it. He said that he had read the book so much that the pages were worn. Although Marcus could not recollect the title or author, he knew intimately some of the passages contained within about how to stand and how to be safe when going out and how to keep yourself on the right path. According to Marcus,

> I loved that book. It was about being black in society. It had parts on driving while you was black, it had like, basically it had at least, so many chapters, and it was like so easy to read. When it tells you how to be like a better black person, and what to do when you need to go into the store, keep your hands out of your pockets and all this other stuff. I loved that book, but I just wanted to keep it. You really know what you supposed to do, but you shouldn't do it. It was a famous book. I read that book even though when I first found about it, I said like "phew, that's garbage," but you know, I don't like reading, so I thought I don't want to read that thing. But then when I read it one day, I saw it's not bad, not too many pages, so I got interested, I read a few pages, and then I started going on. I went through like so many chapters before I knew it My dad kept it for me, put a rubber band around it because I had flipped the pages so much that the pages started falling open, and he had to use a rubber band to hold the book together. That book was so nice.

After searching widely, we located the book called "Yo, Little Brother," and took it to Jackson to give to Marcus. His reaction was quite moving; he held the book tightly to his chest and hugged it. If only every teacher could have the good fortune of experiencing this kind of joy in their students for such a seemingly simple gesture of interest. The stereotyped perception that Marcus was an angry black male or disinterested in school (as he had been described by one teacher) vanished because here was an engaged and charming young man who was overjoyed at being reunited with his lost self. Although he admitted that he could get angry, he was determined not to let adverse circumstances bother him too much. Initially, Marcus had been skeptical that bringing distant student groups together could change anything, but in the end he had to admit that he was changed and he thought others could be changed too. He realized, however, that it would take more to change the climate at the school.

> Everybody's gotta be a different person. It's like taking a bad person through and they gotta tell you about everything. They gotta tell you how it is and all that kind of stuff. But then when it comes back up here, it's gotta be a whole new different story. You got your friends that look up to you and your like, "yeah,

yeah", you can't be all this and that and when you go back in here you can be a whole new different person. You can be quiet as a mouse, you talk about everything, but then when you go back out there and you're around your people, it's like being all different. You have to, you have to separate thoughts. Even if you were friends, you understood that separate thought. So, like, small groups, it would probably be easier to figure you know, but, big groups like, it's like they go right back out there. It changes. But it's also, basically, it's not the school, it's the society, when you go outside the school. I don't know. I see a lot of movies, like, have you ever seen East Side High? I liked that movie. I see how he was and then he changed, transformed that school, but that was one of the first, that was inspired. I liked that movie.

Marcus learned to relate better with the Africans that he had met at Jackson and he felt that he could talk to them as a result of his participation in this study. He had been skeptical about finding a way to relate to students he previously had seen as hostile and distant, and in many ways unlike him or his friends. Marcus began to talk to the other students about the book and what great ideas it contained. Another Afro-American male immediately asked if he could read it next. Marcus said that he'd be happy to share with others.

Marcus's reaction was more enthusiastic than we had expected, but when we read the book we understood how important it could be to him. This was a book that was talking directly to him and his experiences and his needs. He could identify with every situation and the advice was relevant, not high and mighty but from direct experience and from a place of encouragement and empowerment. The chapter titles included "street smarts, driving while black, homies, keeping the faith, a time to learn, understanding your emotions, cross cultural, guarding your health, it's your money, common courtesy, your future, and sexually speaking." The book focused on resilience and strategies to survive racism and discrimination. Marcus treated the book as his guide and felt encouraged by its many positive messages of support and respect for the viewpoint of young people. He said he wouldn't do drugs and he wouldn't fight because it wasn't the right path. We had to ask ourselves "why can't we put this book into the hands of every black male youth?" It sure beats "Goosebumps" for Silent Reading time. Valeisha shared with us her vision for extending the reach of the inchoate Afrocentric perspective she was developing to her peers and others in the Jackson community at large:

> If it were up to me, I would write a play and put it in an urban setting where African students were at school. Little do people know that every song that the black man writes here in the city, you know black music and everything, it has the vibe of African beat in it. Whether they think, you know, some of their heritage and things from what they have and the things are passed on from generation to generation to generation. Those children right here are going to be looking in their eyes.

Chapter Summary

In this chapter we described some of the Afro-American students we met and talked with at Jackson, several of whom participated in our study. In the next chapter we explore the relationship between their African origin and its link with the profound befuddlement about perceived racism that the African students encounter in their interactions with their African-American peers as well as in their interactions with their teachers and other school personnel. To understand the confusion expressed by African students related to their initial lack of affinity with Afro-Americans, it is important to set the framework of American-style racism in the context of the experiences of Africans and Afro-Americans pertaining to several hundred years of slavery.

CHAPTER 6

The "White Elephant in the Room," or
How Come Some Students Don't Know They're African?[1]

The country keeps changing the problem's name every few years, like a lion elaborating his excuses. . . . . Only white men have the luxury of ignoring race.[2]

In this chapter we explore the relationship between their African origin and the African students' profound befuddlement over the perceived tensions, and sometimes open hostility, that they experienced in their interactions with their Afro-American peers as well as occasionally in their interactions with teachers and school staff. Initially, African students made no racial distinction between themselves and their Afro-Americans peers. For the African students, "race" had not been a relevant category that they comprehended in any way that correlated with the evolution of racial distinctions that have prospered in America (Gerstle, 2001; Gilroy, 2000; Hacker, 1992). Consequently, the African students were very discouraged when they encountered antipathy from their American peers, or a lack of understanding from their teachers. Their search for explanations for these problematic interactions was compounded by the apparent apathy about Africa that was exhibited by the Afro-American students, and the rejection of their own curiosity about their Afro-American peers.

Despite having taken at least one course in African American studies while at Jackson High, some of the Afro-American students admitted that they still knew very little about Africa. For the most part, they acknowledged that what they had learned was more akin to prevailing stereotypes with which they already were familiar than representative of any real knowledge. Moreover, despite sitting next to African students in their classrooms every day, it had not even occurred to many of the Afro-American students that having an African student in class presented an opportunity to learn more about Africa. Although the Afro-American students were keenly aware that Africans were present in many of their classes the Afro-American students did not know any by name and were unaware of any other information about them. One Afro-American student admitted that she recognized that the African students obviously would know more about the land where they came from, yet she had not talked to any of them to find out more about Africa for herself. Not one of the students in our study had sought to get to know personally an African student until after this project began.

Leaving aside South Africa's more recent emergence from apartheid, most of the African nations have been independent or self-governing since the middle of the last century when the majority of Africa experienced de-colonization, beginning during World War II and in successive efforts through the 1960s (Ayittey, 2005; J. Harris, 1998; Meredith, 2005). In the African students' home countries, therefore, persons in power are Africans like themselves, and the stratification of society predicated on the color of a person's skin has largely dissipated.[3] Unlike the majority in the West Indies and those from other countries having a large population of persons of African descent (Waters, 1999), the African students who arrive in our inner-city classrooms previously have experienced little exposure to the social hierarchies that exist in America based on race[4] (Traoré, 2002).

Race and the American Dream

Sadly enough, despite our avowed enlightenment one of the prominent characteristics that Americans notice about each other is color of skin—a visual as well as political distinction based on Americans' seemingly unquestioned perceptions about "race" as a physical and unavoidable phenomenon. Omi & and Winant (1994) remind us that "one of the first things we notice about people when we meet them (along with their sex) is their race" (p. 59). Race as a conceptual frame, however, has had a variegated history (Isaac, 2004; Mead, 1959/1950; Montagu, 1997/1964; Myrdal, 1996/1944). The concept of race was only a dim and ephemeral one to most Europeans during the Middle Ages and its contours did not begin growing a more distinct meaning until the fifteenth century (Blackburn, 1997; Goldberg, 1993; Isaac, 2004; Malik, 1996). Western ideas about race are of very recent origin, coming to take the form of the treacherous moral quandary that bedeviled the leaders of the American colonies only during the early to mid-eighteenth century[5] (Davis, 1988/1966; Fredrickson, 2002; Johnson, 1999; Jordan, 1995; Morgan, 2003/1975). For many of the colonists who espoused the liberal notions of equality and freedom, it became a difficult proposition to reconcile differences due to race, the continued disparities in the treatment of men of different colored skin, and the demand for liberty from the oppressions felt under British rule (Dain, 2003; D'Souza, 1995, pp. 79-84; Finkelman, 1996; Jefferson, 1984a).

More recently, the principal issue has focused on deciding whether race is a real and objective property of human differentiation, or whether it is a useful categorization at all (Fredrickson, 2002; Hannaford, 1996). Disputes increasingly and predominantly arise over determining whether race as a category limns characteristics that are innate (i.e., essentialism), or it is a creation of Western societies (i.e., social construction). These disputes tend to minimize the continued moral relevance of race and its impact on efforts at integration, as well as its legitimacy in framing public policy. Two schools of thought dominate how race is perceived today and what it may mean as a conceptual framework: 1) race is important and continues to influence the difficulties faced by many persons of color, or 2) there is no biological basis for race and any significance it might once have had in determining a person's beliefs or fortunes has long since diminished (Appiah & Gutmann, 1996; Bell, 1992; Gossett, 1997/1963; Helms, 1990; Jordan, 1995/1968; Rowe, 2005; Smedley, 1999; Smedley & Smedley, 2005).

The fifty year evolution of post-*Brown* efforts to acknowledge differential treatment along racial lines and to attempt to redress any remaining inequities from the 300 plus years of oppression has not accomplished integration, and has led instead to a backlash against further affirmative efforts to equalize the American people. In short, today we seem pre-occupied with resolving the issue of whether race is real at the expense of recognizing the importance of deciding its moral significance (Appiah, 1993; Blum, 2002; D'Souza, 1995). Although it has been argued persuasively that "race" as a meaningful method for distinguishing between humans is without biological foundation (Fredrickson, 2002), the effects of interactions that encompass distinctions based on race as it exists in the hearts, minds, and experiences of people in the U.S. are real and in some instances can be devastating (Cashin, 2004).

> Whether it is articulated in the more specialized tongues of biological science and pseudo-science or in a vernacular idiom of culture and common sense, the term "race" conjures up a peculiarly resistant variety to natural difference. It stands outside of, and in opposition to, most attempts to render it secondary to the overwhelming sameness that overdetermines relationships between people and continually betrays the tragic predicaments of their common species life. (Gilroy, 2000, p. 29)

In the context of the continuing impact of race on contemporary social interactions, a wide range of opinions have attempted to delineate viable explanations for the ongoing disparities in status, health, and various other criteria between caucasians and persons of color (Delpit, 1995; Rodriguez, 1995; Wilson, 1987, 1996). Haymes (1995), for instance, focuses directly on the spatial segregation of blacks and the exoticisation of black culture. He proposes a critical pedagogy of black urban struggle and decolonization. Africans who get situated in urban neighborhoods, either because of family connections or institutional placements, must deal with racism at its most intransigent and its most basic level because not only must they contend with racism from whites but they must also deal with prejudicial reactions, bordering on racism, from other people of color. The negative stereotypes about Africans have taken hold in American society, and within the Afro-American community these have polluted the way in which these two groups interact. For most Americans, the Africans who remain in their home countries are still savages, and therefore they must live in trees with the animals. For their part, the media readily provide familiar and vivid images of starving children and men with guns (Davis, 2001, pp. 171-172; Ferguson, 1998; Gilens, 1999; Kellstedt, 2003).[6] To counteract these pervasive stereotypes, some Afro-American communities have taken drastic measures by providing after-school programs and other positive activities to educate their youth about their African ancestry.

Wilson (1996) connects race-specific policies to the inability of the disadvantaged to make progress toward anything resembling an America Dream. It is no accident that a large proportion of persons of African descent are poor and live in segregated communities (Brooks, 1992; Feagin, 2001, 2003; Franklin, 1997; Hamilton & Hamilton, 1997; Henry & Tobin 2004; Hochschild, 1995;

Oliver & Shapiro, 1995; Robinson, 2000; Shulman & Darity, 1989; Shapiro, 2003; Steinhorn & Diggs-Brow, 1999; Swain, 2002; Wachtel, 1999; Williams, 2003). After their arrival in the U.S., the African students soon discover that DuBois's concerns articulated a century ago still exist; DuBois's declaration that "the problem of the twentieth century [is] the problem of the color line" (DuBois, 1986/1903, p. 10) has yet to be fully confronted or resolved. According to West (1993), in order to "engage in a serious discussion of race in America we must begin not with the problems of black people but with the flaws of American society—flaws rooted in historic inequalities and longstanding cultural stereotypes" (p. 6).

Delpit (1995) explains the need for students to be given the tools to maneuver their way within the "culture of power" (p. 24). She refers to "linguistic forms, communicative strategies, and presentation of self; that is, ways of talking, ways of writing, ways of dressing, and ways of interacting" (p. 25).[7] Those within the culture of power are the least aware of it, but those from without feel the effects. Very much like their Afro-American peers, the Africans feel the adverse effects of the political, economic, and racial stratification that infuses American society and culture. As Harlan Dalton (1995) reminds us,

> so long as race is one of the categories we use to organize our experiences, we will of necessity view each new person of a particular kind against the backdrop of our prior experiences with other of that kind. (p. 38)

In general, African students are completely unprepared to encounter the various forms of overt or more subtle racism that still exist in America. In Africa, people are not perceived in terms of color. Identity is based on the family lineage, location of one's village, ethnic affiliation, or nationality. According to George Fredrickson (2002), "ethnic identity is created by the racialization of people who would not otherwise have shared an identity (Blacks did not think of themselves as blacks, Negroes, or even Africans when they lived in the various kingdoms and tribal communities of West Africa before the slave trade" (p. 155). Upon their arrival in this country, suddenly the African students become "black," "colored," or minority members, not terms that previously formed part of their self-identity. In a dual effort to counteract the insidious effects of prejudice against immigrants generally and to retain a sense of national pride they see themselves as Africans, or as citizens of their particular country or ethnic group. It is only while in America that they get identified as black and begin to experience the negative stereotyping that accompanies that categorization in the U.S. They get identified as "black" by their Afro-American peers (who are identified as black in the census definition) and other persons of color; this unsought, and to them meaningless, categorization confuses the African students (Allen, 2004). They get called black by whites, which confounds them further. On the various administrative forms that need to be filled out once they get to America many Africans list themselves as "other," a reflection perhaps that they do not perceive themselves as any of the available administrative categories with which they might identify. Since Afro-American and Black are most often joined together in the American system, the African students do not consider themselves as being members of either of these categories. The question then becomes, how do they see themselves and what strategies do they develop to survive in the various contexts in which they must learn to navigate the American system? How can this experience be helpful to our understanding of race?

In *Hey, whassup homeboy?*, Ibrahim (1998) observed and interviewed African students in a French-speaking high school in Toronto. Ibrahim reported that the "process of identity formation for African youth . . . is a process of creolization, translation, and negotiation" (p. ii). For these students, race is a point of departure, for negotiation, and Black popular culture becomes a way of crossing the border; the African students become Black, not as a matter of choice, but as a necessity for their survival in a racist society, which already views them as Black. The process of becoming Black has been called "racialization" (p. 36).[8] Africans perceive themselves as their ethnicity or nationality first, and as African second; the process of racialization forces them to become something unnatural to them.

Nigresence

Although recent in its development, much has been written about Nigresence, or Black identity development (Cross, Parham, & Helms, 1991). Nigresence can be a critical tool to counteract the damage done by slavery and the continued oppression of persons of African descent by institutionalized and structural racism in America. Slavery was a process of deracination schemes devised "to mute and disable their Afrocentric perspective" (p. 335). Keto (1994) eloquently mocks the standard American textbook versions of the Middle Passage and the abduction of Africans from African soil when declaring that a

> very disturbing consequence of the hegemonic Europe centered perspective, is the way the trade in enslaved Africans has been described in most history textbooks. American history textbooks tend to celebrate a miraculous social transformation of Africans in the middle of the Atlantic Ocean. In an ocean that was once known as the Ethiopian Sea in the sixteenth century, the Africans commit physical and cultural genocide by disappearing without a trace. They either complete a process that reformulates them into "Negroes" on the coasts of West and West Central Africa or undergo a rapid social metamorphosis to this status at sea. Once the Africans had transformed themselves into slaves, Negroes, and Blacks, they were now ready to play their ascribed peripheral roles as social adjuncts to the Europe centered enterprise whose glorious narrative swept across the histories of the Americas using the grand concepts of liberty, human freedom and the American dream. (pp. 96-97)

Prior to their emigration to the U.S., the students from the African continent had little knowledge about slavery and its effect on the Africans transported to America in the days when slavery was a principal method of importing labor. Families and members of the same ethnic groups were purposely sold apart so as to prevent slave communication and organization, which could lead to uprisings

(Hahn, 2004; Stuckey, 1987). Slave labor provided the foundation for the economic development of the American colonies, most particularly the Southern states following the Revolutionary period, and every effort was made by those who profited from it to ensure that the slaves could not develop a collective awareness (Blight, 2001; Fredrickson, 1987/1971; Mills, 1997; Morgan, 2003/1975).[9] According to Smith (1997),

> the impossibility and immorality of treating fellow humans as things led the administrators of the colonial slave laws into agonizingly tortuous paths . . . [and] by legislating black chattel slavery, Americans . . . gave legal expression to an increasingly racialized sense of their identity so powerful that the very humanity of these outsiders was denied. (p. 64)

Following the practice of slavery being made unconstitutional in the U.S. by passage of the Thirteenth and other Civil War Amendments, the *Brown* decision, the Civil Rights Act of 1964, and similar efforts to redress the humiliations reigned down on persons of color during more than two centuries of slavery, the popular notion today may be that distinctions predicated upon race are a thing of the past (D'Souza, 1995; Tsesis, 2004). A typical attitude expressed by many students (and some of their parents) is that "slavery was a long time ago; why haven't the Blacks gotten over it" (Dickerson, 2004; McWhorter, 2000). In contemporary U.S. society support for developing a Black identity has generally come from outside the school systems or from small learning communities, magnet or charter schools, which are specifically designed to promote the development of a Black identity.

Cross, Parham, and Helms (1991) present a four-stage model of Nigresence/Black identity development. The four stages are: a) recognizing one's current sense of self, b) an event occurs that awakens an awareness of Black identity, c) support for Black identity development, and d) a metamorphosis, a commitment to a Black identity and an 'emerging; new self' (p. 322). Traditionally, Nigresence projected a quasi-pro-white, anti-black frame of reference, but eventually "if a young adolescent is exposed to and indoctrinated with parental and societal messages which are very black in orientation, the reference group orientation initially developed by that youngster might be pro-black as well" (pp. 332-333). In its more updated version Nigresence exemplifies a complex interaction between individual and shared feelings, cognitions, attitudes, and behaviors.

The students in our study were given a number of opportunities to get the information and support they needed to develop an understanding of and appreciation for their African heritage, which in turn could support their developing a Black identity that included the Africans as part of their community. Initially, they had perceived the African students at Jackson as the "other" (Fanon, 1967/1952). Developing a Black identity allows the full expression of their potential. Cross, Parham, and Helms (1991) have described the benefits of "learning to live with ambiguity in juxtaposition with a firm sense of self (blackness) are at the vortex of modern mental health for black people, as it is for most Americans" (p. 330).

Every teacher is aware that high school students are still developing their sense of self. If African and Afro-American students are provided with opportunities to learn about and from one another they can together develop a positive sense of self, a positive sense of being Black. Critical to the research that informs this book was an intervention that provided the students with an experience of their connectedness that then was followed by several opportunities to spend time one-on-one and in this way to discover more about their shared heritage through learning activities, time for reflection, and the support of those around them at school such as teachers, the administration, and other students. What the Nigrescence model provides is an understanding of the stages that are necessary for students to develop a positive Black identity, one that will enable them to

> a) transcend the psychological attacks that stem from having to live in a racist society; b) provide social anchorage and meaning to one's existence by establishing black people as a primary reference group, and c) to serve as a conduit or point of departure for gaining awareness about and completing transactions with, the broader world of which blackness is but a part. (Cross, Parham, & Helms, 1991, p. 328)

In an article entitled "A battle over race, nationality, and control at a Black university," the author described a situation at a state university in which African and Afro-American professors were at odds, and charges of racism were levied in acrimonious terms (Wilson, 2001). "The situation has evolved into a nasty battle in which racial slurs and personal attacks are the sharpest weapons" (ibid.). Although the dispute seemed to be as much between the faculty and the president of the institution as it was ostensibly among the professors, one of the African professors described the situation tersely by using an African saying, "When two elephants are fighting, it's the grass that suffers." [10] The "grass" in this situation would be the students who, of course, are innocent bystanders in this type of dispute among faculty members. However, the relationship between African and Afro-American students at Jackson could easily be described in similar terms of animosity and hostility, with racial slurs and personal attacks being heaped by members of both groups on the other. There are no innocent bystanders in this context, but at Jackson the students are suffering because of the warring elephants that represent the dispute over whether racism still exists in the U.S. or because it is legally outlawed it is a thing of the past (Cashin, 2004; D'Souza, 1995; Williams, 2003).

Since the first encounters between Africa and Europe, the people of African descent have become increasingly preoccupied with race, skin color, and demanding justice. [11] These preoccupations are not a matter of choice; rather, they are the direct product of a history of slavery, colonization, and cultural domination that has beleaguered Africa since the sixteenth century. Each of these acts of humiliation imposed on the African people has generated a flood of emotional energies which have spurred the imagination of Africans determined to regain their self-respect, pride, and dignity. In America, African immigrants find racism a constant companion.

At first glance, many African students seem content in school, almost placid. Underneath their calm exterior, however, there stirs a potent mixture of hurt, anger, disappointment, and disillusionment, all arising from their schooling experiences. In one pragmatic view of the dilemma, Rothstein (1994) explains that a student's silence and anger under these conditions may be a defense against further insult. However, many teachers "take their passivity for ignorance, their anger and aggressiveness for a personal assault on his/her efforts and authority" (p. 170). The African students, like many of their Afro-American peers, initially approach their educational experiences in America wanting to learn, but in time they sadly find the situation untenable. Neither being invisible nor being compelled to become aggressive is a healthy condition for learning.

American Racism and Its Ongoing Impact

Racism is a form of prejudicial thinking or acting that holds that an individual's abilities and moral character are formed by race rather than by the content of character, life choices, and actions. Racism holds that one should be judged not by one's character, but by color of skin, or some other immutable characteristic associated with race, and by the actions of all people who manifest the same characteristic. Racism is premised on an inherent superiority of a particular race, denies the basic equality of humans, and correlates ability with physical type in a global manner unrelated to actual performance. Politically, this can lead to the belief that some people should be governed or controlled by others. Although people can differ because of ideological orientation, Thomas Sowell (1994) has argued that "one of the most used and least defined words in the contemporary ideological vocabulary is 'racism.' The most straightforward meaning of racism is a belief in the innate inferiority of some race or races" (p. 154). Fredrickson (1981) declares that racism

> is a mode of thought that offers a particular explanation for the fact that population groups which can be distinguished by ancestry are likely to differ in culture, status and power. Racists make the claim that such differences are due to immutable genetic factors and not to environmental or historical circumstance. (p. xii)

D'Souza (1995) argues that racism "is an ideology of intellectual or moral superiority based upon the biological characteristics of race," and he adds that "racism typically entails a willingness to discriminate based upon a perceived hierarchy of superior and inferior races" (p. xx). Racism is prejudice coupled with power or dominion over another; it singles out solely for the purpose of making a superior-inferior relationship based on some characteristic that can be dichotomized (Barndt, 1991; Coons & Brennan, 1999, pp. 247-249). Ford (1994) states that "racism is any action or attitude conscious or unconscious, that subordinates an individual or group based on skin color or race. This subordination can be enacted individually or institutionally" (p. 11). According to Hernton (1992/1968), racism includes

> all of the learned behavior and learned emotions on the part of a group of people

towards another group whose physical characteristics are dissimilar to the former group; behavior and emotions that compel one group to conceive of and to treat the other on the basis of its physical characteristics alone, as if it did not belong to the human race. (p. 78)

Racism is not innate, and must be learned. People learn to discriminate, to segregate, to denigrate, or to despise those they believe are in some way different, and therefore inferior in some way. Beliefs are learned from one's cultural environment (Berger & Luckmann, 1966),[12] and racism is an attitude that projects hatred, prejudice, and discrimination against others without consideration of their individual circumstances. At the 2001 World Conference Against Racism held in South Africa, the delegation representing international psychology as a science offered the following statement as preamble:

[r]acism in all its horrific forms is transmitted across generations and is manifested in individual behaviors, institutional norms and practices, and cultural values and patterns. Racism serves simultaneously both to rationalize the hierarchical domination of one racial or ethnic group over other group(s), and maintain psychological, social, and material advantages for the dominant group. Both active racism and passive acceptance of race-based privilege disrupt the mental health and psychological functioning of both victims, and perpetrators, of racial injustice. . . . The causes of racism and related intolerance and the means for their perpetuation are complex, involving legal vulnerability and discrimination, economic and educational disadvantage, social and political marginalization, and psychological victimization. (American Psychological Association, 2001)

According to Blum (2002, p. 98), "[r]acism, racial injustice, racial discrimination, racial insensitivity, and so on, all involve something going wrong because of someone's race." This feature of making distinctions between people based on presumed characteristics that are immutable and readily perceptible has contributed significantly to the pernicious persistence of racism. Making distinctions is a natural human inclination, and forms the basis of all of our systems of communication (Efran, Lukens, & Lukens, 1990). Andrew Hacker (1992) declares, however, that we abhor racism "because it scars peoples lives. The significance of racism lies in the way it consigns certain human beings to the margins of society, if not to painful lives and early deaths" (p. 29). When the circumstances warrant a judgment being made about any of us, then we should be judged by the content of our character and by our actions, and not by the attitudes or beliefs expressed by others, nor by their actions, and certainly not by the color of our skin, or the manner in which we speak, or our gender, or any other quality we did not choose to possess. By its very nature, racism is destructive of human relations, and pollutes the mind that harbors it against others.

Some have suggested that in order to counter the lasting influence of racism we need to confront and overcome the hindrances to its eradication through a grassroots anti-racism movement (Derman-Sparks & Phillips, 1997).

It takes courage and risk to combat racism and to uphold the common brotherhood and sisterhood of the human family. . . . There are many people who would like to see the end of this terrible social monster called racism. But we must first overcome our fears, our apathies, and our reluctance to do something about it. We must refuse to deny the existence of racism. Rather, we must get all the information we need and act quickly to stop racism. We must never forget that every racist act is, indeed, a violation of the freedom and human rights of someone. (Etuk, 1999, pp. 198-199)

This sentiment mirrors that expressed by Lyndon Johnson in 1965 when describing the fallacy of the belief that a history of oppression might be overcome by simple fiat.   President Johnson, having signed the Voting Rights Act into law, recognized that this remedy alone probably was insufficient to counteract more than two centuries of slave relations because

You do not take a person who, for years, has been hobbled by chains and liberate him, bring him up to the starting line of a race and then say, "you are free to compete with all the others," and still justly believe that you have been completely fair. Thus it is not enough just to open the gates of opportunity. All our citizens must have the ability to walk through those gates.[13] (quoted in Steinberg, 1995, p. 113)

In contrast, racist thinking long has championed that the racial consciousness is a primordial, ineluctable component of a person's identity. This is known as "racial essentialism." According to much of the belief system that underscores racism, not expressing this innate human predilection to categorize others by immutable characteristics, and relate to others according to one's position on the hierarchy of superiority would be unnatural (Duke, 1998). Liberal thinking repudiates racial essentialism and contends that racism is a social construction, resulting from the encounter between Europeans and other parts of the world that led to the domination of non-Europeans (Gossett, 1997/1963; Hannaford, 1996).

More than a century ago, Frederick Douglass predicted that "whenever the American people shall become convinced that they have gone too far in recognizing the rights of the Negro, they will find some way to abridge those rights" (Douglass, 1999/1889, p. 727). Feagin (2000) argues that American society must contend with a complex and subtle system that has embedded racism at its core, from the Constitution to the legacy of slavery and de jure segregation as these have contributed to retarding black economic advancement. Reliance on a color-blind ideology only "provides a veneer of liberality" for those unwilling to recognize how racist thinking continues to shape American mores, while those who attempt to construe the experience of Americans of African descent as equivalent to other immigrant groups ignominiously ignore the ongoing impact of de facto racial discrimination. The naive optimism of those who honestly believe that racism has disappeared or that race is less significant as a consideration today is shattered by the permanence of racial concerns and conflicts as experienced routinely by many persons of color (Cashin, 2004; hooks, 1995; Roberts, 1997; Wilson, 1997). Racial disadvantage still exists in many guises, and these continue to make it extremely difficult for many minority individuals, schools, and communities to achieve the American Dream (Doane & Bonilla-Silva, 2003; Feagin, 2003; Shapiro, 2003; Williams, 1997).

Racism, the premiere manifestation of this hegemony of one group behaving as superior in relation to another, has proved adaptable to a wide range of practical expressions. Racist thinking continues to play a devastating role in many social interactions[14] (Bell, 1992, 2004; Ogletree, 2004). Slavery created wealth for some of the early Americans, and later for some of the Southern plantation owners, and this wealth remained concentrated within a few families and institutions, out of reach of most people who did not own land. One need only look around the U.S. today and see the existing patterns of poverty to realize that most wealth created by slave labor was never redistributed when slavery was abolished (Guinier & Torres, 2003). The slave owners considered this wealth their blessing, and even today racism operates as a barrier to economic development for many persons of color. Racism "remains a powerful and pervasive force in American life, often exercising its influence openly, but even more often covertly and in ways that the actors themselves do not understand" (Carens, 2000, p. 97). For example, compulsory desegregation never really succeeded at achieving the objective of integration of the education experiences of our children because white flight from the urban areas left the inner cities with even more segregated schools (Cashin, 2004; Haymes, 1995; Massey & Denton, 1993; Williams, 2003). Consequently, racism remains a significant issue in public school education, as well as many other areas of American daily life (Orfield & Lee, 2004; Rothstein, 1995; Stephan, 1999; Tatum, 2003; Van Ausdale & Feagin, 2001).

The Emotional Costs of Being a Racial Minority in the U.S.

Most Africans do not live in homes in minority neighborhoods out of an affinity for other minority groups, but rather because such neighborhoods are the only ones affordable to them. Low-income and racial stratification operate in tandem in much of this country. According to Noguera (2003), the quality of our schools has declined "partially because there is less money available as the tax base eroded, but also because when household income goes down and the percentage of low-income, single-parent families goes up, the challenges facing schools increase significantly" (p. 18). This leads to growing problems for inner-city schools as the general movement toward suburbanization has expanded over the past decade. Along with this has been increased urbanization of immigrant groups who often are relegated to low-paying jobs that may preclude their having the financial resources to live in the suburbs. Moreover,

> [n]either full citizenship for blacks nor a new black middle class has eradicated racial domination in America. . . . [P]olitical and economic reform cannot by themselves undo American racial domination. Only if blacks and whites come together at long last in a *new* American culture will racial conflict and racial domination cease. (Merelman, 1995, p. 283)

There are Africans in the U.S. who were high level government officials or successful businessmen or professors at a university in Africa, but even when they are fortunate enough to have become employed in the U.S. they often are driving taxis or working in nursing homes simply to survive in the American system. They find themselves living among the underprivileged, often in neighborhoods that are unsafe or riddled with pockets of poverty, and they tragically have discovered that the American Dream is much more than elusive, it is a lie and unattainable for most persons of color.

Waters (1990) shows how privileging ethnic over racial identity can mislead some Americans into believing that there are no longer any ongoing racial inequities in the U.S. Others have endeavored to illustrate that ongoing racist attitudes pervade much of the institutional barriers confronting people of color and hence discourage, or literally obstruct, them in their pursuit of the American Dream (Blum, 2002; Merelman, 1995). In opposition to the belief that ongoing white hegemony may at least partially explain the persisting oppression of persons of color in the U.S. are those who recite the plea that racial discrimination has been outlawed,[15] any residual difficulties experienced by persons of African descent must be self-inflicted, and therefore "we should all just try to get along," as championed by Rodney King in the midst of the turmoil plaguing Los Angeles for several days following the *acquittal* of the police officers whose trammeling of King was purveyed throughout the media[16] (D'Souza, 1995).

Some even push the envelope further and argue that we "live in a post-racist era and that policies based on the assumption that racial prejudice and discrimination are responsible for the current condition of the black population in the United States do more harm than good" (Fredrickson, 1995b, p. 11). D'Souza (1995), for example, acknowledges that some people still hold racist beliefs, but these derive from a discredited biological determinism which attributed the unequal achievements of people of different skin color to innate disparities in the abstract capabilities demonstrated by the members of specific groups. However, the recent popularity among the general reading public of *The Bell Curve* (Hernstein & Murray, 1994), and the resurgence of debate among experts that the controversial arguments in this book precipitated, signals either that there were many curious readers who succumbed to the media attention on the suggestion made in this book that measurable disparities in intelligence are substantially hereditary, or there remains a core constituency of Americans who still believe that blacks are inherently less intelligent than whites and were simply searching for someone to substantiate this belief[17] (Arrow, Bowles, & Durlauf, 2000; Devlin, Feinberg, Resnick, & Roeder, 1997; Fraser, 1995; Jacoby & Glauberman, 1995; Kincheloe, Steinberg, Gresson, 1996; Miele, 2002; Valencia & Suzuki, 2001; Sarich & Miele, 2004)). However, regardless of the origins of this belief in intellectual inferiority among populations of human beings, poverty does not define intelligence or ability; it does, however, greatly circumscribe access of opportunity (Kunjufu, 2002; Pokempner & Roberts, 2001). In the history of the United States, poverty has not been equally burdensome throughout our great land and access of opportunity has never been equally distributed (Bernstein, 2001). These issues are too complex to be resolved easily or for all time (Katznelson, 2005). According to Hannaford (1996), the transformation or transmogrification of individual human beings into groups that have been founded in the past upon prevailing generalizations of racial and ethnic categories may be nothing more than a cruel fiction and a conjurer's delusion . . . All that can be said is that on the basis of genetic evidence and clinical analysis the similarities between human beings, from whatever part of the planet they come, are greater than their dissimilarities. . . . What science does tell us with force and eloquence is that human existence on this planet has not been for any great length of time, and that the span of year allocated to us, whoever we are, wherever we live, whatever the size of our nose, whatever the color of our skin, whatever the current state of our health, whatever the size of our bank balance, is short and very fragile. (p. 399)

Even in their African American studies class at Jackson the African and Afro-American students remained apart and many of the insidious stereotypes they held about each other were left unaddressed. Even though inaccurate and entirely contrary to their own experiences, to be African was to come from the jungle it appeared. Hilliard (1998) argues that Afro-Americans must begin education and socialization by "affirming our Africanness. We must affirm our respect for our ancient traditions. We must begin from our own cultural base, and then extend into the rest of the world" (p. 20).

The stereotypes, myths, and misperceptions of Africa keep them from coming together. Negative stereotypes of Africa and Africans, as well as negative stereotypes of Afro-Americans sustain the distance between these students. According to the students themselves, their school, their homes, and the media all contribute to keeping them apart. The students almost unanimously described a situation in which there is a complete and total lack of interest in Africa on the part of everyone in their lives. Only one student reported having anyone ask her something about Africa that wasn't insulting, and the question was asked by a teacher that she didn't even know. The teacher indicated a willingness to learn something about Africa and the student exclaimed how excited she was that someone seemed the least bit interested.

There is an expectation on the part of the Africans that the American educational system is one of the best in the world and naturally would include extensive information about Africa since Africa is the third largest continent, currently considered the "Origin of Civilization" and, most significantly, the ancestral home of Afro-Americans who comprise a majority of the students in many inner city schools. To their dismay, there is no focus whatsoever in the curriculum or in the day-to-day interactions between the students or teachers that would confirm any of these obvious facts about Africa. To those who have been arguing for its importance in their writings this lack of information about Africa is heretical (Akbar, 1998b; Asante, 1991; Dei, 1994; Hilliard, 1998; Kunjufu, 1987; Nobles, 1991; Shujaa, 1994; Tedla, 1995; White & Johnson, 1985). The persistent neglect of accurate information about Africa and Africans would discourage those who marched for its inclusion in our educational systems more than thirty-five years ago, and further incites those who continue to argue for its importance today.

At Jackson, we found that when brought together and presented with the true story about their connection, the participants in this study were eager and excited to learn more from and about one another. The students could discuss the stereotypes they had of each other as if they were ridiculous. Once identified, the stereotypes seemed no longer to hold the students captive. They articulated that they knew that the stereotypes of the jungle were false and that there was much more to Africa than jungle and much more to each other than they had been led to believe. Over and over again could be heard the phrase, "I didn't know."

Stereotypes perpetrated by the media, the curriculum at school, and often reproduced at home, initially made coming together and sharing a communal history and culture nearly impossible for these students. The misinformation about both Africans and Afro-Americans is the proverbial White Elephant in the middle of Jackson High; everyone is affected by it, but no one seems motivated to acknowledge it or confront how the lack of accurate information about cultural differences reinforces the stereotypes and makes relating equitably and fairly that much more difficult for the students. Despite the efforts of people in the School District and the staff in individual schools, our educational system has failed to provide students with critical knowledge of their history and their culture.

Critical Pedagogy

Although many of the writers who address the issue of cultural relevancy discuss issues of power and hegemony, it is critical theorists like Freire (1985, 1997, 1998a, 1998b), Giroux (1992), hooks (1994), and McLaren (2002) who focus most intensely on issues of oppression in American schools. The critical paradigm is concerned with issues of power and how power functions in human interaction. The goal of this approach is emancipation, liberation. Subjectivity is highly valued, and truth is emancipation. This can only come when those who are marginalized and oppressed are free. Critical in this context refers to the affirmative act of detecting or exposing existent beliefs that limit individual or group freedom.

Critical research seeks to uncover the ways in which people are oppressed. For too many students of color, oppression is very real while it seems that their ostensible oppressors would argue that it doesn't even exist in America. Dei (1997), Delpit (1995), Fordham (1988, 1996), and Solomon (1992) have all written movingly about the oppression experienced by Black students in our schools. According to Young (1992), oppression can be defined as any "exercise of tyranny by a ruling group" (p. 174). But it can also be defined as "the disadvantage and injustice some people suffer not because a tyrannical power intends to keep them down, but because of the everyday practices of a well-intentioned liberal society" (p. 176). We may have a well-intentioned society, and we may have well-intentioned schools, but oppression still exists for too many. All education is a political act, according to Freire (1985), and in the U.S. it can be more a means of oppression for young people and most especially, young people of color.

Delpit has concluded that those who think oppression doesn't exist in the United States are most likely members of the "culture of power" (p. 24). According to Delpit, those who hold power are "frequently the least aware of—or least willing to acknowledge its existence. Those with less power are often most aware of its existence" (p. 24). It seems self-evident that schools in the United States are not value-free institutions. Macedo (1994) argues that the U.S. "was founded on a cultural hegemony that privileged and assigned control to the White patriarchy and relegated other racial, cultural, and gender groups to a culture of silence" (p. 44). Fine (1987), Lincoln (1995), and Weis and Fine (1993) vividly describe the effects of oppression in schools as the "silenced" voices of our students.

Anyon (1997), Kozol (1991), and McLaren (1998) are among the proliferation of scholars who have written about the devastation of the inequality in our schools. From the gap in funding (such as suburban schools spending twice as much per child as urban schools), to the gap in environment (absolute deterioration of urban school buildings as opposed to the newest technology centers with gymnasiums and pools for suburban student use), from scarce and antiquated materials to the latest textbooks provided to each student in a suburban school, these are the signs of the suburban-urban gap and it is visible from the moment you approach the different school settings. There are students in some of our poorer districts in this country who must go outside to another building just to access a bathroom. There are schools with no library. There are schools with a computer to student ratio of 1:100.

Some would argue that the "Third World" is here in our inner cities (Massey & Denton, 1993) and that schools can be sites of oppression (Rose, 1990). Thus, some "First World" educators have turned to Freire's pedagogy of the oppressed. Freire (1985) explains his pedagogy of the oppressed as "utopian" and "full of hope" (p. 57). He describes it as a process of "denunciation and annunciation" (ibid.). Freire's methodology requires a dialogical praxis that is a dialogue in action with reflection between the student and teacher while recognizing their respective places in the world. His vision challenges seriously most of today's educators. Can we be full of hope and work in collaboration with our students while denouncing the oppression that we see around us and find ways together to announce a transformation? Can we do it if we do not know where our students are from, what experiences have impacted their ability to learn, their cultural strengths, or how they see themselves? McLaren (1998) proposes a pedagogy that "takes the problems and needs of the students themselves as its starting point" and contends that to accomplish this objective "[c]ritical educators need to learn how to understand, affirm, and analyze such experience" (p. 217).

Results like those from the present study could help teachers of African and African American students be better prepared to understand and affirm them and encourage students to reach out and get to know one another better. Freire sees the incredible possibility and awesome responsibility of education for the liberation of the oppressed. In Freire's pedagogy the learner makes a connection between the word and the world. Bringing African and Afro-American students together around their shared history can help them to make connections between the word and the world, words such as racism, stereotyping, colonialism, and slavery. In the literature, Allport (1954) first hypothesized that prejudice

> may be reduced by equal status contact between majority and minority groups in the pursuit of common goals. The effect is greatly enhanced if this contact is sanctioned by institutional supports (i.e., by law, custom or local atmosphere), and provided it is of a sort that leads to the perception of common interests and common humanity between members of the two groups. (p. 281)

Bowles and Gintis (1976) proposed that "revolutionary educators-teachers, students, and others involved in education-should vigorously press for the democratization of schools and colleges by working toward a system of participatory power ... and fight for curriculum that is personally liberating and politically enlightening" (p. 287). The goal of a critical pedagogy is to recognize the silencing that has occurred in our society and our schools and seek the full expression of those who have been silenced in order to begin to restore the full participation of all and create a democratic society.

Failing Our Children of Color

Yon (2000) argues that race is not a static or predictable constant. How young people construct their identification with a particular racial group is juxtaposed to how they conceptualize their social context, which includes their home and school and the way in which these environments contribute to defining their identity. It is this process of identity development that can lead to the social and emotional turmoil some adolescents experience around their racial/ethnic identification while simultaneously defining their academic path and future objectives.

The African students at Jackson initially believed that the education that they were to encounter in America would be focused on improving one's life and providing the tools to be successful in the American way of life. After some time in the system, the Africans can begin to see and to comprehend why some of the Afro-American students had become disengaged with an educational system which stripped them of their heritage and culture and denied their existence in the story told in American classrooms.[18] Those who have been through the system have begun to understand that public education in America has failed the Afro-Americans, and it likely will fail the Africans as well. The system fails them because "difference" is an asset in rhetoric only, not in the curriculum and not in the day-to-day reality of school for students of African descent. Despite the efforts of people in the Philadelphia School District during the late 1960s and 1970s, and despite the ongoing efforts of some of the staff in individual schools, the system as a whole has failed to provide many students with knowledge of their own history and their culture. And so the oppression continues, unacknowledged, which only adds to the mental distress of people of African descent. Young (1992) laments that "all oppressed people share the same inhibition of their ability to develop and exercise their capacities and express their needs, thoughts and feelings" (p. 175). People of African descent have experienced all of Young's five faces of oppression: "exploitation, marginality, powerlessness, cultural imperialism, and violence" (ibid.).

The greatest contribution of Afrocentric theorists has been an understanding that it is essential to provide an accurate historical context and greater insight into the psychology of oppression, confrontation with slavery, and liberation. Our education is skewed toward a history of the powerful—it is predominantly a wealthy, European, colonizer, white, male history. Precisely because of the legacy of slavery and the enduring patterns of institutional and personal racism in this country, poverty has been painted with a dark face. If poverty really was all Black, then those who hate Blacks need not care about the poor, nor concern themselves with their education. Because of the disgraceful legacy of slavery in this country, Blacks have not benefited nearly as much from an increasing standard of living in this country and because poverty has mistakenly been painted with a Black face.[19] Genuine confusion about discrimination based on race and class persists in the minds of most Americans. James G. Speth, Administrator of the United Nations Development Program once declared that

> we live on a planet, which increasingly represents not "one world" but "two worlds." Far from narrowing, the gap in per capita income between the industrial and developing worlds tripled between 1960 and 1993, from $5,700 to $15,400. Today, the net worth of the world's 358 richest people is equal to the combined income of the poorest 45% of the world's population—2.3 billion people. If current trends continue and are not quickly corrected, economic disparities will move from inequitable to inhuman, from unacceptable to intolerable. (Speth, 1996, p. 166)

Mirroring these sentiments, some of the students offered the following comments:

> Inter.: Regardless of where we live, Africa, America, Central America or South America, is there a common bond?
> Patrick: We all Black. (Afro-American male)
> Fatou: We're all from Africa. (African female)
> Marcus: It's not all black, Africa. (Afro-American male)
> Haja: I don't think that just because you're from Africa you have to be black. It depends where people moved and stuff. I think that everybody has African in them no matter what color you are.

From this perspective, what might be different in our social relations if we all accepted that Africa represents the heartland from which all humans evolved, an in this way there remains some African blood in all our veins? (Johanson & Edey, 1981). How different might our relationships be? The stereotypic traits we heard espoused by the students were nearly all negative (e.g., dirty, lazy, uneducated), suggesting that although people may have specific beliefs about Afro-Americans with dark versus light skin (as designated by verbal labels), it is unclear whether those beliefs simply reflect different evaluations. In addition, people's beliefs about the characteristics that are associated with light-versus dark-skinned Afro-Americans may not represent the actual associations that are spontaneously elicited by an Afro-American with lighter or darker skin. Research on colorism provides evidence that perceivers use group-related physical features in a manner that goes beyond an all-or-none category-based process (Blair, Judd, Sadler, & Jenkins, 2002).

Diversity in Education

For a variety of reasons, the majority of teachers in the U.S. are white, middle class females. There can be positive or negative ramifications from this reality of the educational experiences of a majority of our nation's children of color (Howard, 1999; Waters, 1999). These two factors also have been identified as possible explanations for the disengagement with school manifested by some children of color (Kunjufu, 2002). Furthermore, if only in outward appearance the fact that most teachers in our inner city schools are white tends to reinforce the longstanding racial hierarchy that has dominated the public education system since its inception; and the predominance of middle-class women hints at the historic devaluation of the profession of teaching as public education evolved over time from the expected province of males from the leisure class to a more universally accessible system of learning (Spring, 2000, pp. 27-30).

In addition, although segregation in education has been abolished legally for more than half a century, segregation still exists in some subtle, and not so subtle ways (Olsen, 1997). Moreover, the student population is becoming increasingly diverse. Consequently, white teachers are called upon more and more to discover ways to effectively teach diverse students, as well as how to reach both mono-cultural students who need to learn how to live in a more diverse society, and de facto segregated students who need to find ways to be included into the greater society (Hale, 1994, 2001; Majors, 2001; Moses, 2002; Thompson, 2004). White pre-service teachers may encounter many obstacles to learning how to teach diverse students or mono-cultural or segregated students about diversity issues. Their obstacles are at a very deep level of consciousness. They see themselves committed to good teaching and good teaching means "being fair." To be fair, for many of these teachers in training, means to treat everyone the same, which translates into an effort to become oblivious to difference. Many teachers are deeply committed to this understanding of fairness.

We have heard and experienced first hand the resistance and the explanations as to why "colorblindness" is the only "fair" way and noticing or talking about difference or teaching for difference are all discriminatory practices.[20] Due to the visual apparatuses that humans possess, and the enduring patterns of classifying each other according to idiosyncratic traits, color-blind interactions never have been possible (Bonilla-Silva, 2003; Brown, Carnoy, Currie, Duster, Oppenheimer, Shultz, & Wellman, 2003). Due to this idiosyncrasy in human proclivities, a legitimate perspective that attempts to treat skin color as a neutral factor in human relations is difficult for many to contemplate (Guinier & Torres,

2003; Herring, Keith, & Derrick, 2003; McWhorter, 2000).

"Difference does not matter" has become today's mantra for some teachers. The idea that difference does not matter finds plentiful support in literary, philosophical, and religious authorities. It is one thing, however, to declare that we are all created equal and quite another to look at the history of slavery and racism in America. How these eerily inconsistent ways of thinking and acting have countenanced each other is a large part of the remarkable story of America (Berlin, 2003; Davis, 1988/1966, 1999/1975, 2003; Greene, 1993; Johnson, 1999; Jordan, 1995/1968; Morgan, 2003/1975; Patterson, 1998; Williams, 1994). Most often, attitudes toward people of another culture derive from a collection of stereotypes, which have evolved from prejudice, or fear of people from a culture different from one's own (Harris, 1998). According to at least one group of white middle-class pre-service teachers we know, diversity is found in everything that a high school student is involved with. Diversity simply means variety, and when a group of people come together you are sure to find this variety. Trying to get anyone to see the difference between personal prejudice and institutional racism is not an easy feat. Many books have been written on the importance of preparing future teachers for diverse classrooms (Banks, 2003; Delpit, 1995; Howard, 1999; Irvine, 1990, 2000; Kunjufu, 2002; Ladson-Billings, 1994, 2000; Nieto, 1992, 1999; Sleeter, 1996; Sleeter & Grant, 2002). They are committed to being "fair" which they see as a good thing. So, is it fair that some children get a better education than others? Is it fair that some children are overrepresented in special education and underrepresented in gifted programs? Is it fair that some children get more attention because they behave a certain way?

The children in our low-income, inner-city schools do not experience the same quality of education as the children in the upper-income schools or in the International Baccalaureate programs offered to some children in some inner city schools. A dedication to being "fair" to all students should not become an obstacle for America's teachers. The commitment to being good, even excellent teachers should be sufficient to channel learning, to assist all students to realize their highest potential, to not leave any student to lag behind for any reason (Nieto, 1999). The majority of us ought to agree that a "good" teacher *must* be anti-racist. Making a personal connection with students and making the issues of "fairness" real and personal may just change the way that teachers perceive their role. Teachers need to appreciate the benefits in "seeing" difference and understanding and appreciating difference. It is very important to recognize that difference can, and must, matter but only provided it is balanced with an appreciation for fairness and equity and is color-neutral (Minow, 1990).

Chapter Summary

In this chapter we explained the relationship between African origin and its link with the profound befuddlement about perceived racism that the African students encounter in their interactions with their African-American peers as well as in their interactions with their teachers and other school personnel. To understand the confusion expressed by African students related to their initial lack of affinity with Afro-Americans, it is important to set the framework of American-style racism in the context of the experiences of Africans and Afro-Americans pertaining to several hundred years of slavery, segregation, and oppression.[21]

We initiated our discussion of Afrocentric theory, to be continued in the next chapter, by outlining some of the various areas where African students experienced an emotional or intellectual disconnect between their expectations for the kind of education they might experience in American schools and the reality. We argued that the social context of American schools does not ordinarily provide a hospitable environment for students of color to express an authentic identity, one in which they are permitted to express comfortably their own culture and history both privately and publicly but instead are encouraged, if not coerced, to conform to the dominant culture's version of acceptable identity (Moses, 2002). We argued that for African and Afro-American students alike it is the holistic appreciation for the shared African heritage that better facilitates the emergence of an authentic identity for the students of color, and much of the research on educating minority students supports the implementation of such a culturally sensitive methodology.

In the next chapter, we explain in more detail how the theory underlying Afrocentrism can inform the educational practices used with students in American schools when their heritage harkens from Africa, as well as how an Afrocentric view can be used to broaden the multicultural perspective of students with no ties to Africa but whose perspective on history has been otherwise unfairly distorted.

CHAPTER 7

Afrocentricity: Theory and Practical Implications

This chapter discusses how the principles of Afrocentricity can be used to create exercises that bring together students who at first glance seem divided by longstanding misperceptions and unfair, negative stereotypes about each other. Afrocentricity has been evolving for many years (Abarry, 1990; Akbar, 1991; Asante, 1980, 1998, 2003a; Karenga & Carruthers, 1986; Keto, 1995, 2001; Myers. 1988). DuBois (1986/1903) and Woodson (1990/1933) began building the theoretical foundations for the Afrocentric worldview compiled from the best of the traditional thought of African civilizations. Diop (1974) set the stage for the current blossoming of Afrocentricity in his historic work *The African origins of civilization: Myth or reality*. Many others have argued for Afrocentricity on the basis of the existence of an African worldview. For instance, Gyekye (1995), Jahn (1989/1958), Kershaw (1998), and Mbiti (1969) helped to further delineate the precise elements of an African worldview, and how these might transform the Eurocentric and American world views. Many of these authorities have relied on ancient texts and on the oral tradition of African cultures, which have existed since the beginning of civilization.

Afrocentricity

The evolving ideas that generated a renewed interest in the study of Africa and the cultural heritage that is embodied there attained a principled focus in the United States in 1980, with the publication of Asante's *Afrocentricity*.[1] Asante (2003a) describes Afrocentricity as

> a mode of thought and action in which the centrality of African interests, values, and perspectives predominate. In regards to theory, it is the placing of African people in the center of any analysis of African phenomena. . . . In terms of action and behavior, it is a devotion to the idea that what is in the best interest of African consciousness is at the heart of ethical behavior. Finally, Afrocentricity seeks to enshrine the idea that blackness itself is a trope of ethics. Thus, to be black is to be against all forms of oppression. . . . It challenges and takes to task the perpetuation of white racial supremacist ideas in the imagination of the African world, and by extension, the entire world." (p. 2)

Afrocentricity is the critical element in the most recent research conducted on the empowerment and education of youth of African descent in schools in the United States. Madhubuti and Madhubuti (1994) and Tedla (1995) have argued for the importance of an Afrocentric perspective in studying the schooling experience of children of African descent. Akbar (1998a) calls for "educators who structure learning systems in such a way that children learn to respect who they are and see themselves as allies with the environment rather than the oppressive conquerors" (p. 249). It is not possible to directly address all the elements of an Afrocentric worldview here, but we will focus on a few of the more pertinent ingredients that we believe could contribute to understanding the strained relations between African and Afro-American students in the inner city public schools in the U.S. and how their interactions might be made more harmonious as they participate more fully in their education.[2]

There are four principles of Afrocentric theory which clearly distinguish this approach from the Eurocentric perspective, and which, when properly implemented, could have a dramatic influence on the general climate of learning in urban American schools attended by Afro-American or African students. To be discussed more closely below, these principles include: 1) the general distinction between individualism and the Afrocentric respect for community; 2) the distinction between the liberal democratic "all men are created equal" ethos, and the Afrocentric emphasis on respect for one's superiors in the community; 3) the valorization of "progress" in all things scientific and economic, and the Afrocentric emphasis on the interconnections and interdependencies between all humans; and 4) the pragmatic, commonsense view of the cosmos as expressed in "humanism" which is contrasted with the Afrocentrist's reverence for the spiritual and the eternal.

a. Community

Critical to Afrocentricity is a communal ontology—that is, "we are, therefore I exist." From this primary principle, it follows that Afrocentricity is a holistic view of reality. "Individuals find their worth, and their most sublime expression of existence in relationship to a community, to nature, and in relationship to some supreme idea or being" (N. Harris, 1998, p. 20). Mbiti (1969) explains that an "individual can only say: 'I am because we are; and since we are, therefore I am.' This is a cardinal point in the understanding of the African view of man" (p. 106). Ladson-Billings (2000) describes the basic epistemological difference between Eurocentric thought and African thought as Descartes' aphoristic "I think, therefore, I am" and "Ubuntu," and African nostrum that means "I am because we are" (p. 257). These are two distinctly different perceptions about the individual's relationship to the world.

The African view of man has been ignored in Eurocentric representations of Africa. Africans have been depicted as lacking any philosophy or culture worth studying. As long as a Eurocentric ontology of individualism holds sway in the Afro-American community, one might expect "casual and justified inhumanity" (N. Harris, 1998, p. 19). All eleven African students interviewed asked why they can't work together in school. One African student said, "We are used to working together. We study together. We learn together. We help one another." In their experience it's "all for all" not each person for themselves. This was also obvious when the African students were asked why it's important to get an education. Their answers focused on family, community and nation development, and not individual success.

b. Connectedness

A second key element of an Afrocentric worldview is that we are all connected and therefore deserving of respect. Akbar (1998b) explains that respect

> for the young by the adults and respect for the adults by the young is not simply a matter of "proper conduct," it is an outgrowth of the recognition of the spiritual core or essence in all of us. The manifestation of that spiritual core is primarily in the service one renders to the community. (p. 23)

What strikes the African students when they come to America is the lack of respect of American students for their teachers. Teachers in Africa are considered to be at least as deserving of respect as their parents, and students are quickly punished for the least bit of disrespect in school. Thus, when the African students first come to school in America they are quite submissive in school; however, in time, as adolescents, they begin to conform to peer pressure and imitate the behavior of other students.

When parents are called in to school because their child has disrespected a teacher, in many cases the child will be strongly disciplined by her parents because disrespect is not tolerated. And yet, the African students are exposed to disrespect in an inner-city school at almost every moment. There exists then a conflict between home culture values and school values. The student must learn to lead a double life and keep school experiences out of the home or risk the consequences of school acceptance and home disapproval.

c. Circular

A third aspect of an African worldview is the concept of time and history as circular and not driving towards progress. One's relationship to family, community, ancestors, elders and nature all play a critical role in maintaining harmony in the community.

> Rather than control nature, the search to understand and function consistently with nature's laws is aided by the belief that each aspect of nature has a special, unique role to play in the larger scheme of things (the whole). Each is valued and studied with an emphasis on integration and interdependence. In traditional African culture to be out of harmony, or rhythm, with nature was regarded as harmful to the well-being and survival of the whole. (Myers, 1988, pp. 47-48)

To Africans, people are more important than time. It is important to recognize that in some contexts one would not ignore a friend in need just because of an appointment elsewhere. A friend or family member in need takes precedence. The African students spend a lot of time "socializing" at school. Some teachers have commented that socializing is all that some of them do. Socializing for an African is recognizing their fellow human being. You greet everyone, everywhere all the time in Africa; you do not ignore people. Ignoring people is a sign of disrespect. History is to be studied because there are important lessons to be learned from the past, and the ancestors must be respected because they have much to teach us.

d. Creator

The fourth element is the interconnection between the spiritual and the material. One recognizes the Creator in all things. "In African philosophy, there is a commitment to harmony that some might call spirituality. It is the manifest essence of a search for the resolution of cultural and human problems" (Asante, 1998, p. 188). In an Afrocentric worldview, God is present in all things and many an African student will pray before all things. For instance, at the initial meeting of the African Students Association begun at Jackson High the students wanted to start the meeting with a prayer. In public schools in America, however, beginning with a prayer is not acceptable behavior. I've overheard African students ask what happened to prayer. How can a Christian country not pray before all things? The President prayed before he took the oath of office. They see others pray in public. The guest speaker at the graduation ceremony for a computer training class, an Afro-American minister, thanked God before beginning his commencement address. Black actors and actresses have thanked God at the Essence awards; but in our public schools prayer is not allowed. The students accept that Muslims pray in their language, and Christians pray in another and other religions in another; they accept that God hears many languages.

Afrocentric Versus Eurocentric

Under the best of circumstances, identity development is no small challenge. In the face of perduring racism, however, the evolution of any young person's identity can become exponentially more complicated (Davis, 2001; Moya, 2002). Afrocentricity provides a vehicle for positive identity development. Our study was designed to implement this tool in an urban high school with both African and Afro-American students. In bringing the African and Afro-American students together around their shared heritage, this study provides an excellent opportunity to explore the practical application of Afrocentricity. Despite the media stereotypes, negative images of the jungle environment, half-clothed savages, and pervasive welfare and crime, we endeavored in this study to discover whether our students could get past the dominant stereotypes and see each other as inter-related by providing them with appropriate experiences to facilitate some interconnections between them.

Moikobu (1981), a woman from Kenya, examined the relationship between Africans and Afro-Americans on a college campus in the United States from both a Eurocentric and Afrocentric view. She found that an Afrocentric view was a more positive view of the relationship between these two groups of students, because the Eurocentric view distorted the reality for both the Africans and Afro-Americans. She examined the literature from a Eurocentric view and described how "the Eurocentric view maintains that black Americans and Africans have little in common with one another except their ancestry and color" (p. 15). Moikobu argues for the superior qualities of Afrocentricity in appreciating and explaining what is common to persons of African descent. An Afrocentric view demonstrated that they had much in common and experienced a strong affinity, not limited to their skin color and ancestry, but based on shared values and beliefs and a common struggle against oppression and suppression in a "white-dominated, hostile world" (p. 68). They found shared beliefs in a Creator, the Supreme Being and a commitment to freedom and liberation.

Moikobu's research has demonstrated the failure of the Eurocentric view to adequately present the relationship that could exist between Africans and Afro-Americans. It is white superiority that has created the negative stereotypes of Africans as all living in the jungle and the pernicious view that Afro-Americans all live on welfare and do drugs and engage in crime. But from an Afrocentric view those stereotypes disappear and a more accurate representation can appear from behind the veil of this white hegemony.

Africans and Afro-Americans share a common ancestry, but even more importantly, a common worldview. What might we learn if we could see the world through African eyes; what could be of value to all the world? The allegation that Africans sold their own people into slavery has long made some Afro-Americans resistant to acknowledging a connection with Africa. In turn, the Africans are surprised when they learn that they are blamed by some Afro-Americans for the perpetration and perpetuation of slavery. The presence of Africans in America could be of great benefit to all Americans if there would be an exchange of history, experiences and cultural values. This could be a first step toward the healing of the antediluvian wounds that remain the aftermath of slavery, along with a growing strength in the struggle against continued oppression

The Evolution of Afro-American Studies in the Philadelphia School District

Since 1970, the formal study of Black History has been mandated in the Philadelphia School District for every child. It did not come easily and now, though it may be mandated, it is far from a reality. In November 1967, "several hundred black students from Philadelphia's high schools presented the Board of Education with a list of demands which included the teaching of Afro-American history. The date will also be remembered as the first time that the phrase—Negro or Afro-American History—became linked with student unrest here and in other cities" (Gillespie, 1969, p. 36). The march on the School Board was a major step in seeking a better quality education for Afro-American children in Philadelphia. The student demonstrators were met with violence and afterwards there were accusations of police brutality. An anonymous editorial described the demonstration as "needless" because this particular School Board was "one of the nation's most responsive," and went on to argue that if the violence was excessive it was the fault of the students or those who persuaded them to march in the first place. The author of the editorial declared that the demonstration and ensuing violence was pointless because much already had been done to provide "better courses on Afro-American history and culture" (*Violence – for what?*, 1967). The students who marched, however, knew that they were being denied an accurate representation of people of African descent. They knew their history was an important element in their getting a quality education. They knew that the officially endorsed story of Africa and Africans, the one found in their textbooks, was not the only story.

These students seemed to have made a significant impact by their marching. Changes were immediately made in curriculum offerings and teacher training was developed. Courses were started, workshops were held and curricula were developed. Teachers traveled to Africa; students held celebrations of their history in school assemblies; much work was done to ensure that the students in Philadelphia knew their history.[3]

Much progressive work was done by many people back in the 1970s. But has that work endured? Not only was Black studies considered to be an important subject to teach to Black children but there were those who argued for the importance of Afro-American history and culture for all children. The principal of one elementary school declared that "teaching Afro-American history to both white and Negro pupils would prove an antidote to the poison of prejudice" (Ryan, 1968). Mark Shedd, then Superintendent of the Philadelphia School District, declared at the time that the "more the students in our predominantly white schools learn about the contributions of the Negro in the making of America, as well as his current concerns, the more hope for racial harmony the future will hold" (*Gratz given*, 1968).[4] Afro-American history was proposed as an antidote to prejudice. More recently, Dei (1994) has argued for an understanding of history from many points of view, including the African perspective.

> When a teacher gives voice and space to multi-centric perspectives and other legitimate interpretations of human experiences, every student in the class, African and non-African gains from knowing the complete account of events that have shaped human history. (p. 20)

The myths about Africa have survived despite the serious work of many highly committed individuals. And the commitment to providing all students with a better sense of their history and culture has not been realized. As a spokesman for the Superintendent of Schools said in 1967, "[i]dentity is the problem of many Negro students. . . . Negro history and culture, they feel, will give them an identity which they claim was taken from them when they arrived in this country" (Gillespie, 1967a). Although the importance of more accurate information about Afro-American history made media headlines in the late 1960s, textbooks produced as late as 1995 still were not accurate representations of the events and experiences affecting people of African descent.

Since 1970, when an Office of African and Afro-American Studies was established, there has been a mandate in the Philadelphia School District's policy requiring "every school to provide a well-rounded program in Afro-American studies as an integral part of its total school experience."[5] The story of people of

African descent has not become a part of the fabric of life in America. "Black History" remains an add-on to the understanding of the evolution of the world, is not well-integrated into our society, and remains the only exposure most of our children in most of our schools will ever have to the many traditions and unique qualities of the African heritage. Ngugi wa Thiong'o (1986) has described the process of relegating African history to the add-on subject it has become by noting that the

> effect of a cultural bomb is to annihilate a people's belief in their names, in their languages, in their environment, in their heritage of struggle, in their unity, in their capacities and ultimately in themselves. It makes them see their past as one wasteland of nonachievement and it makes them want to distance themselves from that wasteland. (p. 3)

In late 2004, a specific curriculum on African history was introduced as a pilot project in several Philadelphia area high schools (Woodall, 2005). With the incoming classes beginning in Fall 2005, the Philadelphia School District will establish a combined African and African American history course as a graduation requirement, taking its place among the other required social studies subjects, including American history, geography and world history (Snyder, 2005).

African-Centered Education

Out of a commitment to reach children of African descent has come a movement for African-centered education, which would provide students with a learning environment that is more congruent with the lifestyles and values of Afro-American families. A school based on African values, it is believed, "would eliminate the patterns of rejection and alienation that engulf so many Afro-American school children, especially males" (Epps, 2000, p. vi). Another way that Black parents and teachers have addressed their concern for the education of their children is to create supplementary education centers. Supplementary means "in addition to" not "instead of" the required school programs. These programs take place after school, on weekends, or in the summer, as in the Freedom Schools, which were a

> signature project of the Children's Defense Fund's (CDF) Black Community Crusade for Children (BCCC). Established as part of the voter registration and community mobilization effort during the summer of 1964, Freedom Schools provide a way for students, parents and community leaders to come together to strengthen both educational opportunities and the fabric of neighborhoods, as well as achieve equality through advocacy and community organizing.[6]

According to Kifano (1996), "[i]ndependent Africentric supplementary schools . . . have assisted public and private schools in meeting the intellectual, social, and cultural needs of Afro-American students for the past three decades" (p. 217). In these supplementary programs students are taught African languages, traditions, values and history. Programs are designed to immerse the students in African and Afro-American culture and thereby center themselves in their African ancestry (p. 215). Kifano argues that Afrocentric supplementary schools are based on the ability to meet the academic and cultural needs of Afro-American students and "serve as valuable resources for effectively supporting Afro-American students' academic achievement" (p. 217). Students are taught African languages, traditions, values and history. "Proverbs, poetry, plays and other games and activities rooted in African and Afro-American culture are used extensively to impart values that teach students to serve their community" (p. 214). The Nguzo Saba principles are both taught and practiced. Programs are designed to immerse the students in African and Afro-American culture and thereby center themselves in their African ancestry (p. 215). Although six of these schools were established in California in the 1960s and 70s, only four remain viable today. One of the major impediments to their viability has been funding.

Culturally Relevant Education

Much has been written about the importance of a culturally relevant curriculum. The mainstream curriculum, or what E.D. Hirsch would describe as "Cultural Literacy," is based on the European version of the world. Although Hirsch has his supporters such as Diane Ravitch, Chester Finn and others, there are many Afro-American scholars such as Delpit, Hale, Irvine, Ladner, and Ladson-Billings who have written profusely to counter this attempt at cultural hegemony. There are similar approaches taken by Latino/Latina scholars such as Sonia Nieto (1992, 1999) and Pedro Antonio Noguera (2003). Each of these scholars focuses attention on the power relations that exist in schools and how minority status is defined by the lack of access to this power.

For example, Lisa Delpit amplifies the voice of the teachers of color who feel that they know the students and what they need, but are struggling in a system designed to keep children of color at the bottom, a system which does not invite nor respect their views. In her chapter, "Cross-cultural confusions," Delpit makes the point that there are differences in culture and they are to be celebrated rather than minimized, dismissed, or even worse, attacked. According to Delpit (1995),

> [i]f we are to successfully educate all of our children, we must work to remove the blinders built of stereotypes, monocultural instructional methodologies, ignorance, social distance, biased research and racism. We must work to destroy those blinders so that it is possible to really see, to really know the students we must teach. (p. 182)

In her study of eight successful teachers of Afro-American children, Ladson-Billings (1994) found that it is not that teachers must be Afro-American to be culturally relevant, and it's not that being Afro-American makes one culturally relevant to Afro-American children. Rather, it is the commitment to "honor and respect" the culture of others that makes one a culturally relevant teacher.

One therefore has to recognize, call forth, and celebrate the cultures of the students in their classes. But you cannot celebrate what you do not know.

Ladner (1998) focuses on the values that she learned from her family which have provided her with the necessary preparation to succeed in life. The values "molded the character of a people who fought their way out of slavery and the poverty that followed in the rugged years after emancipation" (p. 8). These values are based on four basic principles: a) the power of self-identity, b) the power of the extended family, c) the power of the community to determine its future, and d) the power of the past to influence the present. Ladner explains that

> our ancestors brought some of these values from their old cultures, others originated during and in response to the Middle Passage and slavery. Still others developed in response to the twentieth century and were severely tested in a national environment of legally recognized segregation. Taken together, they constitute a living legacy. (pp. 11-12)

This living legacy must be passed on to the next generation. If not, the consequences, according to Ladner will be "selfishness, slothfulness, materialism, an inability to cope and a fragility of the soul" (p. 6). Ladner has focused specifically on adolescence as a time of identity development and calls upon the entire community to assist the youth in developing strong identities, a call that includes teaching black history.

Although understood to be a site of enculturation, schools cannot succeed in isolation. Students have lives outside of the classrooms and teachers cannot ignore that fact. Home culture can be looked upon as an asset or a deficit. When the home culture is viewed as a deficit, the school sets up an oppositional relationship with the student, their family, their community, their ancestry, and their heritage. Viewed as an asset, the home culture can assist the student in acquiring the necessary tools to succeed in school and in life.

One characteristic of the Afrocentric epistemology is the "transcendent order in the world" (Asante, 1988, p. 21), which combines history, intuition, and immersion and which recognizes the spiritual in the worldly. For true freedom to exist, people of African descent cannot rely on the interpretation of freedom, such as the right to vote, but must focus on the inner change.

Despite the attempts of colonialism, slavery, and the Eurocentric educational system to extirpate African history, values, and culture, the African worldview has been resilient and has been passed down from generation to generation both in Africa and the Diaspora. The song featured in the film "The Language You Cry In" is but one example of the preservation of African culture despite colonialism, slavery, and the seemingly omnipresent Eurocentric educational system.

Chapter Summary

In order for there to be true freedom for people of African descent they must free themselves from a Eurocentric perspective and construct their own identity based at least in part on African philosophical thought. In addition, African high school students, whether in Africa or the United States, are an understudied group. This research project was one small step in the implementation of Afrocentricity as a theoretical framework and methodology. The results from the present study confirm that the principles of Afrocentricity have much to contribute to the understanding of the interactions between African students and their American peers. This understanding could help teachers of African and Afro-American students be better prepared to understand and affirm their students and encourage them to reach out and get to know one another better. In the next chapter we explore how the Afrocentric model can inform the educational practices used with students in inner-city public schools to broaden the multicultural perspective of students with no ties to Africa but whose understanding of world history has been otherwise unfairly distorted.

CHAPTER 8

Making the Connection / Sharing a Heritage

They consider my uniqueness strange	Any praise is preferential treatment
They call my language slang	To voice concern is discontentment
They see my confidence as conceit	If I stand up for myself, I am too defensive
They see my mistakes as defeat	If I do not trust them, I am too apprehensive
They consider my success accidental	I am deviant if I separate, I am fake if I
They minimize my intelligence to "poten-	assimilate
tial"	My character is constantly under attack
My questions mean I am unaware	Pride for my race makes me
My advancement is somehow unfair	"TOO BLACK." (Anon).

In this chapter, we explain how an Afrocentric approach can inform the educational practices used with students in inner-city public schools when their heritage harkens from Africa. We suggest that this same Afrocentric view can be used to broaden the multicultural perspective of students with no ties to Africa but whose understanding of world history has been otherwise unfairly distorted. In this, and carrying over into the final chapter, we also will explore how the underlying themes of Afrocentricity, including community identity, collective responsibility, and knowing oneself, can be useful concepts to infuse into the educational experiences of all of America's children, regardless of their heritage.

The presence of newly arrived African students at Jackson posed a collection of new problems for both students and teachers.[1] There existed plenty of stereotypes maintained by both the African students about America and the Afro-American experience in American society, as well as by the Afro-Americans students and their seeming apathy about Africa or the African students in their classes. These stereotypes unavoidably interfered with the relationships that failed to materialize between the Afro-American and African students. Hostility and ignorance were permeating the atmosphere at Jackson and having significant adverse impact on the learning experiences of all of the students at Jackson.

Premises of This Study

Researchers studying people of African descent must be cognizant of the possible bias of a Eurocentric approach that objectifies interpretations of the experience of Africans. According to Asante (1990), the most legitimate reason for advancing an Afrocentric method is that "Eurocentric methods have been aggressive and violative" (p. 119). The Afrocentric method "suggests cultural and social immersion as opposed to 'scientific distance' as the best approach to understand African phenomena" (p. 27). In our view, an Afrocentric method and framework both in the collection and the analysis of data provided the most promising approach to bridge the gulf that clearly existed between these two groups of students unaware of any common heritage emanating from the African continent.

To know one's history and culture is of paramount importance in an Afrocentric model and is the fundamental principle that informed this study. Despite the concerted efforts expended during American-style slavery to destroy all connection that slaves, and even freed slaves had with Africa, the connection remains vital, if sublimated, today and it can be restored to full vitality (Akbar, 1998b; Hilliard, 1998; Hale, 2001; Kambon, 1992, 1998). Given their history of strained relationships and the negative or denigrating myths, misperceptions, and stereotypes that existed between these two groups of students, however, reestablishing the connection required an intervention that disrupted the status quo (Efran, Lukens, & Lukens, 1990). Nothing in their environment was designed to bring them together around their shared heritage. Although there was one African American studies course offered at Jackson, there was only one teacher for the subject and so the course was limited to fewer than 100 students out of the student body of 2,000. Even though there were both African and Afro-American students in the class, it was not designed to bring the two groups together or adequately address the negative misperceptions they held about each other. The Afro-American students reported that the stereotypes of Tarzan and savages in the jungle were all that they knew about Africa, even after completing the course. For their part, the African students continued to see the Afro-Americans as rude and violent. These stereotypes prevented them from seeing one another as potential allies related by a common ancestry.

Norman Harris (1998) argues that true knowing about a common ancestry must arise from African history and African philosophy, which includes the visible and the invisible, and relates to history as a circular not linear pattern of events. History is different when examined from an Afrocentric orientation because Afrocentricity requires a holistic view of reality. In other words, the principle at the foundation of Afrocentric thinking is not to promote the Western capitalistic and American individualistic ideals of acquire more, more, more; rather, it is be more, live more, and relate more. No study of people of African descent would be appropriate if it did not let their voices be heard and follow the beat of their worldview.[2]

We started this project by analyzing the existing relationships among African and Afro-American students at Jackson from the perspective of a mixed group of students who were struggling to establish common grounds to relate. We then developed a number of Afrocentric activities to bring these students together in an attempt to bridge the gaps in their understanding of each other. Finally, we documented the impact of these activities from the perspectives of the students themselves. Our purpose was to bring together African and Afro-American students apparently at odds and out of sync, and to provide them with several opportunities to learn from and about one another and their shared heritage.

The first step was to identify the sources of the strained relationships that existed among these two groups of students, and to this end we tried to understand the misapprehensions between these students who seemed to have much in common but who appeared unaware of the existence of any commonalities between them. We documented the existing situation through observations, interviews, and focus group interactions. Then we set the tone for the "bringing together experiences" by first having the students view the film entitled "The Language You Cry In: The story of a Mende song." This hour-long documentary depicts the life experiences and the shared heritage of a particular African woman and her Afro-American counterpart, unknown to each other and separated by thousands of miles, who are emotionally bonded through the vehicle of the words to a specific song each had learned from her respective grandmother. The film conveys the network of connections between two cultures separated by hundreds of years of hardships, pathos, and unforgotten memories. The students were then encouraged to verbally share their experiences following the film, and to write reaction papers. These activities comprised the students' introduction to Afrocentricity. The goal of this initial process, as indeed it was the primary objective undergirding this entire study, was to facilitate, understand, and document the generative activities and sharing of reactions that would encourage the students to undertake a "crossing over" to the way things were being perceived by the other students. This was intended to break down stereotypes, to bridge the gaps in experience and knowledge that kept them from seeing each other as equals, and to facilitate the students' developing an appreciation for their shared African heritage.

Student Voice

Until quite recently, student voice has been missing in most studies of the schooling experience of our youth, but over the past decade and a half, much has been written about the "silenced voices" of students (Fine, 1987; MacLeod, 1991; Weis & Fine, 1993). Delpit (1993), for example, writes that

> We must keep the perspective that people are experts in their own lives. . . . They can be the only chroniclers of their own experience. . . . We must believe that people are rational beings, and therefore must always act rationally. We may not understand their rationales, but that in no way militates against the existence of these rationales or reduces our responsibility to attempt to apprehend them. (p. 139)

Crucial to the outcome of this study was documenting the students' views and experiences as well as the historical basis for those experiences as expressed by African and Afro-American students. Asante (1990) stresses that "projection conceals diversity and imposes an epistemological perspective contrary to the unique attributes of other people" (p. 150). To mitigate any projection it was necessary to do member checks and verify their responses. The students were asked to comment on what they had learned, describe their experience during this project and make recommendations for the future. A conscientious effort was made to use the students' own words and to let their words speak for themselves.

It was a significant factor to the outcomes of this study that most of the African students had been in the U.S. only a few years and had not yet completely adapted to or not yet been co-opted by American culture. Although they were not immune to the colonialism and cultural hegemony imposed on them in their educational systems, they are still connected to life in Africa, their extended families, their elders, their ancestors, and their experiences growing up. They have much to share about everyday life in Africa today, although they, too, may need to learn more about their own history.

Working with a small group of African students who have not yet acculturated as "American" but are still connected enough to being African provides an important context because they can assist in the process of developing Afrocentric activities and are still committed to promoting a positive image of Africa and Africans. The American influence, although compelling, had not yet taken hold of this group of African students. There are several generalizable lessons to be learned from our results, principally an appreciation for the many ways in which stereotypes keep groups apart due to misunderstandings or ignorance. Our own knowledge of Afrocentricity, experience in many countries on the continent of Africa, and a commitment to Afrocentricity and an appreciation of the value of the African worldview was, of course, a remarkable feature of the unique qualities of this study, but we believe that these characteristics are not so unique that very similar activities presented to another group of students would produce similar outcomes, provided the guiding force of the teacher is willing also to evolve along with the students. We realize that the presence of students recently arrived from the continent of Africa is not the norm in most schools, but the Afrocentric principles discussed in Chapter 7 are life-affirming for human beings generally, although we concede they may have a special attraction for students of African descent. Given its place in world history and its potential to influence world events, understanding more about Africa should be required of every student.

Through observing the African American studies class, as well as interviewing and listening to the students interact in many different situations—from the halls to the cafeteria to the gym—we started to comprehend some of the underlying reasons for how they perceived one another and how their perceptions were impeding any of their efforts to connect with each other. Nothing in their environment was planned or designed to bring these two groups together, or to provide an accurate representation of Africa; this was not rectified by the information presented in the lone, elective African American studies class, which in some very subtle ways merely reinforced the standard misperceptions about Africa and the African people. Although they would walk beside each other, sit in classrooms together and share the same cafeteria, nothing was in place to bridge the great divide of misinformation and stereotypes about Africa, Africans, and Afro-Americans. Once the fundamental connection was made—the African connection—everyone was on a path to learn more. Yes, there is a much longer journey to take into deepening the connection to Africa, but when the desire is there the journey can begin. With no desire, no interest, the information, of course, goes nowhere and every teacher has experienced the student apathy that ensues.

We initially found the Afro-American students to have little interest in Africa. The African students had been told not to associate with the Afro-Americans or they would be changed, and not for the better. We believed that both stigmatizing, unreflective mind sets could benefit from some liberating experiences. What ultimately changed for the participants in this study was their interest in each other. They began to see each other as connected by a common heritage, common ancestors, a history and culture that belong to them. Each activity built on the last activity, always looking for ways to expose the myths, misperceptions and stereotypes that were keeping the students apart. In just a few activities distributed over ten weeks during a school semester, the students had the opportunity to connect with their shared African heritage and develop new, positive images of Africa, Africans and Afro-Americans. In the end, they could articulate the value of seeing the world through an Afrocentric perspective.

Getting Past the Stereotypes—The Students' Journey

The activities we selected were intended specifically to redress the misperceptions and stereotypes that were underneath the feelings that were keeping these students apart and we used activities that were focused on the connection to Africa and to one another as people of African descent. The first activity addressed the need for new images of Africa and Africans; the second activity reconnected the students to Africa; the third activity allowed them to make a personal connection to each other; the fourth activity addressed the stereotypes and their shared values and finally the students had the opportunity to converse with Molefi Kete Asante, the Afrocentrist scholar most prominent for his zealous advocacy of Afrocentric education. Dr. Asante embodies the African connection and both the African and Afro-American participants were moved by his presence, his speaking, and his obviously deep appreciation for his African heritage.

Each of the activities chosen derived from our commitment to provide the students with the opportunity to take a deeper look into their African heritage and our own understanding of Afrocentricity and the African worldview. They were asked to reflect on the intervention and group activities, communicate what worked and make recommendations. The first step in the process of implementing Afrocentricity was to bring the African students together and to build a network of support for them. At the request of a small group of African students, we helped them form an African Students Association, draw up some basic agreements, enroll members, elect officers, and organize our initial activities.

a.   The Language You Cry In

In the film "The Language You Cry In," which we selected for its dramatic story of connecting an American with her African past, the narrator begins by talking about the "non-history," the silent history" of the Afro-Americans and their connection to Africa. This film traces the generational transmission of a song preserved by the descendents of those enslaved in the American South to the village of its origin in Sierra Leone. It follows the paths of two families, separated by thousands of miles and connected only by the words of this particular song, who are reunited in Sierra Leone, despite war and other difficulties. Two women, one in Georgia, the other in Sierra Leone, have kept the same song alive without even being aware of the existence of her counterpart's similar efforts. The women and their families finally meet in Sierra Leone and are reunited in an emotional embrace.

The voice of the narrator is strong and tells the students that "memory is power." The message is that we need to remember our connection to Africa. Africa has much to teach us. Our connection is real. Although it has been left out of the textbooks and their life experiences, it is real and can be accessed through following the journey of Mary Moran and Bendu Jabati, the two protagonists in the film, who connect after hundreds of years of slavery, war and misinformation. The film visualizes the notion that there is power in memory and amnesia is the loss of that memory.[3] The film opens ominously with the narrator's voice saying:

Africa–18th century

A young woman is snatched from her village by slave traders, forced apart forever from her mother, her motherland, her language, her identity.

This is the non-history of millions of Afro-American women and men, a wall of silence, a mysterious past that memory fights to preserve from the onslaught of time, but which ends up shrouded in darkness.

The mixed group of students who participated in the discussion following the film requested several things: a) an assignment that would require them to interview and learn about each other, b) small group activities that required them to work together, c) exchanging more information about each other, and d) the opportunity to learn some African languages and more about the various African cultures—even the African students wanted to learn more about Africa. All agreed that the large assemblies do not work in bringing the students together. They are too impersonal and they are too readily influenced by peer pressure. Peer pressure is strong and even if they want to learn more about one another they won't if their peers reject it. The students requested that more students at Jackson have this experience of coming to the film in a small group. It would be necessary to reach a critical mass of students to effect change. Everyone noted that there had been booing at the last multicultural assembly and that hurt when you are the one trying to share your culture and the response is so negative. Everyone agreed that small group interactions with opportunities for one on one work were critical to bringing the students together.

This film opened their eyes and made the connection so real, so visible, so valid and at the level of the heart. The next plea speaks loudly for how much it meant to at least one Afro-American student, though her comment was echoed by others, who remarked that having had their eyes opened, they wanted to know more. They did not want to remain ignorant of their heritage, their ancestry, their culture, and their connection. They wanted to reclaim it. "I want to know the truth. I'd rather give up all the benefits of technology and live in a village in truth." Valeisha experienced the sense of community, the connectedness, the importance of the ancestors, and spiritual values as opposed to materialism through the film. She went home and wrote a play and included these elements of the African worldview. For the African students, one of their major complaints was how they had been treated here in America, and in particular, how they had been treated by the Afro-Americans. The film provided graphic images of the reception of the Afro-Americans in Sierra Leone. The African students in the study reinforced the film by talking about how they would treat any and all Afro-Americans in Africa. As in the movie, they would be welcomed as family. In fact, they would be treated even better than family. They would be considered as a member of the family who had traveled and who returned with knowledge and is worthy of respect. And yet, the Africans find themselves treated as less than, much less than, when they come to America. According to the students it is much more hurtful to be rejected by a Black American than a White American, because the Black American is family. White Americans are strangers. Their ignorance can be tolerated, but to be mistreated by members of your family is much more degrading.

> Hamed: If Black Americans go to Africa they will be treated well. If you go to Africa you will be welcomed. Not like here. Some people are ignorant to us here. How would you feel if people treated you badly?
> Sylviane: I'd probably cry.
> Miriam: We need to be united.

After the film had ended, there were stunning reactions on the part of both the Africans and the Afro-Americans. The students led a discussion in which both Africans and Afro-Americans had a chance to speak to each other from a new and different place, that is, the place of shared heritage which is the focus of the film. Something unexpected happened during this discussion: An Afro-American female asked to speak first and she said that she had had the opportunity to travel to Senegal recently and she had been welcomed there as if she were long-lost family. She could never forget the wonderful way that the Africans treated her. And then she apologized to the African students who were present for the behavior of the students at Jackson toward the African students. This provided the opportunity for the African students to talk about how they felt about how they had been treated—the harassment, name calling, teasing, mocking and even violence that they have experienced at the hands of their Afro-American peers and how they would prefer to be treated. Everyone participated in a discussion about what could be done to improve the situation. Many of the Afro-American students expressed the desire to learn more and in small groups. They complained about the one-day or one-week multicultural assemblies organized at school because they were too big and ineffective. It was easy to be unaffected in large groups. They admitted that they had ridiculed some of the presentations at the assemblies, but now they wanted to know more.

Near the end of the time for the discussion, some of the participants started spontaneously singing the Sister Sledge song from the 1970s, "We are family. Brothers and sisters are we." While the formal discussion had to end in order to get the students back to school on time, the participants continued to talk to each other as they left the room and started to head back to school or home. Many students were not content to have the discussion end there. They continued talking on the trolley back to school and the conversations continued until the school year ended. One question they asked was "What can we do to help set the record straight for more students at our school?"

One African student informed us that her experience that day already had improved her life at Jackson. Apparently, the day after seeing the film with the group, she and some of the other Afro-Americans who had been present, were on the same bus going to school. They greeted each other and one of the Afro-American girls asked the African girl how to greet in Mende, the girl's home language and also the language spoken by the villagers in the film. They talked, and since then they are no longer strangers, but sisters, from a common ancestry, related by a shared experience and walking a similar path. The African student said that her Afro-American friend now "knows where she is from now and it's no longer strange to her. Now we can talk and get along. I really hope we can take more students to the film so they can see where they are from. Then we can learn from each other." The African student said that she looked forward to school again so that she could get to know this friendly student better and hopefully meet others after they see the film too.

b.   The Balch Institute

In October 2001, the Balch Institute, located in downtown Philadelphia, showcased an exhibit entitled "Extended Lives: The African Immigrant Experience in Philadelphia." This exhibit displayed, through a variety of media, the lives of the various groups of Africans residing in the area, both those who had come as refugees and those who immigrated to this city. As an interactive exhibit it transported the observer into the lives of the city's African immigrants including their social, cultural, religious, work and day-to-day lives, and even featured some pictures of students and teachers at Jackson High, which made it all the more compelling. The focus was to present a celebration of the presence of the Africans and their contributions to the vibrant life of this metropolis. It was the embodiment of the descriptions offered by Rong and Preissle (1998), and demonstrated that Africans are working, worshiping, shopping, creating, living, and contributing to Philadelphia. They are neighbors, friends, customers, clients, and employers. They are still connected to Africa and can bring their traditions, stories, tales, music, knowledge, worldview and culture to share with those of us in America. They have much to offer. They are rich in their life experiences. This is the message of the exhibit, a message not readily available elsewhere but because it is in such an official place as a museum, it is received by the students as "true" and "real." It is more real to them than what they have seen on television. It counteracts the myths and misperceptions and replaces them with images that cannot co-exist with those stereotypes.

The four elements of the African worldview were clearly manifested in this exhibit. One of the creative features of the exhibit is a bridge, which shows, through the use of various artifacts, the African immigrants' connection to Africa and the ways in which they maintain that connection. Even the title of the exhibit, "Extended Lives" refers to the ways in which the Africans continue to be connected to their lives back in Africa. They remain connected to their families, their communities back in Africa and make new connections here in America. Their connections are about community and circular in nature. The exhibit promotes the idea that the African connection remains strong no matter how far Africans may travel from their homeland.

The stories dramatized in the exhibit are about families, extended families, communities; this is not an exhibit about individuals. A centerpiece in the exhibit is a video presentation of the importance of religion in the lives of the African immigrants. There are clips of Africans in churches and mosques in the Philadelphia area. The Afro-American students could recognize many of the various religious expressions of the Africans. Their spiritual connections became more obvious to all of the students who attended the exhibit.

After arriving at the institute we were ushered into a room with some pictures on the wall and a map of Africa. The Instructor for the workshop asked everyone to gather close together at the map of Africa. She asked the students, "How many countries are in Africa?" One African student answered "50." The instructor said, "You're close. The current generally agreed on number is 53." Then she asked, "How many countries are in the United States?" Several students responded together, "50." "Oh no," said the instructor, "There are 50 states in the United States, not countries. The U.S. is one country, with many states." She continued, "One of the first things we want to recognize is that Africa is a continent, not a country." Then she went on to explain the size of the continent of Africa and how the United States, China and Europe can fit inside the dimensions of the continent of Africa. Next, the Instructor asked what people think of when they hear the word Africa. The students responded with, "Jungle, animals, desert." She went on to explain that some of the world's major cities such as Cairo and Johannesburg are in Africa and that only a small percentage is jungle. "There are cities with high rise buildings and so much more." One of the African students said, "Everything you can find here, you can find there."

Every conversation and interaction that occurred seemed to be heightened in intensity and seriousness because we were in an academic "institute." We might have been able to hold similar discussion in a classroom at Jackson, but the students said it would not have had as profound an impact simply because an institute is a site of 'official' knowledge, or as one student said, "We know it's important if it's in a museum." Their school, on the other hand, is a site of the conflict and negative stereotyping and boredom for many students.

We were escorted to a room full of artifacts of immigrants to America.

There were pictures of all kinds of people coming to America, most of whom struggled to survive. The instructor pointed out many of the artifacts from various groups of immigrants in American history, including the Irish, Germans and the Chinese. She asked them if they could tell her why and how people had come to America. The students talked about immigrants wanting jobs, wanting a better life, and wanting an education. They talked about coming by boat, by plane, as a refugee, as an immigrant, as a child, as an adult. The distinction of slavery was made; it was not immigration but forced transport of human beings for forced labor as distinct from indentured servants which was another way that people came to America. She talked about the slave trade, the Middle Passage and the effects of slavery.

After describing various ethnic groups throughout American history who had come to America, the Instructor talked specifically about the African immigrants and she asked the Africans in the room to tell her where they were from. She handed out the booklets about the exhibit and had the students read that in Philadelphia, "there are an estimated 40,000-55,000 African immigrants . . . from almost every African country . . . the largest communities are from Nigeria, Liberia, Ethiopia, and Ghana" (Extended Lives, p. 3). She asked the students to read along with her as she identified the communities of African immigrants in Philadelphia—"Angolan, Eritrean, Ethiopian, Ghanaian, Guinean, Ivoirian, Liberian, Kenyan, Mauritanian, Malian, Nigerian, Senegalese, Sierra Leonian, Somali, and Sudanese." As she read she asked if there was anyone in the room from that country. When she called Guinea, two students raised their hands. When she called Liberia, five students raised their hands. When she called Sierra Leone, two students raised their hands and when she called Senegal, one student raised his hand. We pointed out that at Jackson we also had students from Eritrea, Ethiopia, Ivory Coast, and Sudan and a teacher from Mauritania. Even the African students did not know that there were Africans from so many different countries living in Philadelphia. A little known fact was highlighted in the presentation by the staff of the Balch Institute. "Immigrants from Africa have the highest educational levels among all immigrants to the United States. They have on average over three years of college and over half are college graduates" (p. 3).

We then watched a film of various African religious services. Religion held a prominent place in this exhibit; the Creator also plays a major role in the Afrocentric worldview. Africans recognize the Creator and the role played by a Creator in sustaining life on this planet. The film included clips of a Coptic service, prayers at the Mosque, a Baptist and Methodist Church service and others. Several students in the room could recognize the languages being spoken, which were not always English, and this brought up the question of languages. After the film, the Instructor asked the students which services were similar to their own and which were different and then asked the students which languages they could speak. As a student identified a language not yet mentioned, the Instructor counted the total languages spoken by the students in attendance as eleven different languages.

Then we ventured to another part of the exhibit where the students became quickly engaged with the computer displays of the lives of Africans both here and in Africa, a music station with the sounds of Afro-Artists, clothing, family photographs, a taxi that tells the story of the Africans who transport people all over Philadelphia, a bridge that demonstrates the continued connection to loved ones still on the continent and the photo displays of entire families' life experiences.

Students commented that the exhibit made the people real to them. At one point there were students dancing to the music and there were African and Afro-Americans together. Two females were walking arm in arm and they were an African and an Afro-American and the one could be heard asking the other, "Tell me about this picture." Now the African students were the experts and could explain things to their Afro-American peers.

The comments shared by the students when they returned to school prompted others to request to be included on the next trip. Perhaps the best tribute to the trip's value was that more than a few students wanted to go again and there was soon an extensive waiting list for another trip. The students began to more actively interact while at the exhibit, and their interactions continued; there were friendships developing.

We discovered that the questions that the Africans most frequently got from students who had been to the exhibit were questions based on their experience of the exhibit and not the usual "negative" stereotypes of the media. The conversations then derived from a shared experience based in reality, no longer based on Tarzan and the jungle images.

This workshop provided all the participants, including the chaperones, with a point of departure for a meaningful conversation about Africa and Africans. We overheard quite a lot of "I didn't know that" as we walked around the exhibit with the students. Both Africans and Afro-Americans were learning something about the real lives of Africans in America that could transcend and correct the information formerly provided by school, home and the media.

c. Breaking Through the Stereotypes

Prior to joining this study, the African students who participated believed that the Afro-Americans just didn't want to know anything about Africa. One commented that "some people don't want to know the truth." The African students did not know that their Afro-American peers had had no access to the information. The myths perpetrated by school, home and the media are powerful images of negativity and the students have little to no access to more appropriate images of Africa.

The students were surprised to discover that they had little to no knowledge of Africa except stereotypes. The following table illustrates their efforts to uncover the ways that they viewed each other based on their lack of real knowledge.

Table 8.1– Stereotypes and Preconceptions

Africa	Africans	Afro-Americans
All jungle	Stink	Live in nice cities
Just tribes	Are dirty	Think they know more
Animals in the wild	Stupid	Welfare
A violent continent	Eat raw animals	Rude
There's hunger	Sleep on floor	Violent
No houses	Mostly naked	Lazy
Africa is poor	Are not civilized	There are no rich
	Have no cars	
	No cable TV	
	Live in the jungle	

What is immediately noticeable from this catalogue of characteristics is the number of stereotypes applied to Africa and Africans, while the Africans could list only a few stereotypes of Afro-Americans, and they are predominantly negative characteristics regardless of origin. For many of the Africans, they have only global, amorphous stereotypes about Afro-Americans before coming to the U.S. Some have seen American films and have images of gangsters, criminals and drug dealers but others, not only don't have any images, they may not even know that there are Black Americans. One African female told the story of how she was surprised to find all these Black students at her school on the first day. "I expected them to be white." What is interesting to note is that "violent" appears on both lists. That Blacks are violent by virtue of the color of their skin is the stereotype that distinguishes the Africans as immigrants from other immigrant groups and gives them qualities of the involuntary minorities (Ogbu & Simons, 1998). They are judged by the color of their skin, first and foremost. Merely because of their shared skin color, Africans and Afro-Americans share the burden of the American-type racist notion that to be Black is to be violent.

What is also illuminating is the stereotype that all Afro-Americans live in nice houses. Most African students might have inquired "Doesn't everyone in America live in nice houses?" The Africans participating in this study characterized their neighborhoods in America as not being nice, of actually being worse than they could have imagined. Some of them described themselves as living better lives in Africa

It was important for the students to have time to reflect first on their own values and then hear from a member of the other group and compare and contrast. What was interesting was that there was no contrasting, only sharing what they had listed in common. At no point did anyone question the other about his or her values. When they shared their lists the response principally was, "Oh, that was important to you too?"

As outlined in Table 8.1, both groups shared the image of being "stuck up" or "knowing more." One of the key activities, therefore, was having the students interview each other. Following the interview, one Afro-American student said, "We have a lot of the same interests. I didn't know that." There were similar responses and similar comments of "I didn't know." Sylviane an Afro-

American female asked Haja an African female what values she had brought with her and had not given up since she had come. Haja talked about the respect she has for her parents, for all elders and how she could never talk back to an elder, even if they made her angry. Sylviane commented how she could understand that if you were brought up that way it would be hard to see all the ways in which the students at Jackson seemed disrespectful and how hard that must be when it is so opposite to your culture. This was the beginning of a discovery and discussion of cultural values. The students were beginning, on their own initiative, to touch on the four elements of the African worldview, community, connectedness, circular and Creator. Needing a sense of community, their connection to their families, the importance of their faith and their recognizing their ancestors or those who came before were mentioned when the students talked about what is important to them.

Table 8.2 – Typical Value Preferences

Individual Values – Male

Damon – Afro-American male	*Musa – African male*
Basketball talent	My family
Getting an education	Intelligence
Going to college	Learning
Making it to NBA	Being good
Life	Education
Friends	Family unity
Family	Being in college
Money	Having good grades
Striving for the best	My country
Learning more	My friends
Time I have on earth	My future

Individual Values – Female

Sylviane – Afro-American female	*Fanta – African female*
My mother	My family
Life	My life
God	My goals
Family	My mom
Jobs	My honesty
Being in control	My education
	My friends
	My country
	My traditions
	Accept my mistakes

As illustrated in Table 8.2, the students in general recognized many similarities, but only similarities. We saw some exceptions, as money was not a value listed by any of the Africans, but it was listed as the most important by one of the Afro-American males. The students, however, did not focus on exceptions. They talked only about what they shared. What was interesting was watching the students as they shared their lists of values with each other. They could be overheard talking about what was the same like religion and God, mom and family, and education and future. They didn't talk about differences; they focused on what they had in common. What was common to all the students was the importance of their families, their religion, their education and their hopes for the future.

As a culminating activity four of the students created a chart of American values and African values. Table 8.3 shows how the students listed American values as seen in the larger society, not their personal values.

Table 8.3 – Stereotypical Social Values

Societal Values

American Values	African Values
Money	Community
Food	Unity
Do for yourself	Respect
Look forward	Education
Success	Prayer
No respect	Creator
Romantic Love	Ancestors
Crime	Loyalty
Entrepreneurial goals	

The individual charts reflected the students' personal values, yet the societal chart speaks loudly about how the African and Afro-American students see American values. Neither the Africans nor the Afro-Americans argued over any of the values when they were shared with the group. There was general agreement about these values. In general, they found that they had very similar interests and values on their individual charts, although the chart of "American" values could be considered quite different both from the African and their own individual charts.

We did not have a lot of time to discuss this chart with the participants, but it was obvious from the way that they generated this chart that they were more critical of the American values. Their initial comment about the chart was that the African values were more positive. The African values listed by the students included two of the key elements of Afrocentricity explicitly—community and Creator. The other two elements—circular and connectedness—were alluded to in the value of the ancestors, unity and respect. These values were considered by all of the participants to be positive, desirable and shared.

d. Molefi Kete Asante—Embodied Afrocentrism

The final activity of this study included a visit from Dr. Molefi Kete Asante. The presence of Dr. Asante put a human face to Afrocentricity and the promise it holds for both Africans and Afro-Americans. An Afrocentric view of history supports people of African descent in developing a positive self-perception and therefore, Afrocentricity has been proposed as a tool for improving the self-esteem of Afro-Americans. Dr. Asante dispelled myths, argued for the connection with Africa and its benefit for both Africans and Afro-Americans, and challenged the students to learn more. He told them to be proud of being someone of African descent whether they came from the continent recently or are descendents of those brought here against their will. He emphasized that Africa has a rich heritage, which remains available for them to claim. Dr. Asante admonished that the young people would need to seek out information actively and to discover more about that rich heritage. He specifically addressed the African value of community. He said that "the person is significant because of the community. A person is not significant except in the collectivity. We laugh at the idea that I am important in my own self. How does that make any sense?" Dr. Asante also addressed the African connection to nature. He explained that "trees have life and if you cut down a tree you are cutting down a part of life. You need to recognize our connection to all living things. The goal is to live in harmony with nature."

Questions for Dr. Asante were prepared in advance by the students and submitted early so that we could maximize his time with the students.

Dr. Asante: Hotep – I greet you in peace, in the most ancient Kemetic language along the Nile Valley.

First Student Question: What got you interested in Africa?

Dr. Asante: I could look back now and I say, I'm African, that's what got me interested in Africa but I can tell you that when I was about 11 years old I knew that I was not from Georgia. It was only a stopping place for me. I used to pick cotton. I was picking in the hot cotton fields of Georgia and I knew that something wasn't right.

It was when I was a freshman in college that I met someone from the continent of Africa, my first African friend. He was from Nigeria and I fell in love with African food. It was first the food. I loved African food. He used to cook all the time at his place. Then I met a whole community of African friends at the University of Oklahoma where I went to college. We went to parties; we ate together. But I still didn't yet have an understanding that I was African and would go to Africa, although my family was strong in Pan Africanism. They saw themselves as committed to self-determination, self reliance, self definition; they were Garveyites. My whole family was like that, my father was like that although I never thought about the continent at that time.

Finally, I went to Africa and I kissed the earth. My people left here 250 years ago and I have returned. I visited the slave dungeons in Ghana and I went in there and I poured libations to the ancestors. I said, "We went through the door of no return, but I have returned. I have come back. I curse you, the door of no return. I have come back." I poured libations. You have to understand that all of us as African Americans carry that ancestry. They took Africans from Africa and brought them here and took them to Brazil and the Caribbean. You have to understand that we carry all that with us, all the emotions, all that history. I understood the connection to the African continent.

Africa is quite large. I have traveled to Ghana, Zimbabwe, Cameroon. You can't say one word and explain African. I like the majesty of the mountains in Malawi, in Congo. I like the desert: the Kalahari and the Sahara. I like the colors. I like the music. The music connects everything. It's a fascinating continent, an incredible variety and incredible power of a people. My people, millions of them came from the continent.

I also traveled to Brazil. Did you know that there are twice as many Africans in Brazil as there are in the U.S. There are 70 million Africans in Brazil and 35 million in the U.S. We are in the Caribbean, Cuba, Jamaica. Then sometimes we forget, but I didn't forget. It was in my memory because I believe in the old scholars who talked about African redemption.

Nkrumah got his ideas from here. He was educated in Philadelphia. He went to Lincoln University. Pan Africanism started here. He developed his ideas here. He had the idea of the United States of Africa. You can do it. You can figure out how to create a United States of Africa. How can we resolve the ethnic issues? If Africa were powerful then we could unite.

Second Student Question: How did you get your name?

Dr. Asante: I was born Arthur L. Smith Jr., in Georgia and named after my father. But do I look like Smith to you? Do I look like an Arthur? Do I look like an Englishman? It was when I was in Africa that I was given my name. I was going to UCLA and I had a friend. He had a name Kete and it means "one who likes musical instruments." And then Molefi means "One who keeps the traditions" in Lesotho and I liked that too. In Ghana they told me that I am Asante so in 1973 I changed my name to Molefi Kete Asante. I had written 5 books under the name of Arthur L. Smith. I had to write them to connect the Arthur Smith to Molefi Kete Asante. I've written 46 books since. My son was born in Zimbabwe so we named him Molefi Kumalo Asante. Kumalo is a name from Zimbabwe.

Third Student Question: How did you come up with Afrocentricity?

Dr. Asante: I am a reflective person and I was living in Buffalo and it gets really cold and I had time to think. How could African Americans not have an understanding of Africa? I was thinking about the social dislocation of African Americans. When we were taken from Africa we were taken from our center. We had our language taken away; our identity; our birthplaces. We don't know if we are Mandingo, Dan, Yoruba, or Igbo. Africans came here and they were enslaved. They weren't slaves on the continent. They were farmers, rice growers, musicians, dancers, traders, blacksmiths, merchants, members of royal families; they were African people, not slaves. There weren't a group of people called slaves waiting to be picked up and taken as slaves; they were Africans.[4] We had names like Camara, Diop, Ba, but we were given English names. Most of us have been here 6 generations now and our names are lost. I'm not really Smith. That's the name that was given to my ancestors who were enslaved.

You look at someone like Allen Iverson. Iverson, that's not an African name. How did an African man come up with a name like Iverson. That's how slavery created our names. Slavery changed our names.

I created the theory of Afrocentricity in 1980, and it says, "To discover the truth about African people, in America or in Africa, in the Caribbean, or in South America, the only way to discover the truth about African people is to look at African people as subjects of our own history, as agents in our own historical experiences." You must look from the African perspective, not Africa on the margins of Europe or as defined by Europe.

"Classical Africa," one of my books, is the first time that this word was connected to Africa. This is the first time that you have classical and Africa together in the same book. I took Classical which Europeans think refers only to European civilizations and connected it to the history of the continent. Africa is itself Africa; it does not have to be on the margins of Europe or connected to Europe in any way.

Fourth Student Question: Why do most African Americans not seem interested in Africa?

Dr. Asante: The reason that most African Americans are not interested in Africa is because they don't know anything about Africa and what they know about Africa is negative. And the reason it's negative is the American media. If you look at American television for one week, you probably will see nothing about Africa. Take one week and look at what is on TV about Africa. If there is a story it will be negative. Africa is the richest continent on the earth. The genetic diversity in Africa is as rich on that one continent as the entire rest of the world combined. You wouldn't know that if you weren't studying science. The history of Africa is extremely ancient. The earliest examples that we know of a monarchy is in Nubia, in Northern Sudan and Egypt. You wouldn't know this; it's rare to be exposed to this information. We are raised to favor and love Europe, not Africa. Europe becomes the model for all that we think and do. Africa is out, Asia is out.

That is what has happened. How could anyone know anything about Africa? Who is going to teach that? Well they ought to be interested because they are Black, one might say. Who reinforces that? But how does this get passed on? You might run into a professor like me at college who can teach you, but there aren't professors like me everywhere. It's not just African Americans who need to learn about Africa, but also continental Africans do too. I just had a student from Guinea in my class who wrote and thanked me for exposing him to the truth about his history that he hadn't learned elsewhere. Sitting in your class, reading your books, for the first time I truly understand my culture. People on the continent need to learn about Africa too. America is not going to teach you Africa; they will teach you Europe.

The great resistance in this country has been pushed by the African Americans. All the freedoms have largely been pushed by African Americans. African Americans are the vanguards of resistance to racism. You give respect to the African Americans. Martin Luther King, Marcus Garvey, Malcolm X fought for freedom for people of African descent. Ida B. Wells Barnett fought against lynching. In this country they could drag you out of your homes and lynch you if you tried to vote or did something that they didn't like. Ida B. Wells single-handedly fought against lynching. The African spirit in the African American made them fight against racism. To help us with the unification of people of African descent we need African Americans to travel to Africa and Africans to travel here and those of us in all the different areas to come together. On the continental side, the more Africans to travel outside would be good for a possible unification. Some African Americans go to Africa and come back unchanged but most come back with a changed perspective.

Dr. Asante's vision for the future includes a United States of Africa, a coming together of all people of African descent, from those in Haiti, to those in Brazil, to the Afro-Americans, and those on the continent. According to Asante, the greatest obstacle to a United States of Africa is that "there is nothing in the Afro-American community that consistently gives consciousness about Africa, nor is there a consistent response to the same symbols, curricula, information and media in the general community."

Dr. Asante told the students that "I'm African and I'm proud to be African." He then challenged the students to learn more about who they are and where they are from and congratulated them on their coming together. The students were adamant about the need for other students to hear him. "Everybody needs to hear him" (Sylviane, Afro-American female) and "We need to bring him back for the whole school" (Aminata, African female). The students were unanimous in their appreciation for his visit.

The Students' Reactions and Responses

Although upon first entering Jackson we had been struck at what seemed a daunting task to bring the African and Afro-American students together, after only a few short activities, this task became a joyous experience. During the initial interviews, we observed a range of reactions to our invitation to join some group activities designed to bring the students together. Some seemed predisposed and some seemed skeptical about getting together, but most seemed neutral at first. The majority of the students seemed amenable to getting together, but were not sure how that could work. Those who were pre-disposed had at least one friend from the other group and were open to learning more about the other on a person-to-person basis, not necessarily on a shared heritage basis. They could understand how you could make a friend in the other group but weren't sure that the groups could come together. Those who were skeptical considered it highly unlikely that the groups could get together. They thought it might be possible to meet a member of the other group, one on one, but not as friends and not as a group. All the participants participated because they were invited and they stayed because they believed they were benefiting from the experience—they were accumulating no credit, and some of the activities were emotionally challenging so their perseverance was an indication that they saw value in this enterprise.

Hilliard (1998) delineates various aspects of African indigenous pedagogy and stresses that teachers who educate African students "must take into account two realities: 1) the African cultural tradition and 2) the political and economic environment within which people of African descent are situated—especially for the last four centuries (p. 107). He argues that "a part of what it takes to function as a powerful ethnic group is a clear memory and a clear view of our culture" (p. 99). The students in our study became eager to learn more about and from one another. They were eager to learn more about Africa. The students had found ways to see each other in a new light and interact with each other from a common ground. Focusing on their shared heritage facilitated this process. Providing positive images of Africa and Africans and retelling the story of their missing connection through the powerful images of the film enabled the students to begin to see each other from their shared heritage, not as "other" but as related. Sharing the rich oral tradition of African proverbs during discussion groups added a level of value to their discovering their African heritage together. Identifying and letting go of stereotypes, and replacing them with more appropriate images, was critical to their being able to identify with each other and with Africa. Interviewing each other made this experience personal. They were not only connected in a general sense as descendents of people of Africa, but they shared common values in the here and now. Bringing African and Afro-American students together around their shared heritage stimulated the opportunity to support students of African descent in coming to "Know themselves."

Aminata, an African female, summed up the experience: "Well, we brought Africans and Afro-Americans together and it was fun." Several students, both African and Afro-American, asked if we could continue for the whole school year. Aminata remarked that "we could do this until the end of the year. Really. We could be here until the end of the year." Each of the students talked about the importance of the trips to the exhibit and the film at the local university which gave them new information and a new experience outside of the school environment.

> I think it was wonderful because we went on the trip to the museum. It was good because we saw good, good stuff, like the pictures, and in the groups we had the chance to express ourselves. We learned from each other. (Aisha)

All of the participants commented on the importance of meeting in small groups and talking face to face. Musa, an African male, emphasized that in meeting one-on-one, they had the chance to develop more enduring and personal relationships. A major benefit to him was gaining new friends. "Now I have Afro-American friends and we are closer. They know that they are from Africa." Haja, an African female, explained, "Before I used to think that they [Afro-Americans] didn't care and they didn't like us. Now I don't think that." Damon, an Afro-American male, explained the impact on him as a willingness to include the Africans. "Usually I just look at them [Africans] as kinda different, I don't know why. Now I talk to them. I don't exclude them anymore."

Surprisingly, neither group of students had anything negative to say about their experiences, except that more students needed to be involved. The students were unanimous in their request that more students at their school participate to free them up to act upon this new learning. The students told us that peer pressure would prevent them from being able to act consistently with their new understanding of themselves and the other group. The students were univocal in saying that everyone needed to know; everyone needed to see the film in a small group. Everyone needed the chance to work together in small groups, face to face and work through their misconceptions of each other.

It took only a few simple activities together to convince the students that they were not getting the true picture about one another from school, from their homes or from the media. Now that they knew a more balanced view of Africa and their connection, they couldn't keep this information to themselves. They had to make it more widely available Valeisha, an Afro-American female, proposed the following to the group, and all the participants agreed with her that more must be done.

> We need to do a panel for the school. We need to address these issues. We need to talk about this in front of the students. We need to bring out the stereotypes and talk about them.

The students all agreed that smaller group interactions were better because they provided more opportunities to share their experiences, but they also hoped that more people would be able to participate. As more than one student declared, "Everybody needs this!" The importance of the face-to-face contact was mentioned again and again by the students as a key to increasing their appreciation for each other. Brandy put it succinctly: "We can't learn in a crowd. This group wants to learn something, but not in a crowd." There was general consensus that interviewing each other was very helpful. They learned each other's names and more specific information about one another, including common worries and hopes they shared. One of the biggest benefits was that they had made one or more friends and saw the potential for more friends and even more learning together in the future. Their willingness to participate when there was nothing for them to gain except getting together and learning more about Africa was inspiring. For instance, they each took a book about Africa or Afro-Americans. All of them said that they had read at least some of the book. Two students gave full oral reports about their books. They read for no credit. They came for no credit. They participated for no credit. They valued the time we spent together and asked for more.

These students had the opportunity to explore their connection to Africa and to each other in new and exciting ways. The participants did not keep this ex-

perience to themselves; they shared it with friends and families. They enthusiastically wanted to share it with their peers at school in a formal presentation.
They wanted to do a panel for the school addressing this issue of the "African"
in African American.

We doubt that there is a teacher anywhere in the world who would pass on
the opportunity to have worked with these students. They were delightful, respectful, interested in the prospects, and actively engaged and thinking about the
sessions, activities, and discussions. They came and stayed engaged; they
wanted to know more. This was "good, good stuff" (Aminata, African female).
Initially, nothing in the students' environment had seemed designed to bring
them together around their African heritage. We had multiple opportunities to
be with the students as they brought the walls down that had stood between them
and as they began to inquire into their connection with Africa and with one another. The activities helped the students make the African connection. Do they
need to know more and is there more to know? Yes, there is a much longer
journey to take. Our schools should be a place where that connection is made
and nurtured routinely.

Where is the motivation to learn about this connection for other students in
America? Where is the impetus? Where is it manifested in what the students
see everyday that would make learning about Africa and their connection to Africa a priority? The silence about the rich history of Africa and the silence about
the devastation of slavery and racism in America are not items to be put into a
few sentences of a textbook and resolved. These are issues to be discussed.
That someone of African descent cannot find himself or herself in any part of
what happens in classrooms in America despite his/her presence here for hundreds of years is not a slight omission, it is an indicator that racism is not yet
dead.

That any student can go to an American school and not learn about African
history and culture as an integral component in the development of the world's
story is denying all of us an understanding of the past that has much to teach us,
and abnegates so much of the experience of globalization that infuses our present times. Because the eradication of connection to one's life, history, family,
culture, religion, language can be emotionally devastating, re-connecting to
one's identity is a not a minor event.

Students at Jackson cannot find their history in the curriculum as presently
compiled. They are not being supported at this critical time of identity development with the connection to their roots that could help them develop strong
identities. Desmond Tutu of South Africa has warned that "One of the ways of
helping to destroy a people is to tell them that they don't have a history, that
they have no roots" (Stewart, 1997, p. 15). Africa and the painful legacy of
slavery are part of who these students are and without the knowledge of their
heritage the educational system is stripping them of their roots.

An African proverb describes the lack of knowledge of one's history as a
tree without its roots blowing in the wind; it cannot bear fruit. We are not just
denying the Black students; we have denied the white students too. Without the
connection to Africa, they too are being denied the chance to see the world from

another perspective, one that maintains the connectedness of human beings to each other and to their ancestors and to the Creator.

From the outset the information that was provided by the media had not motivated the Afro-American students to want to learn more, but the new images provided by the film and their personal interactions had changed their views. "This was the real thing" and that's what had been missing. When asked, "Do you want to learn more?" Brandy responded with an enthusiastic, "Yeah! Yeah! Like I got more respect for it. It made me want to learn."

Restoring the Connection—Finding A Bridge

Some proponents of Afrocentric education have extolled social change that "calls for transformation among its target audiences, black people on the continent, and the diaspora" (Dei, 1994, p. 5). Dei argues that "education has, for the most part, not cultivated our self-esteem and pride as Africans. Even today, in many circles, Euro-American education continues to distort, misappropriate, and misinterpret many African peoples lives and experiences" (p. 3). One major objective of Afrocentric education is to "'move' or 'bring' all peoples of African descent from the margins to the center of postmodern history" (p. 5). Our initial observations at Jackson High confirmed that there was significant lack of connection between the Africans and the Afro-Americans students there.

As a prelude to more sustained interactions we considered the best approach was to engage the students indirectly by viewing with a small group the film "The Language You Cry In: The Story of a Mende Song." This film provided us with the context to illustrate for the students the missing link between them because the film takes the story of the Afro-Americans back to the time before slavery and makes the connection between Africa and America at the level of heart and soul. We elected not to hold the initial screening in an auditorium because we wanted the students to have the opportunity to be a "captive audience" to their own reluctance to engage with each other. We wanted to provide a different setting, a setting of greater importance, a different context for their interactions, in hopes that an environment of higher stature would help put the experience in a more prestigious light and help them change their attitudes toward each other as well.

The film brought up emotional and historic issues for both Africans and Afro-Americans. We enlisted three vehicles for them to express themselves after the film: 1) a discussion immediately following the film that was videotaped, 2) a class discussion in the Afro-American studies class a few days later, and 3) a written assignment in the Afro-American studies class which asked the students for their thoughts and feelings about the film. The film is the story of a song that had been preserved since slavery and had been passed on from generation to generation, even though it could not be understood in Georgia, as it was in an African language. Because of the visceral power of its contents and the story it conveys, we provide below the text of its opening prologue. This story of an African song resonates with the students despite their lack of knowledge about their heritage. It was a treasure that was finally discovered and traced back to Africa. The connection between a family in Georgia and a family in Sierra Leone is made and they are reunited after generations of separation caused by slavery and war. Haja, an African female student wrote this about the film:

> I went to the local university to watch a documentary about how two people from different continents were brought together by a song. It all started during slavery when the white man came to Africa, they were taking people, and inspecting them like they were animals checking their hair, skin, and their private body parts for any sign of sickness. Then, they were branded and put on a ship to America. They were stripped naked and chained together to the ship's floor. During the trip many of them did not make it.
>
> Because they were chained together they had no room to breathe. If the ship hit a storm they were thrown on top of each other. They would excrete on themselves and each other. It was a nightmare. It looked just like what we saw in the movie "Amistad." One of these slaves brought over from Africa passed a song on to the next generation. Years after slavery in a small town in Georgia, there lived a family that had not forgotten the song. This song, even though those singing it did not understand the words, had been passed down from generation to generation.
>
> One day this woman named Amelia Dawley was heard singing the song. It was the 1930s and Professor Turner discovered this song and recorded it. He decided to try to find the meaning of the words of the song. Turner went all over the country to find someone that could interpret the song. Finally he found a student that went to some college who knew the meaning of one or two words of the song, but not all of it. This young man was from Sierra Leone and identified a few words as Mende, a language spoken in Sierra Leone.
>
> Many years later in 1990 another researcher found the song, was hypnotized by the song and wanted to find the origin of the song. So he found someone that could translate the song. He and his assistant went to Sierra Leone to hopefully find any one that could remember the song. They went all over the country and nobody knew the song. Just when they wanted to give up, they tried one last place and the women started singing along with the recording. The researchers were ecstatic and relieved. They asked them what the song was about. They said the song is part of the tradition at a burial. Women have to sing the song to let the soul to go in peace.
>
> Dawley's great, great granddaughter May Moran enjoyed singing the song to her grand kids. One day, the researcher came back with good news for her that the song had originated in Sierra Leone and she was invited to go and visit Sierra Leone. But because of the war her trip was cancelled. Years later, she was able to go and meet one of the women that remembered the song. Mary and her family were welcomed with arms wide open. She visited all the nice places of Sierra Leone and she had a great time.

Other written comments about the experience by the participants illustrated the emotional content of the issues addressed in the film, from slavery and the Middle Passage and the destruction of the African culture in America, to the devastation of the war in Sierra Leone and the welcome the Americans received at every level from the Head of State, to the seat carriers in the village. The film brought up many different emotions for both Afro-Americans and Africans.

> This film makes me feel angry. I have to sit and watch what whites did to our people. Some of the things they spoke of were inhuman. I learned a lot from the film. (Afro-American male)

> I think the movie was beautiful and too emotional. I like the reaction that took place when Mary Moran visited Bendu Jabati in Sierra Leone. (African female)

It became clear from the African students' reactions and even some of the Afro-American students that they had not been aware previously about the era of slavery and its impact on all of America's people, but particularly the Afro-Americans who endured its devastation. Much in the same way that the Afro-Americans were treating the Africans as second-class citizens, the African students did not understand the Afro-American students. They were shocked at the images and were just beginning to understand why their peers might not know where they were from. An African female wrote that the "island where they took the slaves was a very bad place where they treated people like animals, burning them with iron and marking them for life. That was very wicked." One Afro-American male student wrote, "Who came up with the idea of slaves? Did they not feel for the African, cause it made me feel bad what they did?" An African female wrote, "I was uncomfortable when they started talking about how the slaves were chained, inspected and sold." Many of the students seemed never to have heard about the complete destruction of connections to Africa that occurred in slavery. Although the film vividly portrays the horrors of slavery and the destruction of the connection to Africa, it is also the story of a joyous reunion. One student summed up the feeling of pride that many students gathered from the film.

> I feel so proud for the African people and the Afro-Americans. People are trying hard to trace their roots. I feel very sorry for those who do not know where they are from. There are big similarities between Africans and Afro-Americans even though there was a long lifetime between. The similarities were very incredible.

The film was a media event that showed without a doubt the misinformation that had been previously available to them. "I do not like how the white people treated the Africans and messed up our culture and brought the Africans here and treated them like dogs" (African female). Now, they knew they were connected at a level that could not be denied. The connection was made on many levels, not just intellectual, but emotional as well. The following written reactions to the film show the breadth and depth of thought and emotions elicited from the participants.

> I almost cried when they talked about the war in Sierra Leone and how it affected Bendu and her village. (African female)

> Even though slavery happened so long ago, the pain of the Africans in slavery still hurts. (Afro-American female)

I feel sorry because they were treated with no respect. I felt happy at the end because she found her roots. I was happy to see the people joyful once again once they were reunited. (Afro-American male)

I felt many emotions, sadness, pain, joy and anger. Sadness for what they did to our ancestors and joy because everything was revealed. (Afro-American female)

This film elicited many strong feelings and the students' reactions point to the complexity of this situation. There are 400 years between the slaves being captured in Africa and these students meeting today at Jackson High. And their story is not the story told in schools. It is not told in the media. It is not told in most homes. Although it has been told in the past, and the necessity and importance of telling this story has been chronicled by many (Kunjufu, 1987; Nobles, 1991, 2004; Shujaa, 1994; Tedla, 1995; White & Johnson, 1985), it is not yet readily available to the students at Jackson High, nor, we would argue, in most schools in America today. Valeisha, an Afro-American female, was quick to say that although she knew she had been misinformed that it was thanks to her father's intervention that she had some more accurate information available to her.

I never really believed in those stereotypes of Africa because I thought, you know, they were going in the bush where they have monkeys and take pictures. They don't live like savages however they advertise it on TV. This picture we have in our minds, we think of Africa, we think of dirt hills, and you know monkeys, trees and all that other stuff. African, that's my cultural background. That's where I came from. There's a connection.

This student wrote the play we mentioned in an earlier chapter in which she dramatized the story of an Afro-American female who travels to Africa to fulfill her dying grandmother's wish that she visit her homeland. In the play, the young Afro-American female benefits greatly from her visit to Africa and returns with a greater sense of who she is. The value of this knowledge is self-evident with RP. She is clear about who she is and when she talks, others stop and listen. She has a presence about her that cannot be denied. She knows who she is and where she is from and she acknowledges her father and an African friend, in her former school who became her best friend and taught her much about Africa. Although the film was graphic in the portrayal of the horrors of slavery, many students left excited by the connection that was made between the two families.

I am happy that they found the origin of the song and the two groups of people that helped make the union between the two people possible. I am happy to see that just one song could mean so much. (Afro-American female)

This was a good film for us to look at so we can see where our ancestors came from. (Afro-American male)

What this student doesn't say is "and I'm not ashamed to be of African descent."

The film helps the students take the shame out of being of African descent. This student became excited when he realized that perhaps he too could be Mende.

> The story to me is sad but at least I learned something about the Mende song. Maybe I could be from that tribe. It was a song to help people deal with the death of their loved ones and it's a shame that we were enslaved like that. I would like to learn that song. (Afro-American male)

For the discussion following the film, the students went into another room and their discussion was videotaped. The following are some excerpts from the transcripts of that videotaped discussion

> Fanta: I was thinking that I know some of my roots. Most people don't know their great, great grandparents. Even me, I don't know.
> Haja: The movie was kind of sad. It has a message that no matter where you are you can't forget about your culture or your roots. I think it was touching the way the two cultures could reconnect and have such a strong feeling about it

The following interaction between two African students demonstrates the value of this film experience for them.

> Haja: I have a question. Was anyone from Sierra Leone touched when they saw their country? Does anyone have any memories from that film?
> Fanta: I have a lot of feelings too because people here, some people, not everyone thinks Africa is like just bushes. Like in the beginning of the movie, those houses actually we call that place the interior part, the rural part of Africa where they have their houses, with their huts and all that stuff. Later on we saw the President Ahmed Kabah of Sierra Leone and we saw the city. Some people were surprised because they all think that it's all bush. It showed what people do, where they sleep, what they eat. Even you could see in the rural part of Africa in Sierra Leone the people have customs, traditions. It was a little civilized. They are not country. My feelings were that I was actually happy for people to see that Sierra Leone is not a big place with lions running around the street. It showed that there were no lions around or like that. It brought old memories back. That's Africa. That's my home.

The mood in the room during this videotaped discussion was serious. There was little to no chitchat or side commenting. The participants sat in a circle facing each other. The videotaper was outside the circle standing; this was Hamed, the president of the African Students Association, familiar to all the participants, which appeared to help put them at ease. The moderator was a Teaching Assistant at the school originally from Haiti. In this next question from the moderator, the responses demonstrate the range of information about Africa from little to nothing to positive coming from the African students. This was not the place for the stereotypes to be presented. The film had just put those stereotypes to rest.

> Aliya: Did this change your views about Africa? (Moderator)
> Marcus: Some people didn't have a view. I didn't know how it was.

Fanta: It's different in Africa. We really respect trees, mountains, everything.
Hamed: It's my motherland.

The students grappled with the issue of skin color; it was not resolved. They left the topic to talk more about the film and how they felt about it. Some of the questions left unanswered were: Is the connection just skin color? Is there more to this connection to Africa? Is there a shared heritage? The students continued to engage in this question of the connection made in the film.

Hamed: How did you feel about the movie?
Sherry: It was sad how the different cultures got separated on two different continents and then were brought back together. It was happy how they reacted when they got back together.
Sylviane: I felt it was sad when they had people on top of people shipping them from Africa.

Another student shared an experience that had disturbed her. She hoped that by coming to view the film together the Afro-Americans present will see themselves as connected to Africa.

Well, let me see now, I was so happy that Black Americans came to see the movie because a lot of Black Americans believe that they are not part of us. My sister and I were on our way to get our little sister and we met a group of Afro-Americans who wanted to fight. We said, "We don't want to fight. We are all Africans. You are Black and we are Black." They said, "No, you are African; I'm American." I said, "You have red blood. I have red blood. I was also created by God and you were also created by God." They said, no they have blue blood. (Everyone laughed). Then they said they wanted to fight. We said, "we don't want to fight; you can go your way." A lady came and take us with her car and then she take us home. (Rosalie, African female)

For the Africans, the connection was more obvious. They wondered why the Afro-Americans didn't see a connection. Although they may have heard about slavery, the impact of slavery in destroying the African connection was not understood. The film, though, provides a clue as to why the connection to Africa is not as clear for the Afro-Americans. Slavery sought to destroy the connection. The film helped the Africans understand better why the connection is not clear to the Afro-Americans.

The movie was kind of sad. It has a message that no matter where you are you can't forget about your culture or your roots. I think it was touching the way the two cultures could reconnect and have such a strong feeling about it. (Aminata, African female)

The strong feeling could be felt in the room at the end of the film. It was a different feeling than before the film. The connection was made. The film contained the four elements of the African worldview. The students could feel the community, see the spiritual connection, and see the importance of the ancestors and knowing one's history and the acknowledgement of the Creator in every activity from the singing in the church the singing of the song. DB, an Afro-American female said, "I didn't know they [Africans] were so tight. They eat together, sing together, and do things together." She saw the community that is the African tradition. All the students saw the honoring of the ancestors and the spiritual connection in the singing of the song preserved for so many years. The song is a burial song meant to help pass someone on to the next life.

One of the most striking comments about the importance of their experience of the film came from Fatou. It is disheartening given the work in the 1960s that today in the year 2002 the information is still not available in this school, nor many other schools in America, no doubt. According to Fatou, "we need our parents to be teaching this. We can't just depend on the school." Why can't the students depend on their schools to teach them their history, to provide them with a more accurate understanding of Africa and how they are connected to the continent of Africa?

The Africans are not savages sitting next to the Afro-American students in their classrooms, nor were the Afro-American students actual criminals or rude people sitting next to the "well behaved and respectful" Africans. We sought out conversations with Afro-American students and found many students who thought the project sounded "cool." Some of the other teachers, as well as the staff, began to exhibit a new-found respect for these young people and their evolving sense of pride and identification with their African heritage. We began to see that the issue was more than African-American history, or the subject matter, or the way material is presented. Although it was necessary in the 60s and 70s to fight for African American studies classes, now it is time to fight for the truth of the history of Americans which includes slavery and the taking of people from Africa by force and using them like "animals or machinery" for many years. This is not just Afro-American history; this is American history. This happened in America even though the people had been taken from Africa. This is the Africa-America connection that must no longer be denied. All Americans need to learn about Africa and slavery and the mistreatment of human beings based on the color of their skin.

We will never heal the wounds of racism until we tell the truth. It can not be one sentence in a history book, or a month of remembrance, or an isolated pilgrimage. It warrants much more than a re-working of our history books. True liberation from the shackles of our efforts to ignore or rebuke history demands much more. We must stop ignoring slavery and our relationship to the continent of Africa. In slavery, it was Americans who brutalized other human beings. In the film, the narrator reminds us:

> Three generations ago, the parents of our grandparents lived in the era of slavery. Slave owners knew that to master a human being, no matter what his race or color, all you need to do is to strip him of his identity, his land, the strength of his culture, and the memory of his ancestors. Memory is power. We can't rewrite the history of humanity, but we can rekindle memory or at least a part of it. Neither time nor centuries of oppression have been able to erase America's African heritage. Forty million Afro-Americans live in the United States today and in this nation searching for its past, some of them can show theirs.

Everyone deserves the chance to know his or her heritage. To deny someone a history is to attempt to annihilate them. Ali Mazrui, a Kenyan scholar and the producer of the film, "The Africans" admonishes that a "people denied history is a people deprived of dignity" (Stewart, 1997, p. 15). The first President of Tanzania, Julius Nyerere, once declared that

> African people cannot be read out of history. Not to know what one's race has done in former times is to continue always as a child. The African himself expresses the thought in saying "knowing thyself is better than he who speaks of thee." Not to know is bad; but not to wish to know is worse. (Stewart, 1997, p. 15)

We did not wish to know until we were shown so clearly by the students themselves how wrong we had been about them, how judgmental, and how little we really understood about how magnificent they could become. Each week as we approached Jackson we became excited with anticipation about what we would discover on this day through our interactions with this group of young people who were re-discovering the joys of learning about their lives. The way we saw the students change, as we learned more about them as individuals and as group members, was one of the grandest lessons a teacher can learn. Watching them interview each other and listening to them laugh together or ask a touching question, moved us profoundly. We were unaware initially about how many of the most mundane stereotypes we had about the Afro-American students, but by the time we facilitated the last of our sessions together, Jackson had become a home to us.

Students who had at first seemed disinterested in school were asking us to borrow another book and telling us enthusiastically about the one they had just finished reading. They were excited. Each week there was something new to discover. At the beginning, school, home, and the media had not enkindled in them the desire to learn about their history and their heritage, but now, at least, school was becoming a place of some true learning activities. The students found their connection to Africa and to each other through the film and the other activities we had shared and from there they could not be stopped. They wanted to know more. The film was a useful tool that if more widely viewed, could be a catalyst for making a connection to Africa and regain the memory that was lost.

We suspect that the greatest gift a teacher will ever experience is having the opportunity to work with an enthusiastic learner. The students in this study were a joy to work with, and by providing them with the opportunity to connect to Africa and to each other at the level of heart and not just intellectually, they saw something that didn't know they didn't know and they just wanted more.

Chapter Summary

In earlier chapters we provided profiles of the group of African and Afro-American students who participated in this study and described some of their observations about the differences between educational experience in Africa and America. The students described their reasons for electing to discuss these issues with us, some of their concerns, and the sources of information they had about Africa and Africans as well as the extent of prior interactions they had experienced with students from the continent of Africa or from the U.S. In this chapter we outlined the arguments to support our contention that the key to incorporating multicultural values in American classrooms where African and Afro-American students interact is to have an understanding of the principles underlying Afrocentricity and the African worldview and to use these principles to inform activities that will reconnect the students to their shared histories. While the administrations at other schools that experience these same issues of adversarial relations between student groups may call in mediation counselors or conflict resolution experts, the success of this study suggests that a shared history, shared cultural approach, was more appropriate and more effective because it provided a valuable learning experience for all the students.

A major lesson learned from these students was that they could not make changes in their behavior without having more students made aware of their interconnections with each other. The students who participated in this study themselves requested permission to work with the entire student body in small groups to educate them about what they had learned. Surprisingly, they took this step in order to put peer pressure on their side, to use it to ameliorate the tensions between the African and Afro-American students. In the final chapter we attempt to explain why conflict resolution may result in superficial emolument for some of the strained relations that can arise between African and Afro-American students, but sharing stories and experiences may provide a more lasting interconnection that can resolve many of the tensions that arise recurrently between divergent groups of students in our schools.

CHAPTER 9

Afrocentricity and Education Reforms

In this chapter we attempt to explain why some of the efforts expended to reconcile students in disharmony may result in superficial emolument of strained interactions. Our research suggests that sharing personal stories and experiences can provide a more lasting interconnection that can resolve many of the tensions that can arise between divergent groups. How the students arrived at their misunderstandings and rancorous interactions was the focus of the earlier chapters. We then explored the tenets of Afrocentricity, and listened in on the groups of African and Afro-American students as they recounted both what they knew or had experienced about the other group but also what they believed the members of the other group thought about them.

We started our research from the premise that if Afrocentricity constituted a valid way to construe their relations, both the African and Afro-American students should come together around a shared history and a shared worldview. Bringing the African and Afro-American students together at Jackson created an opportunity to share their histories, to present a more contemporary image of Africa, to develop a better understanding of the Afrocentric worldview and values, and thus this process enhanced the possibility of a shared educational experience at school.

In this chapter, we also will explore the benefits of incorporating multicultural principles in other contexts where negative stereotypes influence the interactions between various groups of students. We end with some recommendations for making the Afrocentric approach an integral component of all multicultural education programs, regardless of the student composition. We offer some practical advice on how to engage students in the types of interactive processes that made this study such a success at one inner-city high school.

The key to incorporating multicultural values in American classrooms where African and Afro-American students interact and share educational experiences is first to have an understanding of the principles underlying Afrocentricity and the African worldview and then to use these principles to inform activities that will re-connect the students to their shared histories. Although where similar disruptive difficulties may occur between these two groups, or there is evidence of problems deriving from adversarial relations between particular groups of students, some school administrators may consult with conflict resolution experts to devise a resolution, the success of this particular study suggests that a shared history, shared cultural approach is more appropriate and should be more effective because it provides a valuable learning experience for all of the students and creates a bridge for them to continue to share their experiences in more positive ways.

The students understood implicitly that any enduring changes in attitude would require a critical mass of acceptance from other people so they expressed some urgency to have the other students at Jackson also become aware of their own interconnections with each other. To our delight, the students independently requested permission to work with the entire student body in small groups to educate them about what they had learned. They recognized that they might be better able to effect some change if they used peer pressure to their advantage, to help ameliorate the tensions between the African and Afro-American students by promoting a positive image to the active pursuit of knowledge about African and their African heritage.

The idea that merely sharing a few experiences together could help a group of adolescents at odds to transcend some very insidious cultural stereotypes and to discover a way to bridge the apparent gap between one contingent that harnessed the energy from a community spirit and another that relied on rugged individualism to comply with social expectations was perhaps overreaching on our part. But we were undaunted in our conviction that the very thing missing, an emotional or cultural connection between these two groups who ought to have more in common than the color of their skin, was the most likely catalyst to set right a bonding relationship that the history of the past three centuries had assiduously and diligently tried to eradicate.[1]

Preserving a Connection

Adolescence can be a tough time of life generally. Among other challenges, it is the time of the young person's enduring transition to adult identity (Cross, Parham, & Helms, 1991). The experience of coming together gave the African and Afro-American students in our study the opportunity to learn more about themselves and about each other. They began to see from their encounters with each other the true extent of the misinformation that had been endorsed at school, their homes, and in the media. The Africans had never learned much about slavery or its devastating effects and therefore had little or no empathy for the plight of Afro-Americans who had struggled so arduously and for so long to overcome the after effects of slavery. For their part, the Afro-Americans had only heard about the jungles of Africa and other degrading portrayals of Africans and they therefore had no expectation of anything worthwhile from the African students themselves. Neither group of young people viewed the other as worth engaging until they were brought together purposefully and saw things from a new perspective, the one provided by the activities in this intervention which introduced them to the power of Afrocentricity. Centering oneself in African history, culture and worldview holds power as it provides the person seeking the truth with a perspective not readily available in school, home or the media. Rosalie, an African, described her experience of seeing the "Language You Cry In" with her Afro-American peers,

> So I'm just happy that Black Americans were able to watch this movie. I believe from this moment they will believe that they are from Africa although they are not Africans but from the movie they should know that they are African. And

they will go back to some of their friends and say we are all Africans. We should love one another. We are all Africans.

The roots of the strained relationships between the Africans and the Afro-Americans at Jackson were negative stereotypes and a lack of accurate information about Africa, Africans and Afro-Americans. The activities selected for our study were specifically designed to provide more up-to-date, accurate information about Africa and Africans and to give the students the chance to develop new images about each other that could replace these outdated and inappropriate stereotypes. The Africans needed to learn more about the experience of the Afro-Americans and the Afro-Americans needed positive images about the African continent.

When initially asked what might help bring the two groups together, both the African and the Afro-American students identified some combination of "working together," "interviewing each other," "getting to know each other one on one, face to face." Thus, each of the activities included time for the students to be paired and talk to each other one on one, or talk together in small groups, face to face. When stereotypes or misconceptions arose, the students challenged them. For example, when Fanta said, "Afro-Americans don't care about Africa," Valeisha responded, "I care. It's not true that all Afro-Americans don't care. Some don't, that's true. Maybe even many don't, but some of us do. Some of us are trying to learn more."

Former generalizations had a more difficult time persisting when the students were face to face and placed in an environment where they shared some common experiences in the here and now. For many purposes visual images play an important role in our understanding of the world. Because we recognized that the students held such negative images of each other, the activities we used had to provide some new, more positive images for the students to experience. The context and content of past experiences also play an important role in how students see their world. We realized that the students needed new experiences to replace those that had generated the negative images or it would have been more challenging to keep them engaged in a process that required them to confront some unpleasant stereotypes that they could alter only for themselves. This explains how we decided on the specific activities:

The exhibit provided new images of Africans as contributing members of our society.

The film provided positive images of both Africans and Afro-Americans and etched into the hearts of the viewers the undeniable connection between Africa and Afro-Americans. The images were positive and powerful and strong enough to replace older images of jungle and Tarzan.

The stereotype activity gave the students the opportunity to articulate the images and see them as ridiculous. When they interviewed each other they interacted and this experience gave them a new place from which to talk about themselves and each other. They had shared information about themselves. They saw connections that hadn't been obvious to them.

In the values activity they could distinguish African and American values and they could see how they shared many values.

Finally, Dr. Asante's visit was the chance to see the embodiment of an Afrocentric perspective. Dr. Asante is an Afro-American who has discovered the benefits of understanding and promoting his African heritage. Both the African and Afro-American students commented how great he made them feel. Both African and Afro-American students talked about how proud they felt when they listened to Dr. Asante.

We used a series of events to awaken an awareness in the students of a self that is descended from Africa while ensuring that there were many positive images of Africa presented to free the participants from the negative stereotypes that they had been subjected to previously. Similar pedagogical approaches to those used in this study could help teachers of African and Afro-American students be better prepared to understand and affirm their students and encourage them to reach out and get to know one another better.

Afrocentricity and the Education of Students of Color

This study was designed to ensure that the students were grappling with the questions about their relationship with the misperceptions and stereotypes about the opposite group while engaged in a more personal relationship with students from both groups. We provided the students with multiple avenues for self-expression and discussion about what was keeping them apart and how they could come together. They talked to each other during the trips, they shared classes at Jackson and focus groups. The activities were designed to provide time to reflect individually, but also interact with their peers. They shared experiences with the exhibit and the film; they reflected; they talked together; they listened to each other; they wrote about their experiences, and they interacted actively. Thus, the study provided us with an unusual amount of insight into the process of identity development using Afrocentricity.

Furthermore, it is important to remember that most of the African students had been in the U.S. only a few years and had not yet completely adapted to or had not yet been completely assimilated into American culture. Although they were not immune to the distorted version of African history imposed on them in their original educational systems, they still felt connected to life in Africa, their extended families, their elders, their ancestors, and their individual experiences growing up which they can readily contribute to classroom discussions about contemporary Africa. They had experiences of the rich oral African tradition; they could recount stories of the elders sharing tales or their parents teaching them proverbs and stories.

As a more personal example of the impact of maintaining ties with the African continent, the lead author is the mother of two African children (Laye, now 21, and Hamed, now 5), adopted following her marriage to Laye's Liberian father, Mohamed, and we have witnessed the value that Laye derives from knowing his heritage, his culture, and his history (and we hope to bear similar witness to Hamed's development). Laye, who is African born, came to the U.S. when he was eight years old. He started school in the third grade in a predominantly white school in the suburbs. He quickly lost his accent as he tried to fit in. His presence was seen by other students and some teachers as "exotic." From Laye, his class learned some facts about Liberia, his birthplace and other things he shared with them about his life. However, other than the international festival each year and the rare mention in geography class, the students had no opportunity to learn more about Africa. His first homework assignment was truly enlightening. It was a "fill in the blank" phonics exercise seeking words with a long vowel sound and silent final "e"— some of these examples included "ET phone ___ " and " ___ that tune." Having just arrived from Africa he could not have been expected to know "ET phone home" or "name that tune." This is one of the more humorous ways in which the acculturation processes of the American educational system works, because not having shared these "icons" of American culture, Laye was not able to answer these questions correctly.

Laye might have lost his culture completely if he hadn't had the chance to return to Africa for his middle school years. For three years he attended school in Africa, studied Africa and had African friends. When he returned for high school the American influence again became strong. But at one point, during his junior year he elected to return to Guinea to visit his family, all of whom had fled the war in Liberia and gone to Guinea. This time, the African values were more noticeable to him and he made a commitment to keep them alive no matter what influence American values and norms would try to impose on him when he resumed his life in America. African values of community, harmony, spirituality and respect now are important to him because he sees the contrast with American values. He can now make choices based on another value system. This is one of the major benefits to an experience of African values and worldview. One can choose to see the world in another way.

Laye is proud to be African. He appreciates the freedom of America, but sees the ways in which that freedom has been abused. It was not enough for his family to encourage his African values or even demand that he follow them. Laye had to experience them for himself. In one of his college essays he wrote:

> My stay in Guinea was absolutely priceless.
> There are no toilets to use as bathrooms and the only way to relieve yourself was a hole dug deep in the ground. The flies weren't too friendly as you went to the bathroom, but in about a week I got used to them. There were no showers so I had to use a bucket of water to wash myself. The mosquitoes were very greedy and every chance they got they sucked my blood. All these aspects of the trip were annoying at times, but as I looked around I saw a community of people that was closely bonded, children bursting with so much energy as they played in their yards, and life at its simplest and its best.
> In American society, money is such a big part of life. Getting money and trying to get wealthy take up so much of the time we spend. As I sat in Guinea under the stars that shined in the sky so brilliantly, I believed that even though my family and the families around me weren't rich and didn't have financial stability

they had a bond that was so tight and so right. That night I promised myself that I would stop looking so much at the materialistic part of life and concentrate on being more positive and work hard to have a passion for everything I did. I know that we can't take the wealth with us when we die. It is the way people remember you that is the only wealth that remains.

Before my trip to Guinea I was not as clear about what I was doing with my life. When I saw how people in Guinea appreciate their lives and their families,

I was profoundly touched. They have many more problems than I do in my life, yet, they are so much happier than me. When I came back, I decided to change because I, too, wanted to experience the joy of just being happy to be alive. I have recommitted myself to getting a college education so that I can help my family in Guinea.

Whenever I feel stressed or am confused, I think back to my visit to Guinea and a smile comes on my face. I am a happier person and hungry for an education. I know that I don't have to have everything figured out because life is about experiences and experiences help to develop wisdom. A wise man appreciates life and knows that it is our interconnectedness and caring for each other that brings joy. (Laye Traoré, 2001)

Laye could not see the impact of the subtle forms of enculturation to the American way of life until he re-experienced the African culture. When he could distinguish the values connected to American culture and the values associated with the African culture, he could then make choices.

Perhaps it could be argued that the specific qualities of our study at Jackson were somewhat unique, but anyone with a commitment to helping African and Afro-American students learn about their shared heritage could facilitate a similar process of discovery because the tools to accomplish this task already exist.[2] The presence of students recently arrived from the continent of Africa is not the norm in most schools. However, the power of the film is that it does not require the presence of Africans to serve as a catalyst for the conversation about the Afro-American or Caribbean-American (Diaspora) connection to Africa. One student explained it this way,

I would not want to ever make fun of an African again, but if there are students in the hall who are doing it, I would not be able to do anything different. In fact, I would find myself joining in, even though I now know that it's wrong.

The students lobbied for a continued dialogue and opportunities to learn more. This cannot be an isolated event or done in a large assembly because the learning experience and the best chance to counteract peer pressure are diluted otherwise.

Recommendations

We realized from our initial conversations and interviews with the students that the key issue at Jackson was that not enough effort was expended on accommodating cross-culture and diversity issues. Despite the dedicated efforts of the administration and some of the staff, many of the immigrant students still felt left out by an institution which they had expected to be a safe haven and a place that would help assuage their concerns about ignorance, stereotyping, prejudice, hatred, and humiliation they encountered away from the school. When diversity of background is viewed as an opportunity and not as a problem, life can be more harmonious, particularly in the aggregate culture that is American. Through variety of perspective, if considered as strength and pleasure, we can accomplish a great deal together as a unified body with all the differences that we have still between us. *E pluribus unum* can once again be the principle it was intended by Franklin and this nation's Founders. We could begin to appreciate all the little things that make us different, but also make us unique. The most powerful nation cannot be strong without diversity.[3]

Take away diversity and the strength, the power of a nation or people would diminish. When people begin to realize the beauty of nature, they begin to gain strength and are ready to cooperate to succeed, rather than detract from the community spirit through envy, jealousy, hatred, or violate others' rights. Everyday, there is someone out there that is not accepted for who they are. If we told the truth it would be principally because they are different. Why must we think that we all have to speak alike, look alike, or have the same culture and background? The students who emigrate into any new society can be expected to experience some anxiety about being accepted. They should not have to endure feelings of being humiliated, violated, suppressed, not listened to, or have to confront unspoken prejudice or flagrant racism.

To the Afrocentrist thinker, anyone who feels secure within himself or herself would never feel threatened by another person. Moreover, a secure person is prepared to listen to the ideas others have, to compromise, to try different things, to add to his or her knowledge. Those who feel insecure, however, are always on the verge of recruiting the innocent to prey upon, by projecting on the innocent the insecure feelings that otherwise dominate their lives. We must all learn that ignorance can become a disease which can only be cured by the individual, society or culture involved.

For the true Afrocentrist, the education of Afro-Americans and Africans cannot be left exclusively to the discretion of the individual schools as they are currently structured, most especially in the negative presentation of the lives of Blacks in America. Carter G. Woodson wrote about "the miseducation of the Negro" in 1933 and if he were alive today he would not be comforted by what he would find at Jackson. From the Afrocentric perspective, the textbooks are deficient in that they neglect the most important features of the struggle and contribution of people of African descent. It is true that there are textbooks for Afro-American history; there is even one written by Dr. Molefi Kete Asante that is used in the African American studies class at Jackson. There are even skilled teachers trained to teach African American studies at institutions of higher education throughout this country, like Temple University in Philadelphia.

Notwithstanding outward appearances, however, the connection to Africa is missing for the majority of students at Jackson. Although there are films and exhibits and other resources that would help them make this connection they won't get it in school, most will not get it at home and the media readily available to them will not provide it either. So the severing of the ties with Africa that occurred several centuries ago with the introduction of slavery and colonialization, and the persistent denigration of all things African by the media, will continue to undermine the self-esteem and identity development of many of the students at Jackson. And now it will begin to destroy the identity of those Africans whose parents, guardians and elders still believe in the American educational system and will rely on it for their child's development never realizing that they are developing the African right out of him or her. If they think that the American educational system will prepare the future leaders of Africa, they will be hugely disappointed when their children adopt the American values of independence and start telling them to back off once they reach an age to do so with impunity.

Ladner (1998) describes the Afro-American values that kept her on the right path and those that are being accepted by young people today. She warns parents that if they allow their children to adopt values such as individualism, the "fast" buck and others, they will lose this next generation. Although she is tentative in identifying the values passed on from her mother as African, she alludes to their probable source as Africa and indeed they are African values preserved despite slavery and racism. This should serve as a warning to Africans in America. If you leave the education of your children up to the American educational system you will get Americanized children. The younger children who are arriving from Africa today and entering public schools in the urban centers of the U.S. will, without encouragement, maintain little or no memory of Africa. They will get a distorted view of Africa from the education they receive in the public school. Like the Afro-American students who participated in our study, they will not be interested in learning more about Africa without an intervention of similar magnitude to counter the entrenched apathy of the general populace. They will absorb the stereotypes, myths, and misperceptions that are the only sources of information available to them. Unless the schools change or the parents undertake to educate their children directly, the children will grow up not knowing who they really are. They will feel the shame of their own or their parents' accent, the shame of the jungle stereotype, the shame of the savage image, but they will not know any differently without targeted attention on their heritage.

All schools should reexamine how they present Africa, slavery, the arrival of people of African descent, the contribution of people of African descent, and the viable interconnections between Africa and America. Despite the work of many people to mandate African American studies in the School District of Philadelphia, the students at Jackson have not had any real opportunity to learn about their history and culture in a way that connected them to Africa. The history of people of African descent is a critical element in understanding the world in which we live. The story currently told is not accurate. It leads to the continuation of demeaning stereotypes of people of African descent. Many U.S. history textbooks contain none of the story of the contributions of Afro-Americans, nor the full representation of slavery and its devastating effects on people of African descent. Neither the oppression of people of African descent, nor their resilience and accomplishments, get more than a paragraph in most U.S. or World History textbooks. To cite an example of these lacunae:

> A Dutch ship brought in 20 and odd Negroes [in the 1600s]. The status and fate of these first Africans in the English colonies remains obscure. There is some reason to believe that the colonists did not consider them slaves, that they thought of them as servants to be held for a term of years and then freed, like the white servants with whom the planters were already familiar. For a time, moreover, the use of black labor remained limited. Although Africans continued to trickle steadily into the colony; planters continued to prefer European indentured servants until at least the 1670s, when such servants began to become scarce and expensive. But whether anyone realized it at the time, the small group of black people who arrived in 1619 marked a first step toward the enslavement of Africans within what was to be the American Republic. (Brinkley, 1995, p. 33)

Nothing in this passage provides the reader with a sense of the effect of slavery on the people who were enslaved. The devastation of slavery is not made available to the student reading this in his/her United States History class. That African men, women and children had been captured, thrown into dungeons, stripped of all that they owned, torn away from their families and community, their country and their continent and forced into chains onto a slave ship with little or no food, and taken to America not freely as the European indentured servants to whom they are compared but brutally as animals in a cargo-hold is not apparent. This paragraph does nothing to remind us of the degradation and savagery of slavery. The only other entry related to Africans in this same history textbook explains:

> Masters and Slaves: A small white population, with much of it enjoying greater economic success, and a large African population, all of it in bondage, was a potentially explosive combination. As in other English colonies in the New World, in which Africans came to outnumber Europeans, whites in the Caribbean—fearful of slave revolts—monitored their labor force closely and often harshly. The English West Indians devised, therefore, a rigid set of laws and practices to ensure control over their black labor force. Beginning in the 1600s, all the islands enacted legal codes to regulate relations between masters and slaves and to give white people virtually absolute authority over Africans. (Brinkley, 1995, p. 37)

Students can not possibly discover the truth about slavery when statements such as these are all that is available in their textbooks. The story of slavery is critical in the history of the United States and Africa. Neither the African students nor the Afro-American students could say much about slavery. Only one student, Damon, an Afro-American male, even mentioned slavery as part of what he knew about Africa. When asked "What did you learn about slavery?" He answered, "That it lasted a long time and most of our ancestors were slaves." I then asked him, "Did you learn about how they became slaves?" His response was, "Oh no, I don't remember it." The participants in this study did not have access to their history. They had bits and pieces, but not enough to make a connection that could enrich their lives. Thus far, the continent of Africa has been left out of education except as it relates to geography and nature. It is still treated as if it has nothing to offer the world, no history, no accomplishments, no contribution except landscapes and animals.

None of the African students mentioned slavery until after they saw the film. Memory is power and without the history of and connection to Africa, and a true understanding of the devastation of slavery and the continued struggle for equality passed on from generation to generation, the humanity of the people of African descent is hidden from view on both sides of the ocean, on both continents, for both Africans and Afro-Americans.

The resource list provided in Appendix cites materials currently available that can help parents, teachers, and students begin to break down the stereotypes and make the connection to Africa and the African worldview. African American studies classes need to make the connection at the level of experience, emotion, and heart not just intellectually. The film we showed our students clearly encouraged them to make that connection at the level of the heart. The film needs to be shown across America, not just in schools with African students but in all schools. Brandy, an Afro-American female, argued for a major change in the way that we think about multicultural education and education in general. She was emphatic when she declared that "a crowd don't learn." Small group, one-on-one work, is needed to give the students the opportunity to learn from and about each other. Multicultural assemblies will not accomplish this same experience. It can't be done in large groups.

The presence of even one African student can be an opportunity for increased learning for everyone at a school or in a community. Just recently we were contacted by a high school that has a newly arrived student from Liberia. The school is located in a white, middle to upper class suburb. Several events recently had occurred that could be teachable moments and many more could be developed. For example, within the very early weeks of this student's arrival, while riding the bus, a young girl approached him and made a sexual advance. The Liberian student did not respond in a way that pleased the female and he has since experienced harassment and teasing from this girl and her friends. He's being called "Gay" and other derogatory terms and being told that he can't sit with anyone else. This could provide an opportunity to address cultural difference and how to co-exist in the midst of cultural differences. We recommend first bringing the female student and the Liberian male together and ask them to talk about what happened. This particular student from Liberia has witnessed many horrors including the murder of his father. His life is very different from what is considered "normal" in this suburban community but also very similar to many children around the world who have experienced war, like the youth in many countries even today. When the two students have a better understanding of each other and their different lived experiences, perspectives, and cultural norms, they would be more able to reach out to others and try to understand difference without having to reject it without even understanding it.

Another learning opportunity came to mind when we were informed that the young Liberian student's class had just covered Abraham Lincoln. One aspect that connects the U.S. and Liberia is the fact that when some slaves were freed they chose to return to Africa and many settled in Liberia forming a colony there. This exodus and attempt to establish a safe haven for freed American slaves is the focus of a recent book entitled "The Price of Liberty: African Americans and the Making of Liberia" (Clegg, 2004). Because the Liberian student had little to no education during the war and was reading at a very low level, this book could be an opportunity for students in his class to volunteer to read a chapter to him or read one into a tape so that he could listen to it and the book could provide an enrichment activity to the lesson of Afro-Americans re-silient and undaunted efforts to escape from slavery. This could bring alive the Emancipation Proclamation and Reconstruction period for the present times. The Americo-Liberians are descendents of freed slaves and this connects U.S. history to the history of Liberia. So many more opportunities could be developed if the student from Africa is viewed as someone who has something to offer and that reaching out is of benefit to us all.

Benefits

In addition to the benefits expressed by each student personally, there were benefits to the students as a group and there were positive repercussions throughout the school. The students who participated had the opportunity to have face-to-face conversations with each other and see through the stereotypes that had kept them apart. Recognizing the stereotypes ultimately as misinforma-tion gave them an opportunity to ask more useful questions. They began to see each other through new eyes. They wanted to know more about one another and about Africa. The Afro-American students wanted to know more about their history. The African students wanted to stay connected to their history and learn more about the history of the Afro-Americans in America. Several of the students started sharing books and information. All of the participants started asking more questions.

The African Students Association developed and produced a cultural show, a byproduct of this study, and it provided the Afro-American students participat-ing in this study with the opportunity to appreciate and applaud the African students and their cultural expressions. A multicultural assembly that had been held the previous year had resulted in booing by the audience. This time there was support and applause. The African students felt appreciated for the first time by their Afro-American peers.

The African American studies teacher at Jackson also had the opportunity to see some of his stereotypes disappear as he developed relationships with the African students in his classes and in the African Student Association (ASA) through participating in the cultural show. The school benefited from the many connections that were made between students that have transformed the prior conversation at Jackson from "the Africans are a problem" into "the Africans are an opportunity to learn more about Africa."

The principal of Jackson was very grateful for the work undertaken in this research. Just interviewing both the African and the Afro-American students started a process of inquiry that is blossoming into joint projects, hand holding, an interest in Africa and things African and conversations that would not have occurred had there not been the intervention of this study. A prime example was an Afro-American student who proudly pointed to Guinea on a map of Africa. She now knew where Guinea was, thanks to interviewing one of the African female students from there. Although she was in Afro-American studies class she had not been interested enough before to note even one country in Africa. She added, "Now I want to learn more." At our first meeting it didn't seem important to her to know where she had come from. After Dr. Asante's talk, Sylviane said, "Now I want to learn more about Barbados and about Africa since I realize now that before Barbados, someone in my family came from Africa. I didn't know that before."

A direct consequence of this study was to rejuvenate the interactions between Africans and Afro-Americans in their African American studies class. A few students from each section of this class had participated in our study, and consequently the quality of the conversation in that class was enriched by their presence. Prior to this study, the African students had complained that no one was interested in what they had to say. One articulate student complained "Why should I be there? They don't listen to me." We encouraged him to persevere and continue to volunteer even if his views were not yet appreciated. By the time we had completed only a portion of this study, and the students had put together their cultural show for the student body, this student's views were not only sought but they were valued by his classmates. The atmosphere changed in the African American studies class. The teacher started calling on the African students for their comments and asked them to share their experiences of the various activities involved in this study. What had seemed like a problem became an asset.

We really knew that something significant and perhaps lasting had changed at Jackson when one of the administrators, who originally had seen the African Students Association (ASA) as a problem because it was potentially divisive, asked if the ASA could perform something for the Christmas show. Every time previously that the ASA had needed someone to open the auditorium for our practices, this administrator made it quite evident that they were a nuisance; but when the show was a huge success the Africans became an asset. The African students no longer were treated as intruders, an annoyance, but instead were approached with respect and appreciation and the students noticed the difference too. One African student said, "Now I get called on. Before, I got ignored."

But perhaps the biggest contribution was that the students organized an African American Student Union that planned to work closely with the ASA on a cultural show for Black History Month. The two groups worked together to produce a show. This collaboration was not only unexpected it was unthinkable just a few months earlier. During this study, the African American Student Union invited the ASA to join them in a Kwanzaa celebration. This was a wonderful opportunity for the Afro-Americans to share one of their cultural celebrations with the Africans. Some of the African students had heard about Kwanzaa, however, they were pleasantly surprised when the celebration afforded them the opportunity to talk about the shared values of unity, family, community, service and appreciation for the harvest. They could see themselves in the celebration.

The celebration of Kwanzaa also coincided with the visit from Dr. Asante whose talk with both groups made their connections very clear. Students, both Africans and Afro-Americans said that more students at Jackson needed to hear Dr. Asante, as his message was critical to all of them. Wanting to know more about where they come from is now more important to the students. Both the African and Afro-American students commented about how great he made them feel about themselves. Both African and Afro-American students talked about how proud they felt when they listened to Dr. Asante and were moved by his wisdom.

In connecting the Afro-American students to Africa they have access to a more positive sense of who they are and where they come from. The connection to Africa and the African worldview speaks to who they are and the values they hold dear. They are validated. The students felt "respect" for themselves and for each other. Respecting oneself and others is such a key ingredient to identity development in adolescence. When asked the benefit of the study Brandy, an Afro-American female, replied, "Respect. Respect for myself and respect for others. That's what I got." The connection made through the film, exhibit, interviews and talk by Dr. Asante provided the students with the chance to develop "respect" for themselves, for each other and for Africa and Afro-Americans. For Tony, an Afro-American male, the benefit was a new friend. "I didn't know I had stereotypes. I got to know Amadou (an African male). Now I am friends with him. I didn't know that could happen."

That any student can go to an American school and not learn about African history and culture is denying all of us a history that has much to teach us. All students are being denied a more accurate representation of American history and the struggle for equality and the devastation of racism.

Valeisha was so excited about this project that she went home and wrote her play. The opening of her play entitled "A Dance of Freedom" speaks loudly of the power of the African connection.

> Africa, the beginning of man, the motherland. Knowledge floating in circles of laughter. The A as in Art, the F as in Freedom ride, the R as in the Rage that has come of the years that I have mistaken, the C for the courage that will carry me across the ocean, and A access to all the opening doors. I have a story to tell.

"The rage that has come of the years that I have mistaken" is a great description for the time spent not being connected. Once the connection is made at the level of heart and soul, the world of Afrocentricity opens up for those who are willing to study. It takes courage to access the information that is there to be discovered, and learning about Africa, the motherland, in a world that still depicts Africa as the jungle and Africans as wild savages may be the first step on the long road to freedom for many of our inner-city children and those who teach them.

Another benefit to this study is that the African students, as outsiders in

American culture, could shed some light on aspects of American culture and schooling that we might otherwise not be able to see. The most striking element that distinguishes the two cultures is the communal ontology of the African worldview vs. the individualism of the United States. Another way that this worldview manifests at school is the way in which the African students look out for one another. When a student's mother died, the students collected funds from everyone and went as a group to present their condolences to the entire family.

These African values can be found intact in Afro-American communities in the United States today despite the devastating effects of slavery on black families in America. Ladner (1998) has described her experiences growing up in Mississippi and the "power of the extended family."

> Extended families were a fundamental aspect of black culture. A historical tradition imported from Africa, combined with the economic instability that characterized our lives in the New World, had encouraged and strengthened this family structure. (p. 29)

Ladner makes an excellent argument that there are timeless values that originated in Africa and have been preserved and developed by black families in America despite every attempt to destroy them.

The African students who have recently arrived in the U.S. can help Afro-American students recognize and appreciate the African culture that remains with them. The African students bring with them an appreciation for the world that they left behind. The environment that faces them, including the urban public high school, seems uninviting and unfriendly. Because they are not used to the situation here, they perhaps can provide a fresh outlook, though critical it may be. Their critique could provide a new opportunity to make changes in ways that could not have been imagined before.

The educational system in the U.S. is designed to promote assimilation into the American way of life and promotes American values and a version of American history told from the perspective of the White settlers, the White forefathers and the White government. Although persons of African descent have been an integral part of that story for hundreds of years, their version of history is different from the one communicated in classrooms across America. Thus, Black children do not have the opportunity to learn about their heritage, their culture, their values, their version of history in most schools in America. This has serious implications for the education of Black children, whether they are Africans, Afro-Americans, Caribbean Americans, or any other people of African descent. In this study, African and Afro-American students had the chance to begin to explore their shared heritage and found it to be important to them. They didn't necessarily appreciate having Afro-American studies until they saw the undeniable connection between Africa and America in the film, "The Language You Cry In." This connection opens up a world to them that can serve them in many beneficial ways as they continue to develop their identities. The African connection can be the key to their understanding themselves as complete persons. They are not in America by accident and the ideas that keep them separated from Africa keep them disconnected from useful information about who they are how and what they hold dear.

If the African families living in this country entirely delegate the education of their children to the American educational system the children will quickly lose their African values. With no discussion of African values and African worldview the American value system becomes the only value system; but it is not. The African worldview and values provide an alternative to the values of individualism and linear progression and "making it" that are some of the aspects of life in America that are counter to African values. The presence of African students in schools in America is an opportunity for Americans both Black and White to inquire into the ways in which others see the world. It is an opportunity to learn about a continent that still remains "Dark" for the majority of Americans. Much has been written about the African worldview. Books are available that tell the story of the "arrival" of Africans to America that may be sad and upsetting but more truthful than the story currently told in school. We as human beings haven't learned every lesson without pain or discomfort. The story of slavery is abominable but denying its reality keeps our children in a state of ignorance. The truth can be liberating. Moreover, Africa today is not a jungle. Africans are not savages, and the American version of slavery was a savage mistreatment of primarily Black human beings by other human beings for the economic success of mostly White Americans.

On another level this study was about how students actually learn. It is not a new thought that students need to see the connections between what they know and what they are learning. Dewey (1944/1916, 1997/1938) made the connection between experience and learning long ago. Freire's (1985, 1997, 1998b) work with the illiterate in Brazil and many other countries brought new meaning to the connection between the word and the world. Even having a course in African American studies will not bring the students closer to understanding their heritage unless the connection is made at the level of experience, at the heart, not merely the head. Memorizing the countries on the continent of Africa or the names of the early African empires does little to counteract the official story told in schools in America. The history of people of African descent is rich and full of struggle and has much to teach all of us.

Implications for Teachers

Every great teacher's goal is to help students achieve at their highest level, both personally and academically. Students of African descent have been at an obvious disadvantage in our public schools, even in spite of the progress made as a result of the Civil Rights movement. Any discussion about the history of African or the African culture from which Afro-Americans derive has at best been superficial, at worst incomplete or wrong. When students are given a chance to see themselves as strong and resilient and coming from a history that has positive messages of past accomplishments and strong role models, they can follow that leadership and learn from their past. African American history did not originate on American soil because the history of Afro-Americans evolved from the long and prominent history of the African nations. Today, Africa still offers the world many rich traditions and a connectedness to the spiritual world. Reading ancient texts may have the benefit of touching one's soul and this can inspire a sense of awe and appreciation for life; studying Yoruba spirituality can help ignite a passion for learning and for reaching out to others; the Dogon philosophy speaks softly of the way that we are all one and need to learn from each other. These qualities are among those most absent from American society and many discover that they are hungering to fill the void in their lives by adhering to principles very similar to these but without the immemorial tradition that sustains them.

The Afrocentric worldview has something practical to offer everyone. It helps us to focus on a different perspective, one that is still in touch with our heart and soul and align us with the Creator, not in any religious sense but in the spiritual domain. In Africa it is still possible today to feel more connected to a Supreme Being than most Americans achieve in their daily lives, because in African communities respect for neighbors, elders, and an understanding that with age came wisdom and spiritual maturity remains highly important (Nobles, 2004). There is something spiritual in the way one's neighbors use the earth's resources most efficiently to sustain themselves; in many African communities, there is natural anti-pollution and anti-waste policy because the people still recognize their dependency on the fruits of the land they need for their survival. Family and neighbors are the first priority; there is always time to help a member of the family or a neighbor in need. Greeting everyone, everywhere all the time is an everyday occurrence, something absent from most inner city dwellings in America and in short supply in many of our small towns. Spending time listening to the elders is considered an efficient use of one's time and energies. Listening to the stories and proverbs rich in life lessons is simply perceived an essential step to becoming an educated person.

Africa today remains a continent rich in history, tradition, wisdom, and human and physical resources. However, for Africans it is not the land resources that are the most valuable, but the wisdom of the ancient texts, the elders' stories and the everyday experiences in people's lives that recognize the connection to the ancestors and future generations; and it is the caring among family and neighbors, a family that extends so much further than the nuclear family of American society. Currently, life in Africa is very diverse; there are big cities and rural villages; there are skyscrapers and families living in poverty. There are wars and hunger; there is struggle for a place in the world, a demand for self definition and self sufficiency. There is resiliency, having survived years of colonial domination and imposition of government, culture, and religion through education and force. There are instantaneous celebrations and moments of appreciation for the small things such as the sharing of tea (hattai) with friends and family. There is a view of the West from the outside that can help us better understand ourselves.

What Teachers Must Do

To assist *all* students in better understanding Africa and people of African descent, teachers need to use materials that are based in the truth about the history and culture of Africa and Africans. Today, there are many materials produced by people of African descent that communicate the story more accurately than our current textbooks that contain little to no information. A representative list of some resource is included in the Appendix.

An important question for any concerned educator to ask is, "Where are the people of African descent in our telling of history?" Some proponents of Afrocentricity have argued that as the oldest existing civilization, predating Greek and Roman societies, the story of Egypt needs to be acknowledged as a study of Africa (Asante, 1990; Karenga & Caruthers, 1986). Because Egypt remains part of the continent of Africa, Egyptian accomplishments are African accomplishments as well. Early Greek philosophers have given credit to the education that they received in Egypt and in this way Egyptian scholars helped prepare the Greek philosophers (Hilliard, 2004).

The history of "African American" really began when innocent people were abducted and brought to America to be used as slave labor in the development of America (Davis, 2003). Much of the incredible expansion of early America, and the rapid economic growth of the plantation milieu as the bulwark of the capitalist enterprises that made early America a rising power, must be seen as being built on the backs of people of African descent dragged in chains to America (Brooks, 2004; Robinson, 2002). The negative attitude about people with darker- colored skin is not a universal response toward persons whose genetic phenotype differs from the European norm. Racism must be identified as an ideology that was developed to justify the domination of people of African descent both for colonialism and for slavery. Racism has continued to exist as a rationale for the abuse of people of African descent. This persistence in the very visceral antipathy toward persons of African descent is an integral part of our common history. Racism will not simply disappear until we have told the truth about its origins and the reasons for its continued presence today in the inequities that influence where a family can purchase a home, what career paths may be possible, and where our tax dollars are channeled to provide public school education for our children.

White privilege remains a reality in American society (Rothenberg, 2001; Swain, 2002; Williams, 2003). The African students recognize this fact soon after their arrival in the U.S. They are quick to understand the place that they occupy just because of the color of their skin. They also are quick to point out that they thought this was the home of the brave and the land of the free with liberty and justice for all, but it is not as equal as they thought. And the hypocrisy inherent in this inconsistency does not elude them. They see racism from a different view; they see how it affects them in where they can live, where they can work, where they can go to school, and what value their education holds in defining the opportunities that may be available to them for the remainder of their lives. They see the effect it has on their parents who must work long hours in mostly menial jobs to provide for their families. Their fathers, some with college or graduate level education, end up working in parking garages; their mothers, with college degrees, work in maintenance jobs in nursing homes. Defending her disengagement in school, one student declared: "My father is a slave here. What difference does an education make? Why should I even bother?"

Teachers can encourage all students to know who they are and where they are from. Sharing their stories with each other is one way that African students can help American students be more educated about the world. Africa is not just animals or jungle or desert or the Nile River. It is so much more. Africans are not jungle bunnies or illiterate villagers. The literature that has been produced by continental Africans and Africans in the Diaspora is rich in lessons for all human beings, not just Africans or Afro- or Caribbean-Americans. Today, there is a vast array of history texts that tell a more accurate story of Africa and African peoples and a wide selection of both fiction and non-fiction that shares the wisdom of the continent. Teachers can access some of the wealth of benefits going completely untapped by using more African-centered materials, telling a more African-centered story, making available the accomplishments of people of African descent, and learning more themselves about the continent and its people, not just its land masses and natural resources, but its human resources.

One beginning resource we know about is entitled "Africa is Not a Country"—which is one of the most common misperceptions of the African continent. The Peters projection map displays the size of the African continent more accurately; it is the second largest continent—China, the U.S., and Europe all can fit within the borders of Africa. Most students are shocked when they see this map juxtaposed this way. They think of Africa as an insignificant part of our world. It is neither insignificant in size, nor history, cultural influences, spirituality, and contributions to our world as it exists today. The students we came to know at Jackson were on the whole seriously disappointed with what they found to be the reality in America. They had been led to believe that this was the best educational system in the world but their experiences here have left them only with a sense of being excluded as young people with a rich cultural upbringing and with a wealth of experiences to share. How could the best educational system in the world promote such blatant negativity about an entire continent and its people? How can the U.S., which seems to aspire to such high moral ideals, still be relegating people to lower status based on their race? How can where you live, what school you attend and what jobs you can anticipate accomplishing still be so influenced by one's race? How can having an accent be considered a detriment in a country founded by immigrants? How can the wealthiest nation still have people living on the streets and going through garbage cans to find food? Why are people killing each other on the streets where we live? These are some of the questions that the students asked. What we might ask do we have to learn from these students? They have lived different lives and view life very differently. Some of them came from war-torn countries, others came from peace. Those who came from war-torn countries knew a life of peace before the war and wonder what explains the violence in America.

They understand war but as one student from Sierra Leone asked, "What is it here that explains the hostility and apathy evinced by Americans?"

It is a tragic reality of our human predicament that shamefully there are beggars in some cities in Africa, but people there usually do not find that they must scour through garbage bins to find food if their neighbors have some to share. In general, someone in need in most of the countries on the continent not directly impacted by the devastations of war, would be taken care of by their community. Every African student who shared with us during our study admitted that they know more about America than any American they met knows about Africa. One might argue that that makes sense because America is "more important" or "more developed" than Africa. But it makes no sense to the African students who sees their lived experiences in Africa as "more important" or "more developed" from a humane or egalitarian perspective. They see Americans as passing each other by, ignoring others, being too busy to take time to be together, disconnected from their families and friends, too materialistic and missing out on what is important in life – the connection to each other, to the ancestors and to the Creator.

APPENDIX

African-Centered Resources

"Extended lives: The African immigrant experience in Philadelphia." Philadelphia, PA: The Balch Institute for Ethnic Studies, Oct. 2001–Apr. 2002, described at http://www.balchinstitute.org.

Accompanying Materials

Extended lives: The African immigrant experience in Philadelphia—A Balch Institute community profile. (2001). Philadelphia, PA: The Balch Institute for Ethnic Studies.
Extended lives: The African immigrant experience in Philadelphia—Educational guide. (2001). Philadelphia, PA: The Balch Institute for Ethnic Studies.

Films

Toepke, A. & A. Serrano (1998). *The language you cry in: The story of a Mende song*. California Newsreel, http://www.newsreel.org/films/langyou.htm.

There are many African and Afro-American films available from California Newsreel.

Textbooks/Curriculum

Asante, M. K. (2001). *Afro-American history: A journey of liberation*. Saddle Brook, NJ: The Peoples Publishing.
Prescott, F. (1992). *SETCLAE, High School: Self-Esteem through culture leads to academic excellence*. Chicago, IL: African American Images.
Rivers, F. A. (2003). *KMT: Our African heritage*. Lansing, MI: Sankofa Publishing. This is one in a series of books available from Sankofa. Other materials provide Language Arts and Mathematics Curriculum at http://www.sankofapublishing.com.

Afro-American Books with High Interest for Youth

Abrahams, R. D. (1999). *African-American folktales: Stories from Black traditions in the new world*. New York: Pantheon (originally published 1985).
African American literature (2001). New York: Glencoe McGraw-Hill.
Alexander, A. (2001). *Fifty Black women who changed America*. New York: Citadel.
Appiah, A. (Ed.) (1990). Early African-American classics. New York: Bantam.
Browder, A. T. (1996). *Survival strategies for Africans in America: 13 steps to freedom*. Washington, DC: The Institute of Karmic Guidance.
Bryan, A. (2001). *Ashley Bryan's ABC of Afro-American poetry*. New York: Aladdin.
Burroughs, T. (2001). *Black roots: A beginner's guide to tracing the Afro-American family tree*. New York: Fireside.
Canfield, J., M. V. Hansen, L. Nichols, & T. Joyner (2004). *Chicken soup for the African American soul*. Deerfield Beach, FL: Health Communications.
Davis, A. C. & J.W. Jackson (1998). *"Yo, little brother". . . Basic rules of survival for young Afro-American males*. Chicago: Afro-American Images.
Hill, L. C. (2003). *Harlem stomp! A cultural history of the Harlem renaissance*. New York: Megan Tingley Books.

Igus, T. (Ed.) (1997). *Great women in the struggle: An introduction for young readers.* East Orange, NJ: Just Us Books.

Johnson, D. J. (1995). *Proud sisters: The wisdom and wit of Afro-American women.* White Plains, NY: Peter Pauper Press.

Johnson, L. A. (2000). *Go down, Moses! Daily devotions inspired by old Negro spirituals.* Valley Forge, PA: Jordon Press.

Karenga, M. (1998). *Kwanzaa: A celebration of family, community and culture.* Los Angeles: University of Sankore Press.

Kearns, F. E. (1970). *The Black experience: An anthology of American literature for the 1970s.* New York: The Viking Press.

King, C. & L. B. Osborne (1997). *Oh, freedom! Kids talk about the civil rights movement with the people who made it happen.* New York: Random House.

Medaris, A. S. (1994). *The seven days of Kwanzaa: How to celebrate them.* New York: Scholastic.

Mullane, D. (1993). *Crossing the danger water: Three hundred years of African-American writing.* New York: Anchor Books.

Newman, S. P. (2000). *The African slave trade.* New York: Grolier.

Newman, S. P. (2000). *Child slavery in modern times.* New York: Grolier.

Newman, S. P. (2000). *Slavery in the United States.* New York: Grolier.

Vanzant, I. (1993). *Acts of faith: Daily meditations for people of color.* New York: Fireside.

Wright, R. (1941). *12 million Black voices.* New York: Thunder's Mouth Press.

African-related Books with High Interest for Youth

Abrahams, R. D. 1983). *African folktales: Traditional stories of the Black world.* New York: Pantheon.

Achebe, C. & C. L. Innes (1985). *African short stories: Twenty short stories from across the continent.* Portsmouth, NH: Heinemann.

Angelou, M. (1996). *Kofi and his magic.* New York: Clarkson Potter.

Clarke, J. H. (1993). *African people in world history.* Baltimore: Black Classic Press.

Diouf, S. A. (2000). *Kings and queens of Central Africa.* New York: Grolier.

Diouf, S. A. (2000). *Kings and queens of East Africa.* New York: Grolier.

Diouf, S. A. (2000). *Kings and queens of West Africa.* New York: Grolier.

Diouf, S. A. (2000). *Kings and queens of Southern Africa.* New York: Grolier.

Fayemi, A. O. (1999). *Voices from within: Photographs of African children.* Plymouth, VT: Albofa Press.

Feelings, M. (1972). *Moja means one: Swahili counting book.* New York: Dial Books.

Feelings, M. (1974). *Jambo means hello: Swahili alphabet book.* New York: Dial Books.

Froebenius, L. & D.C. Fox (1999). *African genesis: Folk tales and myths of Africa.* Mineola, NY: Dover.

Grifalconi, A. (1986). *The village of round and square houses.* Boston: Little, Brown & Co.

Grifalconi, A. (1992). *The flyaway girl.* Boston: Little, Brown & Co.

Hughes, L. (1960). *An African treasury: The power, agony and glory of the Black experience.* New York: Harcourt, Brace, Jovanavich.

Koslow, P. (1997). *Senegambia: Land of the lion.* Philadelphia, PA: Chelsea House.

Laye, C. (1954). *The dark child: The autobiography of an African boy.* New York: Farrar, Straus and Giroux.

Lewin, A. (1996). *Africa is not a country. It's a continent.* Milltown, NJ: Clarendon.

Moore, G. & U. Beier (1998). *The Penguin book of modern African poetry*. London: Penguin.

Musgrave, M. (1976). *Ashanti to Zulu: African traditions*. New York: Dial Books.

Nelson Mandela's favorite African folktales (2002). New York: W. W. Norton.

Nzekwu, O. & M. Crowder (1963). *Eze goes to school*. Ibadan, Nigeria: African Universities Press.

Onyefulu, I. (1993). *A is for Africa*. New York: Puffin.

Owusu, H. (1998). *Symbols of Africa*. New York: Sterling.

Rivers, F. A. (2000). *Becoming: A creation story*. Lansing, MI: Sankofa Publishing.

Spider and the sky God: An Akan legend. (1993). Memphis, TN: Troll Associates.

Stewart, J. (1997). *African proverbs and wisdom: A collection for every day of the year, from more than forty African nations*. Seacaucus, NJ: Carol Publishing.

Wisniewski, D. (1999). *Sundiata: Lion king of Mali*. Boston: Clarion.

Reference Books

Akbar, N. (1994). *Light from ancient Africa*. Tallahassee, FL: Mind Productions.

Anyike, J. C. (1991). *Afro-American holidays: A historical research and resource guide to cultural celebrations*. Chicago: Popular Truth Publishing.

Asante, M. K. (1994). *Classical Africa*. Maywood, NJ: The Peoples Publishing.

Davidson, B. (1966). *African kingdoms*. New York: Time-Life.

Hilliard, A. G. (1993). *50 plus: Essential references on the history of African people*. Baltimore: Black Classic Press.

Hughes, L. (1960). *An African treasury: The power, agony and glory of the Black experience*. New York: Jove.

Kunjufu, J. (1987). *Lessons from history: A celebration in Blackness*. Chicago: Afro-American Images.

Masrui, A. A. (1986). *The Africans: A triple heritage*. Boston, MA: Little, Brown & Co.

Rogers, J. A. (1989). *Africa's gift to America: The Afro-American in the making and saving of the United States*. St. Petersburg, FL: Helga M. Rogers.

Serequeberhan, T. (2000). *Our heritage: The past and the present of African-American and African existence*. Lanham, MD: Rowman & Littlefield.

Smith, J. C. (Ed.) (1994). *Black firsts: 2,000 years of extraordinary achievement*. Detroit: Visible Ink.

Tedla, E. (1995). *Sankofa: African thought and education*. New York: Peter Lang.

Brain Quest Cards

Black Heritage Brain Quest--Afro-American History (Decks one and two) (1996). New York: Workman Publishing.

Other Resources

African/Afro-American Studies Department, School District of Philadelphia, http://www.phila.k12.pa.us/ll/curriculumsupport/aastudies/africa-resources.

African Readers. Evans Publishing Group, http://www.evansbooks.co.uk.

Altman, L. J. (2004). *The American civil rights movement: The African-American struggle for equality*. New York: Enslow. Young adult. Discusses some of the less familiar events that triggered and then carried out the Civil Rights movement of the 1950s and 1960s.

"The Day of the African Child—June 16" commemorates the day in 1976 when the school children were massacred in Soweto, South Africa.

Edwards, A. & C. K. Polite (1992). *Children of the dream: The psychology of Black success.* New York: Doubleday. Focuses on professionals who have discovered particular strengths and skills that have enabled them to overcome racism.

Ford, C. W. (1994). *We can all get along.* New York: Dell. Young person's guide to work toward ending racism.

Fuchs, L. H. (1990). *The American kaleidoscope: Race, ethnicity and the civic culture.* Wesleyan University Press. Discusses the changing culture and racial and ethnic group compositions in the United States.

The Great Blacks in Wax Museum, located in Baltimore, MD, http://www.greatblacksinwax.org. Contains a slaveship exhibit, lynching exhibit, and ancient Africa exhibit, as well as models of many important figures in Afro-American history up to the present time.

Internet Resources on Africa, http://www.africa.upenn.edu.

Macmillan Books for Schools Catalogue, http://www.macmillan-africa.com.

Rowan, C. T. (1993). *Dream makers, dream breakers: The world of Justice Thurgood Marshall.* Boston: Little, Brown & Co. Biography of Thurgood Marshall, civil rights advocate and first African American to sit on the United States Supreme Court.

Schreiber, A., & Casella, J. (1993). *Resources: Africa.* UNICEF, http://www.unicef.org.

Shomberg Center for Research in Black Culture, 515 Lenox Ave. New York, NY, 10037, http://www.nypl.org/research/sc/sc.html. Phone: 212-491-2200

UNESCO catalogue of videos from and about countries on the continent of Africa, http://www.unesco.org/education/catalogues/sitevideo/regions/afr.

Watts Library, http://www.publishing.grolier.com. Lists numerous African and Afro-American books for students in elementary, middle and high school.

Wilson, A. (1992). *Discrimination: African Americans struggle for equality.* Vero Beach, FL: Rourke Corp. Young adult level. Discusses the struggle of African Americans for equality in education, employment, and other areas.

Preface

1. To establish the contours of the life journey of the lead author, whose dissertation research was so integral to the conceptual predicates that inform this book, Rosemary's personal reflections are offered here as frame of reference. A more complete exposition of Robert's path to co-writing this book is reserved for another venue because it is less instructive for present purposes.

2. Jackson is a pseudonym for the inner city high school that was the site for our study.

Introduction

1. "Education is the American answer to the European welfare state, to massive waves of immigration, and to demands for the abolition of subordination based on race, class, or gender" (Hochschild & Scovronick, 2003, p. 9).

2. According to some theorists, the goal of education is the "moral and spiritual training of the nation," which can only be accomplished by "deriving everything from an original principle," "relating everything to an ideal," and then unifying the principle and ideal into a single process for perpetuating society (Lyotard, 1984, pp. 32-33). Modern deconstructionist thinkers may rebel against this type of conformist indoctrination as the principal objective of education, but most American theorists, being pragmatists by nature, converge around the principle that education should prepare youth to become adults who can contribute to the common good of American society (Anderson, 1988, pp. 79-80; D'Souza, 1995, p. 337; Spring, 2000, pp. 6-20; Waters, 1999, pp. 253-254). The "common" objectives of public school education were launched during the Jacksonian period in the nineteenth century with the intention to "better maintain social order and increase material production" (Nasaw, 1979, p. 4). According to Macedo (2000),

> It was out of this complex mix of motives—a variety of prejudices, not unreasonable anxiety, and a genuine hopefulness about the potential for a common civic life—that the impetus for common schooling emerged and spread. The ethnic and religious diversity that increasingly characterized American cities in the second quarter of the nineteenth century contributed powerfully to calls for an institution that could inculcate a common culture, the English language, and republican sensibilities by educating the children of different faiths and classes in one institution dedicated to forging a shared citizenship. (p. 63)

Lieberman (1993) acknowledges that the traditional rationale was that public education "effectively fosters basic skills, scientific and cultural literacy, civic virtues, and desirable habits and attitudes toward our society and its institutions" (p. 1). In Lieberman's pro-market-inspired assessment, however, public education today is moribund and no reforms will revive this traditional rationale for public education. Unfortunately, in an entirely market-driven system of public education the first educational ideals to become obsolete would be the inculcation of civic virtues and cultural literacy since these evanescent components of the traditional rationale have no discernible means of economic commodification (Allen, 2004).

3. Except where we quote from the interviews conducted for this study, or where quot-

ing or citing a published text, we will follow the convention advocated by a number of race reformers to distinguish persons of color who were born in Africa from those who were born in the United States or elsewhere. Orlando Patterson (1997, p. xi), for example, argues that "Afro-American" should be used to refer to persons of African descent who are not direct immigrants from Africa. Patterson objects to the use of the term "African-American" to refer to this group of persons because it is misleading and because it stresses the African at the expense of the very real American status of persons born in the United States. We hold no conviction on which term should take precedence, but for sake of simplicity, we will identify newly arrived students from Africa as Africans (who may become Americans), and persons of color who already are citizens of the U.S. we will identify as Afro-American. This will allow us to place greater emphasis later on the shared "African" heritage that can connect these youngsters emotionally and intellectually without having the "African" heritage confounded by the African-American heritage. We also have adopted the convention of using the appellations "Black" or "person of color" to denote non-caucasian students where there is no justification for distinguishing students other than that they are not caucasian.

4. The principles of Nguzo Saba were developed by Dr. Maulana Karenga, the founder of Kwanzaa in the mid 1960s. The Joseph Littles-Nguzo Saba charter school remains in operation in West Palm Beach, Florida, and is based on the seven principles (nguzo saba) of Kwanzaa which utilize Kiswahili words: unity (umoja), self-determination (kujichagulia), collective work and responsibility (ujima), cooperative economics (ujamaa), purpose (nia), creativity (kuumba), and faith (imani). Information on this school is available at http://www.racematters.org/amefikageuka.htm.

5. As a collective, Africans have been denied a culturally appropriate education in their home countries in a manner very similar to their American peers. They have been subjected to a colonial education, be it British, French, or Portuguese, or even the Belgians in former Zaire. Their educational systems were not designed to empower or educate in the liberatory sense (Freire, 1997). They basically are trained to take low-level jobs. Those who are educated overseas in the colonial countries are considered for the high-level positions. Consequently, many African families firmly believe that getting an education in the U.S. will be better for their children, no matter what the hardships to access this education.

6. It is extremely important to acknowledge that a key element that contributed to the outcomes of this research (and some of the more rewarding moments inspired by it) was the background of the lead author, a white woman who embodies extensive knowledge of Afrocentricity, sustained first-hand experiences in many countries on the continent of Africa, a profound commitment to Afrocentricity as a generative approach to understanding people who are of African descent, and a deep appreciation for the value of the African worldview and its commitment to a sense of community and the intertwining relationships between all people. The major insight that became more obvious as this study progressed was that the researchers' presence at Jackson High was itself a positive intervention. Beyond the standard Hawthorne effect that intrudes on all research involving participant observation, no one at Jackson would have had the time to offer the activities for the students encompassed in this study unless they were part of a course or an after school program. Under these circumstances, it is important to remember that the researcher can provide the needed energy, focus, resources, and accessibility to generate and conduct the types of activities described in this book with the students. We appreciate that when the researcher departed from Jackson the students continued to associate

together for a brief time, but only until the end of the school year. What was most remarkable to us, however, was the recognition by the students that they could not change their behavior without the entire school population becoming more enlightened about the commonalities they shared because these students intuitively understood that peer pressure would introduce some resistance to their acting in new ways based on their newfound understanding of each other.

7. For example, in the experience of the lead author, the African people would share their last meal with her even when she was an unexpected visitor stranded by torrential rainfall or a broken down vehicle. It was customary to include strangers but she probably got better treatment because they thought she was fragile, which at the moment she really was, also having amoebic dysentery to compound her miseries.

8. According to Marx (1998, p. 52), "[s]lavery in North America was infamously brutal." Although slavery has existed in many variations throughout the ages, until the introduction of the slave trade in the British and Dutch colonies of the seventeenth century slaves mainly comprised members of a conquered people, and slavery was a practical means to perpetuate their conquest (Blum, 2002, pp. 111-117; Patterson, 1982, pp. 39-45). Although Aristotle believed that some people were born to be slaves, he never contemplated that enslaved people were inherently inferior beings, just unfortunately placed (Aristotle, 1984, pp. 1998-1992 [1253b-1255b]; Blum, 2002. pp. 110-111; Isaac, 2004, pp. 70-74, 177-181). The expansion of slavery in the American colonies, steadily descending in depravity from treating African people first as "heathens" needing religious conversion, to regarding African people as "savages" who needed to be civilized, culminated in the concerted effort to de-humanize the entire African people to ensure they became the subjugated masses of bodies needed to toil on the plantations, and later to become the human fodder for the economic whirlwind following the invention of the cotton gin in 1793 (Blum, 2002, pp. 112-115; Fredrickson, 2002, pp. 64-81). This process of dehumanization reached its crowning iniquity in *Dred Scott v. Sandford*, 60 U.S. 393, 407 (1856), in which the Supreme Court declared that persons of African descent maintained "no rights which the white man was bound to respect." It is the supreme tragedy of our nation that the founders' belief in the natural law that "all men are created equal" was insufficient to overcome the economic rewards available to those of European descent who purchased those rewards by subjugating persons of African descent (Fredrickson, 1987; Morgan, 2003). There remains ongoing debate whether slavery caused American-style racism, or whether racism was imported to justify the forms of slavery practiced in the colonies and in the ante-bellum South (Feagin, 2000, pp. 9-16; Malcomson, 2000, pp. 170-184; Morris, 1996, pp. 8-14). We will discuss some of the contemporary residual effects of the master-slave relationship, and the conscious efforts to de-humanize persons of African descent from the Middle Passage period onward, when we explore the ongoing impact of racism in Chapter 6.

Chapter 1

1. Robinson (1979).

2. "Diversity" can be used as a ploughshare or a sword, depending on its intended effect (DeTocqueville, 2000/1840, p. 412; Goodman, 2001; Parekh, 2000; Schuck, 2003; Todorov, 1993; Wood, 2003). Presuming its positive connotation, declaring that there is diversity in America suggests that having opened our shores and borders, others have felt welcomed to approach and eventually settled here. The appeal of such diversity is a

broadening of appreciation for the differences between people, and a meaningful recognition that despite any differences we all are human beings and therefore have a commonality of existence on this planet (Benhabib, 2002; McCarthy, 1998, pp. 111-122; Nieto, 1999, pp. 132-142). This version of diversity is memorialized in the phrase enshrined on the Statute of Liberty. Under its negative application, diversity highlights otherness and emphasizes what makes distinctions between people in a way that retains and reinforces any noticeable idiosyncrasies that have the potential to divide us (D'Souza, 1995; Hollinger, 1995, pp. 98-103).

3. Waters (1999) makes a similar point about immigrants from the West Indies and notes that there may be distinct advantages, both economic and personal, for immigrant students to maintain a distance from Afro-American peers. It is reprehensible that these ersatz advantages for immigrants oftentimes accrue at the expense of Afro-Americans.

4. According to Moikobu (1981, pp. 198-199), identity is most important

> to provide a sense of continuity, and to explain to each person and to each people where they fit into the scheme of things. A man's self-perception is vital to what he does and his self-perception is still largely the result of his view of history. If African history is to provide the African with this self-perception, and thus play an effective role in independent Africa, it has to correct the distortion and bridge the gap created by the colonial experience in the African historical tradition.

5. Waters (1999) convincingly shows that there is a trade-off for students of color in choosing to identify with a particular cultural heritage. Given the alternatives, in an environment where Afro-American students are in the majority, it would be sensible to identify with the majority even if there is some loss of cultural identity in the process.

6. In Chapter 8, we provide a more detailed description of Dr. Asante's meeting with the group of students. The interaction between the young participants in our study and the acknowledged founder of Afrocentrism comprised one of the more powerful but perhaps non-replicable components of our research.

7. "Perhaps the most graphic illustration of choice in the construction of racial identities comes in the context of passing. Passing—the ability of individuals to change race—powerfully indicates race's chosen nature. Not infrequently someone Black through the social construction of their ancestry is physically indistinguishable from someone White" (Lopez, 1994, p. 47).

8. Perhaps ever since our ancestors converted from hunter/gatherers to farmers/settlers, the inchoate sense of territoriality this transition fostered made it easier to recommend that newcomers to the area "go back from whence you came," but no matter how it may be intended this admonition is hurtful to those newcomers trying desperately to adapt to their unfamiliar circumstances (Mann, 1986, pp. 34-35). In 1781, Thomas Jefferson contemplated repatriation to Africa as the only viable resolution to the "problem" of slavery. According to Jefferson,

> Deep rooted prejudices entertained by the whites; ten thousand recollections, by the blacks, of the injuries they have sustained; the real distinctions which nature has made; and many other circumstances, will divide us into parties, and produce convulsions which will probably never end but in the extermination of the one or

the other race. (Jefferson, 1984a, p. 264)

In 1811, Jefferson proposed Sierra Leone as a suitable location for this effort, but perhaps unwittingly re-invoked the colonizer's motive in doing so: "Going from a country possessing all the useful arts, [the deported, freed American slaves] might be the means of transplanting them among the inhabitants of Africa, and would thus carry back to the country of their origin, the seeds of civilization which might render their sojournment and sufferings here a blessing in the end to that country" (Jefferson, 1984b, p. 1240). Liberia became the site of some emigration by freed American slaves during the period immediately preceding the Civil War and its aftermath in the Reconstruction period (Foner, 1988, pp. 599-600; Huffman, 2004). As counted on in many matters relating to the lives of American Negroes, however, Frederick Douglass tartly denounced efforts by Congress in the 1840s to mandate re-colonization to Africa by declaiming that "[w]e are of the opinion that the *free* colored people generally mean to live in America, and not in Africa. . . . Our minds are made up to live here if we can, or die here if we must" (Douglass, 1999/1849, p. 126). Showing similar fortitude, the African students we got to know during this study were determined to make their "American" education count despite the unanticipated sense of rejection by some Americans.

Chapter 2

1. "In Africa, you don't have the problem of racism."

2. Based on data collected by the school system in 2002, the faculty composition at Jackson was essentially evenly split between Caucasian and Afro-American teachers.

Chapter 3

1. An old African proverb. Maat (Ma'at, Mayet) is the Egyptian goddess of truth and justice.

2. Regrettably, Americans' ignorance about other countries and peoples is not restricted to Africa. Many commentators have reflected that increasing intercontinental access has reached the critical point where Americans' ignorance will now work to the economic detriment of those who willfully remain unaware or unconcerned about the remainder of the universe (Cashin, 2004).

3. Population Reference Bureau 2000, available at http://www.prb.org.

4. "Hegel himself had declared the African sub-human: the African lacked reason and therefore moral and ethical content" (Eze, 1997, p. 9).

5. Tradition holds that in earlier days Americans behaved similarly in their earnestness to succeed in their efforts to acquire an education. When we occasionally became dispirited by the seeming pointlessness of some of our academic subjects or other school experiences, our parents tried to challenge us by declaring that "when I was your age I had to walk __ miles through terrible weather every day to get to school." This tropism rarely had the anticipated inspirational effect or assuaged our anomie. In the colonial period, African slaves risked retribution for their efforts to educate themselves (Berlin, 1998; Morris, 1996; Perry, Steele, & Hilliard, 2003). Some have argued that America's slaves cogently saw that educating themselves to read and write was the most expedient way to

triumph over their oppression (Berlin, 2003, pp, 254-255; Hahn, 2003, pp. 42-43; Webber, 1978). With legal emancipation, and most prominently during the period of Reconstruction following the Civil War, former slaves began to experience increased access to more formal educational opportunities (Anderson, 1988; Fireside, 2004; Klarman, 2004; Watkins, 2001). We will discuss more thoroughly in later chapters whether we believe that the systems in the U.S. have made significant progress over the course of the last century to ensure that all of our students are exposed to stimulating and useful school experiences that might encourage most of them to overcome even great obstacles to become educated.

6. The song featured in a documentary film used in this study, "The Language You Cry In: The story of a Mende song," is one example of how the African culture has been preserved despite colonialism, slavery, and the near ubiquity of the Eurocentric educational system. In Chapter 8 we discuss in more detail some of the incidents portrayed in this film and describe some of the reactions that students and others have reported after experiencing "The Language You Cry In."

7. One white American's compelling recounting of his encounters with some children from Sierra Leone who were victims of war became a "Quote of the Day" in The Washington Post: "When you see someone who projects such happiness and spirituality, you see they have something that we wish we had" (*Quote of the Day*, 2002, p. C3). In 2002, anthropologist Michael Jackson visited Sierra Leone at a time when this West African country was just emerging from a protracted and devastating civil war. In the 1970s, Jackson had lived among Sierra Leone's Kuranko people while he conducted research. He returned to this region to research and compose a biography of the former leader of Sierra Leone's People's Party. In his most recent work, Jackson relates his reactions after having visited several refugee camps, and he describes how some of the refugees survived the tragedies of war. Jackson adverts that violence on the magnitude of a civil war percolates over long periods of time, often in the collective unconscious of a people (Jackson, 2004). By the time the war in Sierra Leone ended in 2002, 50 thousand persons had died and more than a million had been displaced from their homes.

8. Additional information the Core Knowledge curriculum is available on the organization's website at http://www.coreknowledge.org/CKproto2/resrcs/frames/lessons_links.

9. We purposefully have excluded a specific discussion of South Africa because the educational system there has been so dramatically polluted by apartheid that comparisons with the other systems throughout the continent would be disproportionately skewed.

10. We discuss Ogbu's (1974, 2003) theory about the differences between voluntary and involuntary arrival in a new country in more detail in Chapter 4.

Chapter 4

1. 347 U.S. 483 (1954). May 2004 marked the half-century anniversary of the Supreme Court's decision in *Brown*, holding that it was unconstitutional to educate racial minorities separately from the majority white students because "separate educational facilities are inherently unequal." 347 U.S. at 495. To mark this auspicious occasion, a plethora of commentators addressed some of the intervening accomplishments toward desegregating our schools and some of the remaining deficiencies in our efforts to provide equal educational opportunities for all of our youth (Bell, 2004; Black Issues in Higher

Education, 2004; Carter, Flores, & Reddick, 2004; Cashin, 2004; Clotfelter, 2004; Feldman, 2004; Klarman, 2004; Ogletree, 2004; Orfield & Lee, 2004). Kluger (2004) updated his exhaustive disquisition on the history of *Brown*, and Greenberg (2004) also updated his reflections on his own significant contributions both to *Brown* and many of the legal challenges against institutional discrimination brought after *Brown*.

2. Race often acts a proxy for class distinctions (Henry & Tobin, 2004; Lublin, 2004; Shipler, 1998, 2004; Wilson, 1987). The economic disparities that exist in America are more pronounced than ever in our history, with the highest levels of the economic pantheon having few non-caucasian representatives (Cashin, 2004). Class distinction is a salient feature informing the decisions about resource allocations for inner-schools that are seriously under-funded and enroll primarily minority students (Guinier & Torres, 2003; Humes, 2003; Sleeter & Grant, 2002).

3. A recent criticism of some seemingly draconian changes in official U.S. immigration policies provides a backhand acknowledgement to the idealization of our country that persists in much of the world despite some of the more controversial shifts in foreign and domestic policy following the tragic events of September 11, 2001. Elena Lappin (2004), a British journalist who was refused entry at the Los Angeles airport, and who was detained overnight for not having the appropriate visa on a trip to this country some time in 2004, commented about her experience that "in the name of fighting terrorism, [the government's response] has transformed a free, open, inimitably attractive democracy into something resembling an insular fortress of Kafkaesque absurdity." It is useful to keep in mind that any living organism, once seriously harmed or threatened, is likely to engage in a period of self-protective behaviors remarkably more confining in most aspects than any of its previous conduct. A threatened and wounded nation should not be expected to behave differently. This is not offered as an excuse for our government's shift in policies, but rather as a hopeful reminder that, like most organisms that have sustained startling injury to their integrity and survival, the U.S. should ultimately revert to most of its prior ways as a "free, open, inimitably attractive democracy" after it has recovered from the tragedy of September 11, 2001. We are reminded of the closing words to Lincoln's Second Inaugural Address from March 1865, near the end of one of this nation's longest and most perilous challenges,

> With malice toward none, with charity for all, with firmness in the right as God gives us to see the right, let us strive on to finish the work we are in, to bind up the nation's wounds, to care for him who shall have borne the battle and for his widow and his orphan, to do all which may achieve and cherish a just and lasting peace among ourselves and with all nations (Lincoln, 1989, p. 687).

Most of the research that informs the present study occurred during the academic year that had started just prior to September 11, 2001, and we were mindful at the time of the sensitivity not only of the American students but also the African students who were new to the U.S. and who may have experienced strife and traumatic events of a similar nature in their homelands.

4. Tedla (1995) discusses the fundamental spiritual basis of family life in Africa. The contexts of indigenous African education have rarely been presented in any coherent way, or from a traditional African perspective. African education is predicated on all that is positive in local thought and customs. Tedla underscores the need to understand Africans on their own terms, and within the context of African culture, as well as the need to

be judicious about introducing more foreign ideas and institutions to Africa. Otherwise, the cultural and spiritual fabric of the African way of life will be missed or once more subordinated to Westernized pre-conceptions about Africa and its need to be rescued or "saved."

5. An exception to this is the situation of the "lost boys" of Sudan who arrived recently and have been warmly received by groups in various suburbs. The "lost boys" are unaccompanied minors from war-torn Sudan who escaped to refugee camps in Kenya and are being resettled here in the U.S. Their story is different. They have the support of refugee resettlement organizations that are placing them outside the typical low-income neighborhoods that other Africans find as their only possible accommodations. The "lost boys" are receiving special attention not at all provided for the thousands of Africans from Sudan and other African countries, even other war-torn countries such as Liberia and Sierra Leone (Zehr, 2001).

6. The most recent data seem to indicate there may be a narrowing of the multi-decade gap in student achievement. According to government-funded research by the National Assessment of Educational Progress, although there continues to be an achievement gap between white and children of color, "the White-Black score gap in reading narrowed from 1971 to 2004. . . . The White-Black reading score gap for 9-year-olds decreased from 35 points in 1999 to 26 points in 2004" (Perie, Moran, & Lutkus, 2005, p. v). A narrowing, perhaps, but there still remains a considerable divide. Furthermore, there also exists an acknowledged achievement gap between white students in America and the students from a number of other nations, most particularly the Asian and Southeast Asian countries (Noguera, 2003). Many have concluded that public education in America has lost its edge in maintaining the reputation for "excellence" it once may have held (Hirsch, 1996; Ravitch, 2000; Sykes, 1995). Most critics, however, fail to consider the exponential increase in new information that has entered the required curriculum in the last 20 years, making the matter of continued "excellence" a chimerical concept. The question we really should ask is "excellent at what?" It appears that maintaining U.S. superiority in scientific progress is the paramount concern of most of the critics, while cultural and social progress are minimized and all but ignored. This preference can be discerned by the emphasis on evidence that U.S. students generally score lower in math and science subjects than many of the students in other countries, which is used to fuel the recurrent calls for educational reform in America (Cavanaugh & Robelen, 2004).

7. The experience that African students have in suburban schools would be expected to be somewhat different. They are definitely a minority and seen as Black but there is an exotic nature given to them by many others. If they live in the suburbs then they must have some means and therefore some class and this gets them some level of acceptance that being from the lower-income neighborhoods cannot but as Waters (1999) says social class and income level cannot whiten them enough.

8. Immigrants from the continent of Africa have the highest educational levels among all immigrants to the United States. They have on average over 3 years of college, and over half are college graduates (*Extended lives*, 2001, p. 53).

9. Cognitive dissonance may occur when "people are driven to maintain consistency between cognitions. Holding two mutually exclusive cognitions produces an aversive state that the person is motivated to reduce through a variety of strategies that aim to adjust the relationship between the cognitions" (Lieberman & Arndt, 2000, p. 701 n.5).

Leon Festinger (1957) described this tendency to reinterpret information that conflicts with internally accepted or publicly held beliefs in an effort to avoid the unpleasant emotional state or discomfort produced by inconsistent thinking. Festinger found that having incompatible thoughts or emotions can create for an individual an internal sense of discomfort, or dissonance, and people generally attempt to avoid this discomfort or feeling of dissonance when possible by finding justification for the apparently conflictual feelings.

Chapter 5

1. According to Usdan (1998), the "strengths of the American system, at least as they are perceived by the admiring Japanese, lie in its adaptability to local conditions, its openness to new ideas, its fostering of creativity, and a higher education system that (deservedly or not) is the envy of the world" (p. 36). Nisbett (2003) declares that "American scientific success, as measured for example by the number of Nobel Prize winners who live in the United States, helps to sustain an illusion that the American educational system is fundamentally healthy. This illusion is further aided by the fact that American higher education is rightly the envy of the world. And it is helped along by the fact that most Americans believe that, though there may be serious problems with most U.S. schools, the ones their children go to are an exception." (http://www.edge.org/q2003/q03_nisbett.html). In November 2002, then-president of the Council of Graduate Schools, Debra Stewart, proclaimed that "the American doctorate is both the envy of the world and a work in progress." (http://www.carnegiefoundation.org/newsroom/press_releases/00.11.1.htm.

2. In this regard, the No Child Left Behind Act of 2001, Pub. L. No. 107-110, 115 Stat. 1425 (Jan. 8, 2002), addresses only part of the ways in which public education needs to be reformed because it holds individual schools accountable for the test performance of students on standards set by centralized decision-makers rather than intersecting with local needs predicated on local economic deficiencies.

3. http://www.phila.k12.pa.us/ll/curriculumsupport/aastudies/african&africanamerican.

Chapter 6

1 We do not wish to minimize any of the other difficulties that African students may have encountered on accommodating to life at Jackson High. However, except for the color of their skin, all of the other factors that characterize the African students' initial experiences at Jackson would apply to other immigrant students in American schools generally. Language, culture, prior learning experiences, and many of the other differences between the newly arrived student and the resident student are susceptible to the same kinds of difficulties whether the young person who lives in a small town moves to New York City, a freshman leaves home for the first time to attend college, or the family re-locates to another country due to one of the parent's military obligations. We want to distinguish between the "newly arrived" contingent and emphasize the reality of the impact the color of their skin may have had on the African students' experiences of life in America and how this affected their interactions with their Afro-American peers and the Jackson High staff.

2. Powers (2003, pp. 296, 304).

3. This is not to claim that the African nations are without their ethnic difficulties and

class struggles, but only that color of skin is not the predominant factor that arises in most social interactions between Africans as often is the case in the U.S. between caucasians and non-caucasians (Asante, 2003b; Omi & Winant, 1994). Africans do not have a history of interaction with whites treating them as inferior, at least not the generation of today. The elders have a memory of improvements being made when the white man was around that they miss so there is definitely another view of the white man in Africa today. South Africa is different. There are very strong experiences of the oppression of the white man but in too many other countries the experience of oppression has been at the hand of greedy African rulers who take care of their own "tribe" and oppress others. The oppression has been at the hand of a Black man, not a white man, except for those who recognize the economic oppression of capitalism and they are for the most part the intellectual elite. So, the Africans, in general, come here with a positive view of the white man, especially the American and movies have not portrayed racism to the extent that it exists either now or historically. They are very surprised to learn about slavery and all its aftermath. They know that some people were taken long ago but they have no idea of the impact that it has had on African Americans. They think that by being called Afro-American, they know where they are from originally, but so few of them acknowledge this heritage.

4. Afro-American Peace Corps Volunteers have different reactions to being in Africa than their caucasian counterparts. The expectations of local people can be higher for the Afro-Americans. If they are black then locals expect then to speak the local language. If they don't then they are expected to learn it faster than their white peers, but often they do not. The issues of class and culture also affect the Afro-American in a way that it doesn't the white volunteer. The Afro-American volunteer, because he is Black, becomes indistinguishable from the indigenous Africans until he/she opens his mouth. And to him or her, it may not be a positive experience because initially the African is seen as underprivileged, underdeveloped and the Afro-American is reminded of the American stereotypes and does not want to lose his/her higher status as an American among Africans. In time, because they need to survive the two years of their Peace Corps commitment, becoming comfortable in the culture is critical and the Afro-Americans who do adjust can become even more at home than their white peers. The white volunteers always remain outsiders no matter how accepted by the Africans they may become. Some Afro-Americas do not want to be associated with the poverty that exists or the initial viewing of everything as lacking. In the end, the Afro-American volunteer who stays and learns the language and who becomes comfortable culturally is accepted by the Africans wholeheartedly. But we wonder if in the end it isn't the white volunteer who gets more from learning the language and being enculturated because the Africans think that if a white person can do it, it's a major feat but for the Afro-American it simply is expected.

5. King (2004) emphatically and succinctly declares that

> All in all, race is the modern West's worst idea. Despite the modest, medical benefits that may have followed from thinking in terms of race and the remarkable cultural achievements of the racially oppressed, it is hard to think of any idea that has more destructive consequences (p. 1).

6. Demonstrating a startlingly naïve presumption, that may be more prevalent than we surmise, according to the thinking of some American students if Africa was the source of the AIDS virus then all Africans must be diseased or at least contagious.

7. As discussed in Chapter 1, many African students reported that they were advised by white Americans not to lose their accents as to not be confused with Afro-Americans; on the other hand, they experience being mocked by peers at school because of their accents and consequently they do their best to overcome them.

8. For caucasians, a corollary process can lead to one's becoming part of a white "race" (Allen, 1997; Bay, 2000; Dyer, 1997; Frankenberg, 1997; Hill, 2004; Morrison, 1992; Rasmussen, Klinenberg, Nexica, & Wray, 2001; Roediger, 2002, 1999; Ware, 1992).

9. Attempts to prohibit those held as slaves from developing a sense of sustainable community were subverted from the outset by the shared experience of the Atlantic passage. An almost heroic effort at defiance of their condition, an unwillingness to capitulate to the common treachery of being capture and enslaved in their homeland, in conjunction with their having shared the horrors of slave ship transport, tragic losses of kin and comrades while at sea, and the humiliation of being sold as chattel upon disembarking in the colonies, all of these combined to create in these early Africans brought unwilling to the new frontier of America an underground determination and resolution to maintain a viable connection with their own customs and traditions. This resolve almost overcame the pan-African differences that were in place in the African nations in the seventeenth century, and some of which continue in Africa today. According to Stuckey (1987), the

> final gift of African "tribalism" in the nineteenth century was its life as a lingering memory in the minds of American slaves. That memory enabled them to go back to the sense of community in the traditional African setting and to include all Africans in their common experience of oppression in North America. It is greatly ironic, therefore, that African ethnicity, an obstacle to African nationalism in the twentieth century, was in this way the principal avenue to black unity in antebellum America. . . . [S]lave ships were the first real incubators of slave unity across cultural lines, cruelly revealing irreducible links from one ethnic group to the other, fostering resistance thousands of miles before the shores of the new land appeared on the horizon. (p. 3)

10. Available at http://chronicle.com/weekly/v47/i46/46a00801.html.

11. Keto (1994) has described the impact on people of African descent of the denial of the oppression of the slave trade:

> Denial of a connection to previous African culture is a form of cultural genocide that affirms the aquatic Maafa of the middle passage. African Americans lose the historical relevance of this "holocaust" since those women and men who were tossed to the sharks; revolted on ships and committed suicide rather than endure enslavement, were not kinfolk from the Carolinas and Georgia (p. 99).

Prior to their emigration, the students from the African continent had little knowledge about slavery and its effect on the Africans transported to America in the days when slavery was a principal method of importing labor.

12. Kenneth and Mamie Clark were among the first to delineate the progression of racial attitudes as these develop in young children (Clark, 1988; Markowitz & Rosner, 1996; Philogene, 2004). It is also pertinent to recall that it is natural for very young children to experience "stranger anxiety," which is distress they may feel when they encounter peo-

ple who are unfamiliar to them (Mahler, Pine, & Bergman, 1975, pp. 56-58). Infants can begin to experience stranger anxiety as young as six months of age, but it usually begins to be noticeable somewhere between eight and nine months of age. Before this age, most infants will accept unfamiliar people without much distress. As they approach the celebration of their first year of life, children begin to show preference for the people who care for them the most, usually parents and kin. At this time, infants are beginning to realize that all people are not the same, and that the relationship they have with their primary caregivers is special. Stranger anxiety highlights an innate ability to discriminate familiar from unfamiliar; it also confirms that there exists an affective bond or attachment between infant and caregiver (Bowlby, 1982, 1988). As they mature, children become more selective about who they will allow to hold them, play with them, comfort them, and so forth. Under normal development and within the typical social environment, this anxiety around unfamiliar people and places attenuates as a child develops more awareness of surroundings and more facility with negotiating new experiences (Berlin & Cassidy, 1999; Stern, 1985). This entire process can be promoted effectively and appropriately managed or discouraged by the reactions of parents and other adults in the child's life.

By around age two, a child will begin to notice that there are differences in the outer appearance among some people, skin color may be one of these observable differences. Over the next few years, children typically begin to identify with their own racial group (Van Ausdale & Feagin, 2001). At some point, the child forms preference patterns on the basis of the prevailing attitude within the child's preferred group and not through contact with a racially different group (Aboud, 2003; Killen, Pisacane, Kim-Lee, & Ardila-Rey, 2001). Parents are the premier and most potent source of a child's evolving attitudes toward different groups; peers become more influential as children mature (Holmes, 1995; Towles-Schwen & Fazio, 2001).

> Although preschool children do not have well-formed ideas about race, it is among their earliest emerging social categories. By the time they are 4 years old, children appear to realize that race is an enduring feature that is inherited from parents and established at birth. They also seem to be aware that race is a dimension along which humans are arranged hierarchically, but they do not have a clear idea about who belongs to which category. . . . The translation of racial categories into racially based behavior appears to occur after the preschool years. (Shonkoff & Philips, 2000, pp. 64-65)

By the early school years it appears that every child engages in at least some stereotyping (Lewis, 2003). According to some research, a "surprising number of young children are already biased toward those of other racial groups" (Katz, 2003, p. 897). Institutional and cultural prejudices, however, are much more subtle and insidious because they are embedded in unexamined assumptions and established patterns of behavior that are communicated to children, sometimes without their conscious awareness. The roots of these prejudices often are multi-generational and can persist even after years of legislative remedies attempt to discourage or thwart them. It would be tragically ironic if we ultimately discover that this atavistic impulse expressed in infancy as anxiety around strangers was distorted into the adult version of prejudice against the "other" just because of some physical or cultural unfamiliarity (Miller, 1997, pp. 230-232; Nussbaum, 2004, pp. 32-37).

13. Lyndon B. Johnson (1965, June 4). Commencement Address, Howard University: "To Fulfill These Rights." The full text of President Johnson's speech is available at

http://usinfo.state.gov/usa/civilrights/s060465.htm.

14. Karl Mannheim (1985/1936) defined an ideology as a system of thoughts or beliefs which results in behavior that maintains the existing social order. According to Mannheim, "ruling groups can in their thinking become so intensively interest-bound to a situation that they are simply no longer able to see certain facts which would undermine their sense of domination" (p. 40). Moreover, it "is only when the distrust of man toward man, which is more or less evident at every stage of human history, becomes explicit and is methodically recognized, that we may properly speak of an ideological taint in the utterances of others. . . . It refers to a sphere of errors, psychological in nature, which unlike deliberate deception, are not intentional, but follow inevitably and unwittingly from certain causal determinants" (p. 61). Racist ideology comprises a system of understanding and faulty beliefs that classifies people into socially stratified racial categories, and which has become methodically recognized by society. It is predicated on the presumption that members of one group are superior to all others. Sadly, it was evident to us that the Afro-American students reacted toward their African peers in some ways that would be perceived as racist if their positions were reversed, or they did not share similar skin color.

15. Those who contend that racial discrimination has been outlawed often cite the Civil Rights Act of 1964, the Voting Rights Act of 1965, and the Fair Housing Act of 1968 (D'Souza, 1995, pp. 166-167, 196). The law may govern how people act but it is a poor vehicle for trying to control how they think (Massey & Denton, 1993). Personal and ongoing "decisionmaking" (i.e., an integral part of the thinking process) demonstrates repeatedly in the ways in which people of different backgrounds interact that racial discrimination has become less overt but it persists, in every realm of human interaction, beyond the reach of the government to command personal adherence to many of our anti-discrimination laws (Cashin, 2004; Gilbert & Hixon, 1991; Hamilton & Hamilton, 1997; Oliver & Shapiro, 1995; Shapiro, 2003; Shulman & Darity, 1989; Williams, 2003).

16. Following the announcement of the acquittal of the charged police officers there ensued 5 days of unleashed anarchy that was "multicultural, transracial, and transclass in nature" and the thousands of arrests included white and non-white rioters (Asante, 2003a, p. 91). According to Cornel West (1993, p. 1), these events in 1992 marked a "multiracial, trans-class, and largely male display of justified social rage." Approximately half of those arrested during these days of looting and rioting were Latino (Perea, 1995, pp. 967-968).

17. Although it focused primarily on group-based differences ostensibly measured by standardized tests, *The Bell Curve* only marginally was about intelligence per se. The basic premise that smart people generally fare better in socioeconomic terms than do less smart people is generally unremarkable; thinking and similar cognitive activities are fiscally rewarded in our society. Much of the media attention on this particular book concerned the authors' argument about the implications of potential race-based differences in measured intelligence. The authors admitted that "our topic is the relationship of human abilities to policy issues . . . based on aggregated data" (Hernstein & Murray, 1994, p. 19). Consequently, it is clear that they were less interested in any actual measurement characteristics of intelligence than with the predictive utility of tests of cognitive ability, and the authors cautioned that "[c]ognitive ability affects social behavior without regard to race or ethnicity" (p. 125). The authors also acknowledged that "[s]ocially significant individual differences include a wide range of human talents that do not fit within the classical conception of intelligence" (p. 20). Using aggregated data to predict how a

group will perform in terms of future social capital is a mercurial undertaking. Any class that comprises children who score high on standardized tests may indeed be expected to do better in achieving many socially sanctioned benefits than would a similar class comprising children who score lower on standardized tests (pp. 19-20). Similar comparisons can be made with very similar statistical results for a class comprising tall and handsome men in comparison to average and shorter men. It is likely that the latter analysis actually could be a more accurate predictor than intelligence of future social rewards bestowed on the two classifications of human types. For instance, "[b]oth attractive children and adults were evaluated significantly more favorably than unattractive children and adults, even by familiar perceivers" (Langlois, Kalakanis, Rubenstein, Larson, Hallam, & Smoot, 2000, p. 400). That an academic tome by a psychologist and social scientist generated so much heated debate is an indication of the outsized sensitivity of American people to any hint that racial distinctions might be justified (Steinberg, 1995, pp. 215-218). Even its authors acknowledged that books relating to research about intelligence ordinarily fall within the realm of academic material read mostly by psychologists and educators (Hernstein & Murray, 1994, pp. 22-23). Making the New York Times best-sellers list was an accomplishment rare among such ostensibly scientific works. One ponders how many of those who purchased *The Bell Curve* actually read its contents; it now is out of print, but the controversy about whether any link exists between genetic composition and cognitive abilities continues unabated (Gottfredson, 2005; Nisbett, 2005; Rowe, 2005; Rushton & Jensen, 2005a, 2005b; Sternberg, 2005; Sternberg, Grigorenko, & Kidd, 2005; Suzuki & Aronson, 2005).

18. One of the sons of the lead author started school in the U.S beginning with the third grade. Laye quickly lost his accent as he tried to fit in. His presence was seen by both his teachers and peers as "exotic." His class learned some facts about Liberia when he arrived. He would have lost his culture completely if he hadn't had the chance to return to Africa for middle school. For three years he attended school in Africa and had African friends. When he returned to the U.S. for high school the American influence became evident once again. At some point, he agreed to go visit his family and this time the African values were noticeable to him and he made a commitment to keeping them alive. African values of community, harmony, spirituality and respect are important to him now and he sees the contrast with American values. He can now make choices based on another value system. This is the benefit of an experience of African values and worldview. One can choose to see the world in another way. Laye is proud to be African. He appreciates the freedom of America but sees the ways in which that freedom has been abused.

19. The public's perception about who receives public cash assistance has been skewed for many years. Although disproportionately represented on census data at or below poverty income, persons of color are not the most likely to collect public welfare; the data show that white women comprise a larger proportion of welfare beneficiaries (Shipler, 2004).

20. Thucydides observed that fair "is only a question between equals because the strong do what they can while the weak do what they must" (Thucydides, 1972/1954, p. 404). Moreover, in "discussion of human affairs the question of justice only enters where there is equal power to enforce it, and the powerful exact what they can, and the weak grant what they must" (ibid.).

21. As Hochschild (1998) has succinctly declared: "The world we live in—its divisions and conflicts, its widening gap between rich and poor, its seemingly inexplicable out-

bursts of violence—is shaped far less by what we celebrate and mythologize than by the painful events we try to forget" (p. 294).

22. To be sure, there are several other factors that could account for some of the tensions evident in many of the interactions between students from diverse backgrounds, including differing socio-economic status, unequal individual physical, emotional, or learning abilities, and so forth. However, within the structure of the American social system, it is implausible to expect our schools to do more than assist students to use their talents and skills to learn in the best ways they can to become contributing members of the larger society. It is indisputable that how and what public schools can help students to learn is limited by the social context. Because the color of a young person's skin has far more of an impact on what she can expect from the future than can be addressed through education alone, the adverse impact is something that students cannot through any of their educational experiences learn how to change on their own. Because this reality of American social patterns cannot be altered by edict alone, nor through any single person's perseverance and hard work, students must learn how to positively counteract the adverse effects of racism directed at persons of color. We have elected to maximize our attention on racism, therefore, and consequently minimized our attention on some of the other factors, because racism remains a subject that schools generally do not teach our students to confront directly. As a result, schools either tacitly or purposefully perpetuate the stereotypes associated with many of the racist beliefs that prevail in America. Many books have been written about how schools perpetuate these racist stereotypes, but few critics of racist beliefs in our educational system have the temerity to state their real objective, which is to indict white hegemony. Until white Americans come to believe that a multicultural American society must encompass equal citizens of all colors, and until each of those citizens is provided the same access to every privilege heretofore reserved for caucasians, none of the reforms proposed to this point will prove successful in providing equal educational opportunities to all of America's children.

Chapter 7

1. We are not historians and take no position here on the dispute over the anthropological origins or historical implications of Afrocentrism, as illustrated in the ongoing debate in Asante (1998, 2000, 2003b), Berlinerblau (1999), Bernal (1987), Bernal & Moore (2001), Binder (2002), Howe (1998), Lefkowitz (1996a, 1996b), Lefkowitz & Rogers (1997), Moses (1998, pp. 1-17), Ortiz de Montellano (1996), Roth (1996), Schlesinger (1998, pp. 79-104), and Walker (2001). For our purposes, the philosophy and ethos underlying the theory, not its provenance, are what we have found to be most useful in our work. None of the more controversial aspects of Afrocentrism (e.g., glorifying African history without fully reconciling this revisionist history with the absence of a unified "Africa" to have lived such a history) directly interferes with our conviction that the positive images espoused by an African-centered approach to learning comprise some of the strongest remedies for the longstanding negative stereotypes that have accompanied American notions about Africa, Africans, and persons of African descent. Ultimately, we agree with Asante (1993a, p. 143) that "Afrocentricity is the active centering of the African in subject place in our historical landscape." An Afrocentric approach underscores three important propositions about education: 1) Education is fundamentally a social phenomenon; 2) Schools prepare children to take their place in society; and 3) Societies develop schools that are suitable to the common goals of the particular society. If for no other reason than its having resurrected from oblivion a fuller appreciation for the presence and contributions of Africa and her descendents on the world's stage, Afrocentricity has had a

salutary impact on the educational experiences of America's children. For differing opinions on the kinds of contributions the Afrocentric approach can make in American education, compare D'Souza (1995, pp. 360-380, 421-422) and Schlesinger (1998, pp. 96-101) who are skeptical, with the authors in Conyers (2001) and Ziegler (1995), as well as Moses (1998, pp. 239-241) and Spring (1998, pp. 98-102), who are more sanguine.

2. As we remarked in Chapter 4, in a predominantly white, suburban school, the African who arrives can be perceived as exotic, not associated with being Afro-American. He or she can be accepted as a "foreigner" and although the reality of racism in America can still have some adverse impact, general prejudice does not confront them in the same way as in the urban environment where race and class are combined in more devastating ways (Rothstein, 1995).

3. "400 Teachers Begin Study of African History" (Gillespie, 1968a), "Gratz Given Grant to Plan Negro History Curriculum" (1968), "15 Schools Get Grants to Set Up Courses" (Gillespie, 1968b), and "Pupils, Parents Will Study Afro-U.S. History at Sayre" (Dyke, 1967) were just some of the headlines in the Philadelphia Bulletin in 1968.

4. In an article in the local newspaper, entitled "Conventional American Education Hasn't Taught Much More About Africa Than Little Black Sambo—Now Teachers Are Learning With Fascination," Adcock (1968) described the event as "2,000 Negro students went to the Philadelphia School District Headquarters . . . [because] they thought they were being denied a source of self respect." He goes on to describe the benefits of learning about Africa and decries the American educational system which currently "tells students little about these things. Africa is seen mostly as 'The Dark Continent,' full of savage animals and peoples, a land partly civilized by white colonizers and missionaries." Several articles in local newspapers in 1968 and 1969 argued the importance of black history and one student described the ways in which the current curriculum gives white students a "superior attitude towards black people" (Black culture, 1968). The student stressed that "the English literature was irrelevant, the history textbooks deliberately omitted black history, the hygiene texts did not relate to black people's environmental needs, and European languages such as French, Spanish and German were irrelevant to black people's survival" (Ibid.). The stereotypes of Africa were widespread and despite the changes made in the 1970s, many of them persist today. In 1967, a Nigerian spoke at the Henry C. Lea School in West Philadelphia and the speaker said he drew the biggest applause when he told the youngsters, "No, we don't sleep with lions and monkeys—in fact, I never saw a monkey until I came to this country" (Dyke, 1967). In the late 1960s, official guides to Negro History were produced and distributed to all schools; the guides included instructions on teaching about African culture. The introduction to one of these guides states: "Until recently, Africa, to some young people, has been the land of wild animals and 'big game' safari, dense tropical jungles, the home of 'Tarzan,' the birthplace of the slave trade, or a Hollywood movie with the colonial commissioner and his daughter protecting elephants from greedy ivory hunters" (Gillespie, 1967a). Although the particular movie of the ivory hunter mentioned in this article may not be as widely viewed today, many of the other negative stereotypes of Africa do survive.

5. Available at http://www.phila.k12.pa.us/offices/afamstudies.

6. Philadelphia Freedom Schools, John F. Kennedy Center, 734 Schuylkill Avenue, Room 681, Philadelphia, PA 19146.

Chapter 8

1. One exceptionally fortuitous factor that facilitated our presence in the school, permitted unrestricted access to the students and staff at Jackson, and made our research so rewarding was the presence of an Afro-American principal who fully supported this effort and who staunchly believed that in bringing these students together there would be great benefit to both groups and to her school. She had studied enough to know that the stereotypes of Africa are just that, stereotypes. She also had enough confidence in the Afro-American students that they were not so brainwashed as to be unable to grasp what their African peers have to offer. Having the encouragement of a supportive principal is a blessing under any circumstance where the educational processes are under study, but this may not be a factor that can be counted on in other school environments. It was extremely important to the outcome of this study that the principal already was seeking ways to bring these two groups of students together. Having a positive environment in which to undertake the activities chosen was a significant strength of the design of this study because this allowed a great deal of latitude with scheduling events, conducting large group meetings, and using other school resources. Although a supportive principal is highly valuable, activities similar to those we describe here could still be undertaken without this support albeit perhaps in a more restricted manner. The greatest limitation of the present study relates, of course, to its limited scope because we were able to reach only a handful of the students in the large bureaucracy of an inner-city school of more than 2,000 students.

2. Asante (1990) admonishes that "African birth does not make one Afrocentric; Afrocentricity is a matter of intellectual discipline and must be learned and practiced" (p. 115). One does not need to be of African descent to learn and practice that discipline (Akbar, 2003).

3. Wilson (1993) uses "amnesia" to explain what has happened to persons of African descent in the United States.

4. He asked some of the African students in the audience to tell him their names: Ba, Camara, Sambola, Saidou. Then he said that their names would now be changed to Thompson, Williams, Jefferson and Smith. None of the African students wanted their names to be changed. They reacted with obvious disagreement to the thought of having their names changed.

Chapter 9

1. A white American male recounted his emotional reaction after meeting some children who were victims of civil war in Sierra Leone frames this sentiment very poignantly: "When you see someone who projects such happiness and spirituality, you see they have something that we wish we had" (Quote of the Day, 2002, p. C3).

2. The Appendix contains some resources for general use.

3. As salutary ruminations go, it would be very useful for all of us to remember that "the beauty of the world can be seen in Mother Nature. Look at the forest and its composition. Look at the different flowers, the different soil, the moon and the sun, the different animals, the difference in our physical makeup by God, and different texture of clothing. If we can sit for a moment and think about the beauty, the changes in taste that life brings

to us, we can change the world" (Mohamed Traoré, 2004, personal communication).

References

Abarry, Abu Shardow (1990). Afrocentricity: Introduction. *Journal of Black Studies*, Vol. 21, pp. 123-125.

Aboud, Frances E. (2003). The formation of in-group favoritism and out-group prejudice in young children: Are they distinct attitudes? *Developmental Psychology*, Vol. 39, pp. 48-60.

Achebe, Chinua (1958). *Things fall apart*. Portsmouth, NH: Heinemann.

Adcock, Joseph (1968, June 2). Conventional education hasn't taught much more about Africa than "Little Black Sambo" -- Now teachers are learning with fascination. *The Bulletin.*

Akbar, Na'im (1991). Paradigms of African American research. In Reginald L. Jones (Ed.), *Black psychology* (pp. 709-725). Berkeley, CA: Cobb & Henry (3d ed.).

Akbar, Na'im (1998a). Afrocentricity: The challenge of implementation. In Janice D. Hamlet (Ed.), *Afrocentric visions: Studies in culture and communication* (pp. 247-249). Thousand Oaks, CA: Sage.

Akbar, Na'im (1998b). *Know thy self*. Tallahassee, FL: Mind Productions.

Akbar, Na'im (2003). *Papers in African psychology*. Tallahassee, FL: Mind Productions.

Alford, Keith, Patrick McKenry, & Stephen Gavazzi (2001). Enhancing achievement in adolescent black males: The rites of passage link. In Richard Majors (Ed.), *Educating our black children: New directions and radical approaches* (pp. 141-156). New York: RoutledgeFalmer.

Allen, Danielle S. (2004). *Talking to strangers: Anxieties of citizenship since Brown v. Board of Education*. Chicago: University of Chicago Press.

Allen, Theodore W. (1997). *The invention of the white race: The origin of racial oppression in Anglo-America*. New York: Verso.

Allport, Gordon (1954). *The nature of prejudice*. Reading, MA: Addison-Wesley.

American Psychological Association (2001). Psychological causes and consequences of racism, racial discrimination, xenophobia and related intolerances: Intervention of the American Psychological Association delegation to the World Conference Against Racism (WCAR), Durban, South Africa, Aug.31 - Sept. 7, 2001, Preamble, available at http://www.apa.org/pi/oema/wcarplenary.html.

Anderson, James (1988). *The education of blacks in the south, 1860-1935*. Chapel Hill, NC: University of North Carolina Press.

Anyon, Jean (1997). *Ghetto schooling: A political economy of urban educational reform*. New York: Teachers College Press.

Appiah, K. Anthony (1993). *In my father's house: African in the philosophy of culture*. New York: Oxford University Press.

Appiah, K. Anthony & Amy Gutmann (1996). *Color conscious: The political morality of race*. Princeton, NJ: Princeton University.

Appiah, Kwame Anthony (2004). *The ethics of identity*. Princeton, NJ: Princeton University Press.

Arendt, Hannah (1973). *The origins of totalitarianism*. New York: Harcourt Brace (originally published 1951).

Aristotle (1984). *Politics*. In Jonathan Barnes (Ed.), *The complete works of Aristotle: The revised Oxford translation* (pp. 1986-2129). Princeton, NJ: Princeton University Press.

Armour, Jody David (2000). *Negrophobia and reasonable racism: The hidden costs of being black in America*. New York: New York University Press.

Arrow, Kenneth, Samuel Bowles, & Steven Durlauf (Eds.) (2000). *Meritocracy and economic inequality*. Princeton, NJ: Princeton University Press.

Asante, Molefi Kete (1980). *Afrocentricity: The theory of social change*. Buffalo, NY: Ainulefi Publishing Co.

Asante, Molefi Kete (1988). *Afrocentricity*. Trenton, NJ: Africa World Press (rev. ed.).

Asante, Molefi Kete (1990). *Kemet, Afrocentricity and knowledge*. Trenton, NJ: Africa World Press.

Asante, Molefi Kete (1991). The Afrocentric idea in education. *Journal of Negro Education*, Vol. 60, pp. 170-180. Also in William L. vanDeburg (Ed.) (1997). *Modern black nationalism: From Marcus Garvey to Louis Farrakhan* (pp. 289-294). New York: New York University Press.

Asante, Molefi Kete (1993). Racism, consciousness, and Afrocentricity. In Gerald Early (Ed.), *Lure and loathing: Essays on race, identity, and the ambivalence of assimilation* (pp. 127-143). New York: Penguin Books.

Asante, Molefi Kete (1998). *The Afrocentric idea*. Philadelphia., PA: Temple University Press (rev. ed.) (originally published 1993).

Asante, Molefi Kete (2000). *The painful demise of Eurocentrism: An Afrocentric response to critics*. Trenton, NJ: Africa World Press.

Asante, Molefi Kete (2001). *African American history: A journey of liberation*. Saddle Brook, NJ: The Peoples Publishing.

Asante, Molefi Kete (2003a). *Afrocentricity: The theory of social change*. Trenton, NJ: Africa World Press (rev. ed.) (originally published 1980).

Asante, Molefi Kete (2003b). *Erasing racism: The survival of the American nation*. New York: Prometheus Books.

Ayittey, George B.N. (2005). *Africa unchained: The blueprint for Africa's future*. New York: Palgrave Macmillan.

Baker, Lee D. (1998). *From savage to negro: Anthropology and the construction of race, 1896-1954*. Berkeley: University of California Press.

Baldwin, James (1998). *Collected essays*. New York: Library of America (Toni Morrison, Ed.).

Banks, James A. (1997). *Educating citizens in a multicultural society*. New York: Teachers College Press.

Barndt, Joseph R. (1991). *Dismantling racism: The continuing challenge to white America*. Minneapolis, MN: Augsburg Fortress.

Baron, Stephen, John Field, & Tom Schuller (Eds.) (2000). *Social capital: Critical perspectives*. New York: Oxford University Press.

Bay, Mia (2000). *The white image in the black mind: African-American ideas about white people, 1830-1925*. New York: Oxford University Press.

Bean, Frank D. & Gillian Stevens (2003). *America's newcomers and the dynamics of diversity*. New York: Russell Sage Foundation.

Bell, Derrick (2004). *Silent covenants:* Brown v. Board of Education *and the unfulfilled hopes of racial reform*. New York: Oxford University Press.

Bell, Derrick A. (1992). *Faces at the bottom of the well: The permanence of racism*. New York: Basic Books.

Bell-Rose, Stephanie & Frank D. Bean (1999). *Immigration and opportunity: Race, ethnicity, and employment in the United States*. New York: Russell Sage Foundation.

Benhabib, Seyla (2002). *The claims of culture: Equality and diversity in the global era*. Princeton, NJ: Princeton University Press.

Berger, Peter L & Thomas Luckmann (1966). *The social construction of reality: A treatise in the sociology of knowledge*. New York: Doubleday.

Berlin, Ira (1998). *Many thousands gone: The first two centuries of slavery in North America*. Cambridge, MA: Belknap Press of Harvard University.

Berlin, Ira (2003). *Generations of captivity: A history of African-American slaves*. Cambridge, MA: Belknap Press of Harvard University.

Berlin, Lisa J. & Jude Cassidy (1999). Relations among relationships: Contributions from attachment theory and research. In Jude Cassidy & Phillip R. Shaver (Eds.), *Handbook of attachment: Theory, research, and clinical applications* (pp. 688-712). New York: Guilford Press.

Berlinerblau, Jacques (1999). *Heresy in the university: The black Athena controversy and the responsibilities of American intellectuals*. Newark, NJ: Rutgers University Press.

Bernal, Martin & David Chioni Moore (Eds.) (2001). *Black Athena writes back: Martin Bernal responds to his critics*. Durham, NC: Duke University Press.

Bernal, Martin (1987). *Black Athena: The Afroasiatic roots of classical civilization*. New Brunswick, NJ: Rutgers University Press.

Bernstein, David E. (2001). *Only one place of redress: African Americans, labor regulations, and the courts from Reconstruction to the New Deal*. Durham, NC: Duke University Press.

Best, John H. (Ed.) (1962). *Benjamin Franklin on education*. New York: Teachers College Press.

Binder, Amy J. (2002). *Contentious curricula: Afrocentrism and creationism in American public schools*. Princeton, NJ: Princeton University Press.

Black culture courses, more Negro officials asked for city schools (1968, Dec. 26). *The Bulletin*.

Black Issues in Higher Education (2004). *The unfinished agenda of Brown v. Board of Education*. Indianapolis, IN: John Wiley & Sons.

Blackburn, Robin (1997). *The making of new world slavery: From the baroque to the modern, 1492-1800*. New York: Verso.

Blair, Irene V., Charles M. Judd, Melody S. Sadler, & Christopher Jenkins (2002, July). The role of Afrocentric features in person perception judging by features and categories, *Journal of Personality and Social Psychology*, Vol. 83, pp. 5-25.

Blight, David W. (2001). *Race and reunion: The Civil War in American memory*. Cambridge, MA: Harvard University Press.

Bloom, Alan (1987). *The closing of the American mind: How higher education has failed democracy and impoverished the soul of today's students*. New York: Simon & Schuster.

Blum, Lawrence (2002). *I'm not a racist, but...: The moral quandary of race*. Ithaca, NY: Cornell University Press.

Boahen, A. Adou (1987). *African perspectives on colonialism*. Baltimore, MD: The Johns Hopkins University Press.

Boger John Charles & Gary Orfield (Eds.) (2005). *School resegregation: Must the South turn back?*. Chapel Hill, NC: University of North Carolina Press.

Bonilla-Silva, Eduardo (2001). *White supremacy and racism in the post-civil rights era*. Boulder, CO: Lynne Rienner.

Bonilla-Silva, Eduardo (2003). *Racism without racists: Color-blind racism and the persistence of racial inequality in the United States*. Lanham, MD: Rowman & Littlefield.

Boorstein, Michelle (2001, Nov. 22). Africans, black Americans lead separate lives in Harlem. *The Philadelphia Inquirer*, p. A41.

Bowlby, John (1982). *Attachment*. New York: Basic Books (2d ed.) (originally published 1969).

Bowlby, John (1988). *A secure base: Parent-child attachment and a healthy human development.* New York: Basic Books.

Bowles, Samuel & Herbert Gintis (1976). *Schooling in capitalist America: Educational reform and the contradictions of economic life.* New York: Basic Books.

Bray, Mark, Peter B. Clarke, & David Stephens (1986). *Education and society in Africa.* London: Edward Arnold.

Brinkley, Alan (1995). *American history: A survey.* New York: McGraw Hill (9th ed.).

Brooks, Roy L. (1992). *Rethinking the American race problem.* Berkeley, CA: University of California Press.

Brooks, Roy L. (2004). *Atonement and forgiveness: A new model for black reparations.* Berkeley, CA: University of California Press.

Brown, Michael K., Martin Carnoy, Elliott Currie, Troy Duster, David B. Oppenheimer, Marjorie Shultz, & David Wellman (2003). *Whitewashing race: The myth of a color-blind society.* Berkeley, CA: University of California Press.

Bryk, Anthony S. & Barbara L. Schneider (2002). *Trust in schools: A core resource for improvement.* New York: Russell Sage Foundation.

Buchanan, Patrick J. (2002). The death of the west: How dying populations and immigrant invasions imperil our country and civilization. New York: St. Martin's Press.

Burns, Donald G. (1965). African education: An introductory survey of education in Commonwealth countries. New York: Oxford University Press.

Busia, Kofi A. (1968). *Purposeful education for Africa.* Netherlands: Mouton.

Bynum, Edward Bruce (1999). *The African unconscious: Roots of ancient mysticism and modern psychology.* New York: Teachers College Press.

Carens, Joseph H. (2000). *Culture, citizenship, and community: Contextual political theory and justice as evenhandedness.* New York: Oxford University Press.

Carter, Dorinda J., Stella M. Flores, & Richard J. Reddick (Eds.) (2004). *Legacies of Brown: Multiracial equity in American education.* Cambridge, MA: Harvard Education Press.

Cashin, Sheryl (2004). *The failures of integration: How race and class are undermining the American dream.* New York: Public Affairs.

Cassidy, Jude & Phillip R. Shaver (Eds.) (1999). *Handbook of attachment: Theory, research, and clinical applications.* New York: Guilford Press.

Castells, Manuel (1997). *The power of identity. The information age: Economy, society and culture, Vol. II.* New York: Blackwell.

Cavanaugh, Sean & Erik W. Robelen (2004, Dec. 7). U.S. students fare poorly in international math comparison. *Education Week.* At http://www.edweek.org/ew/articles.

Clark, Kenneth (1988). *Prejudice and your child.* Middletown, CT: Wesleyan University Press (originally published 1963).

Clegg, Claude A., III (2004). *The price of liberty: African Americans and the making of Liberia.* Durham, NC: University of North Carolina Press.

Clignet, Remi & Philip J. Foster (1966). *The fortunate few: A study of secondary schools and students in the Ivory Coast.* Evanston, IL: Northwestern University.

Clotfelter, Charles T. (2004). *After Brown: The rise and retreat of school desegregation.* Princeton, NJ: Princeton University Press.

Coleman, James S. (1993). *Equality and achievement in education.* Boulder, CO: Westview Press (reprint ed.).

Coleman, James S., Barbara Schneider, Stephen Plank, Kathryn S. Schiller, Roger Shouse, Wang Huayin, Seh-Ann Lee (1999). *Redesigning American education.* Boulder, CO: Westview Press.

Comer, James P. (2004). *Leave no child behind: Preparing today's youth for tomorrow's world.* New Haven, CT: Yale University Press.

Conley, Dalton (1999). *Being black, living in the red: Race, wealth, and social policy in America*. Berkeley, CA: University of California Press.

Conyers, James L. (Ed.) (2001). *Afrocentricity and the academy: Essays on theory and practice*. Jefferson, NC: McFarland & Co., Inc.

Coons, John E. & Patrick M. Brennan (1999). *By nature equal: The anatomy of a Western insight*. Princeton, NJ: Princeton University Press.

Copeland-Carson, Jacqueline (2004). *Creating Africa in America: Translocal identity in an emerging world city*. Philadelphia: University of Pennsylvania Press.

Cross, William E., Jr., Thomas A. Parham, & Janice E. Helms (1991). The stages of Black identity development: Nigresence models. In Reginald L. Jones (Ed.), *Black psychology* (pp. 319-338). Berkeley, CA: Cobb & Henry (3d ed.).

D'Souza, Dinesh (1995). *The end of racism: Principles for a multicultural society*. New York: Free Press.

Dain, Bruce R. (2003). *A hideous monster of the mind: American race theory in the early republic*. Cambridge, MA: Harvard University Press.

Dalton, Harlan L. (1995). *Racial healing: Confronting the fear between blacks and whites*. New York: Doubleday.

Darder, Antonia & Rodolfo D. Torres (2004). *After race: Racism after multiculturalism*. New York: New York University Press.

Datta, Ansu (1984). *Education and society: A sociology of African education*. New York: Palgrave Macmillan.

Davidson, Basil (1993). *The black man's burden: Africa and the curse of the nation-state*. New York: Three Rivers Press.

Davis, Anthony C. & Jeffrey W. Jackson (1998). *Yo, little brother . . . Basic rules of survival for young Afro-American males*. Minneapolis, MN: Sagebrush Education Resources.

Davis, David B. (1988). *The problem of slavery in Western culture*. New York: Oxford University Press (originally published 1966).

Davis, David B. (1999). *The problem of slavery in the age of revolution, 1770 - 1823*. New York: Oxford University Press (2d ed., originally published 1975).

Davis, David B. (2003). *Challenging the boundaries of slavery*. Cambridge, MA: Harvard University Press.

Davis, James E. (2001). Black boys at school: Negotiating masculinities and race. In Richard Majors (Ed.), *Educating our black children: New directions and radical approaches* (pp. 169-182). New York: RoutledgeFalmer

Dei, George J. S. (1994). Afrocentricity: A cornerstone of pedagogy. *Anthropology & Education Quarterly*, Vol. 25, pp. 3-28.

Dei, George J. S., Josephine Mazzucca, Elizabeth McIsaac, & Jasmin Zine (1997). *Reconstructing "drop-out:" A critical ethnography of the dynamics of black students' disengagement from school*. Toronto, Canada: University of Toronto.

Delgado, Richard & Jean Stefancic (Eds.) (1995). *Critical race theory: The cutting edge*. Philadelphia: Temple University Press.

Delgado, Richard & Jean Stefancic (Eds.) (1997). *Critical white studies: Looking behind the mirror*. Philadelphia, PA: Temple University Press.

Delpit, Lisa (1993). The silenced dialogue: Power and pedagogy in educating other people's children. In Lois Weis & Michelle Fine (Eds.), *Beyond silenced voices: Class, race and gender in United States schools* (pp. 119-139). Albany, NY: State University of New York Press.

Delpit, Lisa D. (1995). *Other people's children: Cultural conflict in the classroom*. New York: The New Press.

Derman-Sparks, Louise & Carol B. Phillips (1997). *Teaching/learning anti-racism: A developmental approach.* New York: Teachers College Press.

DeTocqueville, Alexis (2000). *Democracy in America.* Chicago: University of Chicago Press (Harvey C. Mansfield & Delba Winthrop, Trans.) (originally published 1840).

Devlin, Bernie, Stephen E. Feinberg, Daniel P. Resnick, & Kathryn Roeder (Eds.) (1997). *Intelligence, genes, and success: Scientists respond to the bell curve.* New York: Springer Verlag.

Dewey, John (1944). *Democracy and education: An introduction to the philosophy of education.* New York: Free Press (originally published 1916).

Dewey, John (1997). *Experience & education.* New York: Touchstone (originally published 1938).

Dickerson, Debra (2004). *The end of blackness: Returning the souls of black folk to their rightful owners.* New York: Pantheon.

Diop, Cheikh Anta (1974). *The African origin of civilization: Myth or reality.* Brooklyn, NY: Lawrence Hill Books (Mercer Cook, Trans.).

Diop, Cheikh Anta (1990). *Precolonial black Africa: A comparative study of the political and social systems of Europe and Black Africa, from antiquity to the formation of modern.* Brooklyn, NY: Lawrence Hill Books (Harold J. Salemson, Trans.).

Diop, Cheikh Anta (1991). *Civilization or barbarism: An authentic anthropology.* Brooklyn, NY: Lawrence Hill Books (Yaa-Lengi Meema Ngemi, Trans.).

Doane, Ashley W. & Eduardo Bonilla-Silva (Eds.) (2003). *White out: The continuing significance of racism.* New York: Routledge.

Douglass, Frederick (1999). *Selected speeches and writings.* Chicago, IL: Lawrence Hill Books. (Philip S. Foner, Ed., abridged by Yuval Taylor).

Douglass, Frederick (1994). *Autobiographies.* New York: Library of America (Henry Louis Gates, Jr., Ed.).

Douglass, Frederick (1999/1849). Colonization. In Philip S. Foner (Ed.), *Frederick Douglass: Selected speeches and writings* (pp. 125-126). Chicago, IL: Lawrence Hill Books.

Douglass, Frederick (1999/1889). The nation's problem. In Philip S. Foner (Ed.), *Frederick Douglass: Selected speeches and writings* (pp. 725-740). Chicago, IL: Lawrence Hill Books.

DuBois, W.E.B. (1972). *Black reconstruction in America, 1860-1880.* New York: Athenaeum (originally published 1935).

DuBois, W.E.B. (1986). The souls of black folks. In *Writings.* New York: Library of America (pp. 357-547) (Nathan Huggins, Ed.) (originally published 1903).

Duke, David E. (1998). *My awakening: A path to racial understanding.* Mandeville, LA: Free Speech Press.

Dyer, Richard (1997). *White.* New York: Routledge.

Dyke, Katrina R. (1967, Dec. 12). Pupils, parents will study Afro-U.S. history at Sayre. *The Bulletin*

Early, Gerald (Ed.) (1993). *Lure and loathing: Essays on race, identity, and the ambivalence of assimilation.* New York: Penguin Books.

Efran, Jay S., Michael D. Lukens, & Robert J. Lukens (1990). *Language, structure, and change: Frameworks of meaning in psychotherapy.* New York: W.W. Norton.

Eltis, David (2000). *The rise of African slavery in the Americas.* New York: Cambridge University Press.

Ely, Melvin Patrick (2004). *Israel on the Appomattox: A southern experiment in black freedom from the 1790 through the Civil War.* New York: Knopf.

Entman, Robert M. & Andrew Rojecki (2000). *The black image in the white mind: Media and race in America.* Chicago: University of Chicago Press.

Epps, Edgar (2000). Foreword. In Diane S. Pollard & Cheryl S. Ajirotutu (Eds.), *African-centered schooling in theory and practice* (pp. vi–ix). Westport, CT: Greenwood.

Etuk, Emma S. (1999). *Friends: What would I do without them?: Finding real and valuable friendships in an unfriendly world*. Washington, D.C.: Emida International Publishers.

Extended lives: The African immigrant experience in Philadelphia (2001). The Balch Institute for Ethnic Studies.

Eze, Emmanuel Chukwudi (1997). Introduction. In Emmanuel Chukwudi Eze (Ed.), *Postcolonial African philosophy: A critical reader* (pp. 1-21). New York: Blackwell.

Eze, Emmanuel Chukwudi (2001). *Achieving our humanity: The idea of the postracial future*. New York: Routledge.

Fanon, Frantz (1963). *The wretched of the earth*. New York: Grove (Constance Farrington, Trans.).

Fanon, Frantz (1967). *Black skin, white masks*. New York: Grove (Charles Lam Markmann, Trans.) (originally published 1952).

Feagin, Joe R. (2000). *Racist America: Roots, current realities, and future reparations*. New York: Routledge.

Feagin, Joe R. (2003). *The many costs of racism*. Lanham, MD: Rowman & Littlefield.

Feldman, Glenn (Ed.) (2004). *Before "Brown": Civil rights and white backlash in the modern South*. Tuscaloosa, AL: University of Alabama Press.

Ferguson, Robert (1998). *Representing "race:" Ideology, identity and the media*. New York: Oxford University Press.

Festinger, Leon (1957). *A theory of cognitive dissonance*. Evanston, IL: Row, Peterson.

Fine, Michelle (1987). Silencing in public schools. *Language Arts*, Vol. 64, pp. 157-74.

Fine, Michelle (1997). *Off white: Readings on race, power, and society*. New York: Routledge.

Finkelman, Paul (1996). *Slavery and the Founders: Race and liberty in the age of Jefferson*. Armonk, NY: M.E. Sharpe.

Finn, Chester E., Jr. (1991). *We must take charge: Our schools and our future*. New York: Free Press.

Fireside, Harvey (2004). *Separate and unequal: Homer Plessy and the Supreme Court decision that legalized racism*. New York: Carroll & Graf.

Foner, Eric (1988). *Reconstruction: America's unfinished revolution, 1863-1877*. New York: Harper & Row.

Ford, Clyde W. (1994). *We can all get along: 50 steps you can take to help end racism*. New York: Dell.

Ford, Richard (2004). *Racial culture: A critique*. Princeton, NJ: Princeton University Press.

Fordham, Signithia & John U. Ogbu (1986). Black students' school success: Coping with the burden of "acting white." *The Urban Review*, Vol. 18, pp. 176-206.

Fordham, Signithia (1988). Racelessness as a factor in Black students' school success: Pragmatic strategy or pyrrhic victory? *Harvard Educational Review*, Vol. 58, pp. 55-84.

Fordham, Signithia (1996). *Blacked out: Dilemmas of race, identity, and success at Capital High*. Chicago, IL: University of Chicago.

Frankenberg, Erika, Chungmei Lee, & Gary Orfield (2003). *A multiracial society with segregated schools: Are we losing the dream?* Cambridge, MA: The Civil Rights Project at Harvard University, available at www.civilrightsproject.harvard.edu.

Frankenberg, Ruth (Ed.) (1997). *Displacing whiteness: Essays in social and cultural criticism.* Durham, NC: Duke University Press.

Franklin, Benjamin (1987). *Writings.* New York: Library of America (J.A. Leo Lemay, Ed.).

Franklin, Donna L. (1997). *Ensuring inequality: The structural transformation of the African-American family.* New York: Oxford University Press.

Franklin, John Hope & Alfred Moss, Jr. (2000). *From slavery to freedom: A history of African Americans.* New York: Alfred A. Knopf (8th ed.) (originally published 1947).

Franklin, John Hope & Loren Schweninger (2005). *The search of the promised land: A slave family in the old south.* New York: Oxford University Press.

Fraser, Steven (1995). *The bell curve wars: Race, intelligence, and the future of America.* New York: Basic Books.

Fredrickson, George M. (1981). *White supremacy: A comparative study in American and South African history.* New York: Oxford University Press.

Fredrickson, George M. (1987). *The black image in the white mind: The debate on Afro-American character and destiny, 1817-1914.* Middletown, CT: Wesleyan University Press (originally published 1971).

Fredrickson, George M. (1988). *The arrogance of race: Historical perspectives on slavery, racism, and social inequality.* Middletown, CT: Wesleyan University Press.

Fredrickson, George M. (1995a). *Black liberation: A comparative history of black ideologies in the United States and South Africa.* New York: Oxford University Press.

Fredrickson, George M. (1995b, Oct. 19). Demonizing the American dilemma. *New York Review of Books,* Vol. 42, No. 16, pp. 10-17.

Fredrickson, George M. (2002). *Racism: A short history.* Princeton, NJ: Princeton University Press.

Freire, Paulo (1985). *The politics of education: Culture, power, and liberation.* Westport, CT: Bergin and Garvey (Donaldo Macedo, Trans.).

Freire, Paulo (1997). *The pedagogy of the oppressed.* New York: Continuum (Myra B. Ramos, Trans.).

Freire, Paulo (1998a). *Teachers as cultural workers: Letters to those who dare to teach.* Boulder, CO: Westview (Donaldo Macedo, Dake Koike, & Alexandre Oliveira, Trans.).

Freire, Paulo (1998b). *Education for critical consciousness.* New York: The Continuum (Myra B. Ramos, Trans.).

Furstenberg, Frank F., Jr., Thomas D. Cook, Jacquelynne Eccles, Glen H. Elder, Jr., & Arnold Sameroff (2000). *Managing to make it: Urban families and adolescent success.* Chicago: University of Chicago.

Fyle, C. Magbaily (1999). *Introduction to the history of African civilization.* Lanham, MD: Rowman & Littlefield.

Gabbard, Krin (2004). *Black magic: White Hollywood and African American culture.* Piscataway, NJ: Rutgers University Press.

Gay, Geneva (2000). *Culturally responsive teaching: Theory, research, and practice.* New York: Teachers College Press.

Geiger, Roger L. (2004). *Knowledge and money: Research universities and the paradox of the marketplace.* Palo Alto, CA: Stanford University Press.

Genovese, Eugene D. (1976). *Roll Jordan, roll: The world the slaves made.* New York: Pantheon.

Gerstle, Gary (2001). *American crucible: Race and nation in the twentieth century.* Princeton, NJ: Princeton University Press.

Gilbert, Daniel T. & J. Gregory Hixon (1991, April). The trouble of thinking activation and application of stereotypic beliefs. *Journal of Personality and Social Psychology*, Vol. 60, pp. 509-517.

Gilens, Martin (1999). *Why Americans hate welfare: Race, media, and the politics of antipoverty policy*. Chicago: University of Chicago.

Gillespie, John T. (1967a, Nov. 21). Negro students explain objections to schools. *The Bulletin.*

Gillespie, John T. (1967b, Nov. 30). Guides to Negro history issued by School Board. *The Bulletin.*

Gillespie, John T. (1968a, Apr. 2). 400 teachers begin study of African history. *The Bulletin.*

Gillespie, John T. (1968b, May 15). 15 schools get grants to set up courses. *The Bulletin.*

Gillespie, John T. (1969, Jan. 12). Nun teaches Afro-American history at 3 parochial and 2 public schools. *The Sunday Bulletin*, p. 36.

Gilroy, Paul (2000). *Against race: Imagining political culture beyond the color line*. Cambridge, MA: Harvard University Press.

Ginwright, Shawn A. (2004). *Black in school: Afrocentric reform, urban youth & the promise of hip-hop culture*. New York: Teachers College Press.

Giroux, Henry A. (1992). *Border crossings: Cultural workers and the politics of education*. New York: Routledge.

Giroux, Henry A. (2005). *Schooling and the struggle for public life: Democracy's promise and education's challenge*. Boulder, CO: Paradigm.

Glazer, Nathan & Daniel P. Moynihan (1970). *Beyond the melting pot: The Negroes, Puerto Ricans, Jews, Italians, and Irish of New York City*. Cambridge, MA: MIT Press (2d ed.).

Glazer, Nathan (1997). *We are all multiculturalists now*. Cambridge, MA: Harvard University Press.

Goldberg, David T. (1993). *Racist culture: Philosophy and the politics of meaning*. Malden, MA: Blackwell.

Goldhill, Simon (2004). *Love, sex, and tragedy: How the ancient world shapes our lives*. Chicago: University of Chicago Press.

Goodman, Diane J. (2001). *Promoting diversity and social justice: Educating people from privileged groups*. Thousand Oaks, CA: Sage.

Gordon, David T. (Ed.) (2003). *Education reformed: American education 20 years after a Nation at Risk*. Cambridge, MA: Harvard Education Publishing Group.

Gossett, Thomas F. (1997). *Race: The history of an idea in America*. New York: Oxford University Press (originally published 1963).

Gottfredson, Linda S. (2005). What if the hereditarian hypothesis is true? *Psychology, Public Policy, and Law*, Vol. 11, pp. 311-319.

Gratz given grant to plan Negro history curriculum. (1968, Jan. 24). *The Bulletin*, p. 24.

Gray, Cecil C. (2001). *Afrocentric thought and praxis: An intellectual history*. Trenton, NJ: Africa World Press.

Green, Jay P. (2005). *Education myths: What special interest groups want you to believe about our school—and why it isn't so*. Lanham, MD: Rowman & Littlefield.

Greenberg, Jack (2004). *Crusaders in the courts: Legal battles of the civil rights movement*. Twelve Tables Press.

Greene, Jack P. (1993). *The intellectual construction of America: Exceptionalism and identity from 1492 to 1800*. Chapel Hill, NC: University of North Carolina Press.

Guinier, Lani & Gerald Torres (2003). *The miner's canary: Enlisting race, resisting power, transforming democracy*. Cambridge, MA: Harvard University Press.

Gutman, Hebert G. (1976). *The black family in slavery and freedom, 1750-1925.* New York: Random House.

Gutmann, Amy (1987). *Democratic education.* Princeton, NJ: Princeton University Press.

Gutmann, Amy (2003). *Identity in democracy.* Princeton, NJ: Princeton University Press.

Gyekye, Kwame (1995). *An essay on African philosophical thought: The Akan conceptual scheme.* Philadelphia, PA: Temple University Press (originally published 1987).

Hacker, Andrew (1992). *Two nations: Black, white, separate, hostile, unequal.* New York: Charles Scribner's Sons.

Hahn, Steven (2003). *A nation under our feet: Black political struggles in the rural South from slavery to the great migration.* Cambridge, MA: Belknap Press of Harvard University.

Hale, Janice E. (1994). *Unbank the fire: Visions for the education of African American children.* Baltimore, MD: Johns Hopkins University Press.

Hale, Janice E. (2001). *Learning while black: Creating educational excellence for African American children.* Baltimore, MD: Johns Hopkins University Press.

Hale-Benson, Janice E. (1982). *Black children: Their roots, culture and learning styles.* Baltimore, MD: Johns Hopkins University Press

Hale-Benson, Janice E. (1986). *Black children: Their roots, culture, and learning styles.* Baltimore, MD: Johns Hopkins University Press (rev. ed.).

Hamilton, Donna Cooper & Charles V. Hamilton (1997). *The dual agenda: The African-American struggle for civil and economic equality.* New York: Columbia University Press.

Hannaford, Ivan (1996). *Race: The history of an idea in the west.* Baltimore, MD: Johns Hopkins University Press.

Harris, Joseph E. (1998). *Africans and their history.* New York: Plume (2d ed.).

Harris, Michael D. (2003). *Colored pictures: Race and visual representation.* Chapel Hill, NC: University of North Carolina Press.

Harris, Norman (1998). The philosophical basis for an Afrocentric orientation. In Janice D. Hamlet (Ed.), *Afrocentric visions: Studies in culture and communication* (pp. 15-25). Thousand Oaks, CA: Sage.

Haymes, Stephen N. (1995). *Race, culture, and the city: A pedagogy for black urban struggle.* Albany, New York: State University of New York Press.

Helms, Janet E. (1990). *Black and white racial identity: Theory, research, and practice.* Westport, CT: Greenwood Press.

Henig, Jeffery R., Richard C. Hula, Marion Orr, Desiree S. Pedescleaux (1999). *The color of school reform: Race, politics, and the challenge of urban education.* Princeton, NJ: Princeton University Press.

Henry, C. Michael & James Tobin (Eds.) (2004). *Race, poverty, and domestic policy.* New Haven, CT: Yale University Press

Hernstein, Richard & Charles Murray (1994). *The bell curve: Intelligence and class structure in American life.* New York: Free Press.

Hernton, Calvin C. (1992). *Sex and racism in America.* New York: Doubleday (originally published 1968).

Herring, Cedric, Verna M. Keith, & Hayward Derrick (Eds.) (2003). *Skin deep: How race and complexion matter in the "color-blind" era.* Chicago, IL: University of Illinois.

Herskovits, Melville J. (1990). *The myth of the negro past.* New York: Beacon Press (originally published 1941).

Hill, Mike (2004). *After whiteness: Unmaking an American majority.* New York: New York University Press.

Hilliard, Asa G. (1998). *Sba, the reawakening of the African mind.* Gainesville, FL: Makare.

Hilliard, Asa G., III (2004). The state of African education. Challenging the genius: Excellent education for children. Conference, Sept. 10-12, 2004, Phila., PA. This paper, along with others from this conference, is available at http://www.sankofapublishing.com/Final%20Conference%20papers.

Hirsch, E.D. (1987). *Cultural literacy: What every American needs to know.* New York: Houghton Mifflin.

Hirsch, E.D. (1996). *The schools we need and why we don't have them.* New York: Doubleday.

Hochschild, Adam (1998). *King Leopold's ghost: A story of greed, terror, and heroism in colonial Africa.* New York: Houghton Mifflin.

Hochschild, Jennifer L. & Nathan Scovronick (2003). *The American dream and the public schools.* New York: Oxford University Press.

Hochschild, Jennifer L. (1995). *Facing up to the American dream: Race, class, and the soul of the nation.* Princeton, NJ: Princeton University Press.

Hollinger, David A. (1995). *Postethnic America: Beyond multiculturalism.* New York: Basic.

Holmes, Robyn M. (1995). *How young children perceive race.* Thousand Oaks, CA: Sage.

Holtzman, Linda (2001). *Media messages: What film, television, and popular music teach us about race, class, gender, and sexual orientation.* Armonk NY: M. E. Sharpe.

Honig, Bonnie (2001). *Democracy and the foreigner.* Princeton, NJ: Princeton University Press.

hooks, bell (1994). *Teaching to transgress: Education as the practice of freedom.* New York: Routledge.

hooks, bell (1995). *Killing rage: Ending racism.* New York: Henry Holt & Co.

Howard, Gary R. (1999). *We can't teach what we don't know: White teachers, multiracial schools.* New York: Teachers College Press.

Howe, Stephen (1998). *Afrocentrism: Mythical pasts and imagined homes.* New York: Verso.

Huffman, Alan (2004). *Mississippi in Africa: The saga of the slaves of the Prospect Hill plantation and their legacy in Liberia today.* New York: Gotham.

Humes, Edward (2003). *School of dreams: Making the grade at a top American high school.* Orlando, FL: Harcourt, Inc.

Ibrahim, Awad K. M. (1998). *"Hey, whassup homeboy?" Becoming black: Race, language, culture and the politics of identity: African students in a Franco-Ontarian high school.* Unpublished doctoral dissertation, University of Toronto, Toronto, Canada.

Iliffe, John (1995). *Africans: The history of a continent.* New York: Cambridge University Press.

Irvine, Jacqueline J. (1990). *Black students and school failure: Policies, practices, and prescriptions.* Westport, CT: Greenwood Press.

Irvine, Jacqueline J. (2000). Afrocentric education: Critical questions for further considerations. In Diane S. Pollard & Cheryl S. Ajirotutu (Eds.), *African-centered schooling in theory and practice* (pp. 199-210). Westport, CT: Greenwood.

Isaac, Benjamin (2004). *The invention of racism in classical antiquity.* Princeton, NJ: Princeton University Press.

Jackson, John & Nadine Weldman (2004). *Race, racism, and science: Social impact and interaction.* Santa Barbara, CA: ABC-CLIO.

Jackson, Michael (2004). *In Sierra Leone.* Durham, NC: Duke University Press.

Jacobson, Matthew Frye (1998). *Whiteness of a different color: European immigrants and the alchemy of race.* Cambridge, MA: Harvard University Press.

Jacoby, Russell & Naomi Glauberman (Eds.) (1995). *The bell curve debate: History, documents, opinions.* New York: Times Books.

Jacoby, Tamar (1998). *Someone else's house: America's unfinished struggle for integration.* New York: Free Press.

Jacoby, Tamar (Ed.) (2004). *Reinventing the melting pot: The new immigrants and what it means to be American.* New York: Basic Books.

Jahn, Janheinz (1989). *Muntu: African culture and the western world.* New York: Grove (Marjorie Grene, Trans.) (originally published 1958).

Jarrett, Alfred Abioseh (1996). *The under-development of Africa: Colonialism, neo-colonialism and socialism.* New York: University Press of America.

Jean, Clinton M. (1991). *Behind the Eurocentric veils: The search for African realities.* Amherst, MA: University of Massachusetts Press.

Jefferson, Thomas (1984a). Notes on the State of Virginia. In Thomas Jefferson, *Writings.* New York: Library of America (pp. 123-325) (Merrill D. Peterson, Ed.).

Jefferson, Thomas (1984b). Letter to John Lynch, Jan. 21, 1811. In Thomas Jefferson, *Writings.* New York: Library of America (pp. 1239-1241) (Merrill D. Peterson, Ed.).

Jencks, Christopher (1972). *Inequality: A reassessment of the effect of family and schooling in America.* New York: Basic Books.

Jensen, Robert (2005). *The heart of whiteness: Confronting race, racism and white privilege.* San Francisco, CA: City Lights.

Johanson, Donald C. & Maitland A. Edey (1981). *Lucy: The beginnings of humankind.* New York: Simon & Schuster.

Johnson, Walter (1999). *Soul by soul: Life inside the antebellum slave market.* Cambridge, MA: Harvard University Press.

Jones, Reginald L. (Ed.) (1991). *Black psychology.* Berkeley, CA: Cobb & Henry (3d ed.).

Jordan, Winthrop D. (1995). *White over black: American attitudes toward the negro, 1550-1812.* Chapel Hill, NC: University of North Carolina Press. (originally published 1968).

Kamalipourt, Yahya R. & Theresa Carilli (Eds.) (1998). *Cultural diversity and the U.S. media.* Albany, NY: State University of New York Press.

Kambon, Kobi K. (1992). *The African personality in America: An African-centered framework.* Tallahassee, FL: Nubian Nations Pubs.

Kambon, Kobi K. (1998). *African-black psychology in the American context: An African-centered approach.* Tallahassee, FL: Nubian Nations Pubs.

Karenga, Maulana & Jacob H. Carruthers (Eds.) (1986). *Kemet and the African worldview: Research, rescue and restoration.* Los Angeles: University of Sankore Press.

Katz, Michael B. (1995). *Improving poor people: The welfare state, the "underclass," and urban schools as history.* Princeton, NJ: Princeton University.

Katz, Phyllis A. (2003). Racists or tolerant multiculturalists? How do they begin? *American Psychologist,* Vol. 58, pp. 897-909.

Katznelson, Ira (2005). *When affirmative action was white: An untold history of racial inequality in twentieth-century America.* New York: W.W. Norton & Co.

Kelley, Robin D. G. & Earl Lewis (Eds.) (2000). *To make our world anew: A history of African Americans.* New York: Oxford University Press.

Kelley, Robin D. G. (2002). *Freedom dreams: The black radical imagination.* Boston, MA: Beacon Press.

Kellstedt, Paul M. (2003). *The mass media and the dynamics of American racial attitudes.* New York: Cambridge University Press.

Kershaw, Terry (1998). Afrocentrism and the Afrocentric method. In Janice D. Hamlet (Ed.), *Afrocentric visions: Studies in culture and communication* (pp. 27-44). Thousand Oaks, CA: Sage.

Keto, C. Tsehloane (1994). *An introduction to the African-centered perspective of history.* Chicago: Frontline.

Keto, C. Tsehloane (1995). *Vision, identity and time: The Afrocentric paradigm and the study of the past.* Dubuque, IA: Kendall/Hunt Publishing.

Keto, C. Tsehloane (2001). *Vision and time: Historical perspective of an Africa-centered paradigm.* Lanham, MD: Rowman & Littlefield.

Kifano, Subira (1996). Afrocentric education in supplementary schools: Paradigm and practice at the Mary McLeod Bethune Institute. *Journal of Negro Education,* Vol. 65, pp. 209-218.

Killen, Melanie, Perry Pisacane, Jenny Kim-Lee, & Alicia Ardila-Rey (2001). Fairness or stereotypes? Young children's priorities when evaluating group exclusion and inclusion. *Developmental Psychology,* Vol. 37, pp. 587-596.

Kincheloe, Joe L. & Shirley R. Steinberg (1997). *Changing multiculturalism: New times, new curriculum.* New York: Open University Press.

Kincheloe, Joe L., Shirley R. Steinberg, & Aaron D. Gresson III (Eds.) (1996). *Measured lies: The bell curve examined.* New York: St. Martin's Press.

King, Desmond (2000). *Making Americans: Immigration, race, and the origins of the diverse democracy.* Cambridge, MA: Harvard University Press.

King, Martin Luther, Jr. (1963, Aug., 28). *I have a dream.* The text is available at http://www.ukans.edu/carrie/docs/texts/mlkdream.html.

King, Richard H. (2004). *Race, culture, and the intellectuals, 1940-1970.* Baltimore, MD: Johns Hopkins University Press.

Klarman, Michael J. (2004). *From Jim Crow to civil rights: The Supreme Court and the struggle for racial equality.* New York: Oxford University Press.

Kluger, Richard (2004). *Simple justice: The history of* Brown v. Board of Education *and black America's struggle for equality.* New York: Knopf (originally published 1975).

Kozol, Jonathan (1991). *Savage inequalities: Children in America's schools.* New York: Crown.

Kozol, Jonathan (2005). *The shame of the nation: The restoration of apartheid in America.* New York: Crown.

Kunjufu, Jawanza (1987). *Lessons from history: A celebration in blackness.* Chicago, IL: African American Images.

Kunjufu, Jawanza (2002). *Black students - middle class teachers.* Chicago, IL: African American Images.

Labov, William (1982). Competing value systems in the inner-city schools. In Perry Gilmore & Allan A. Glatthorn (Eds.), *Children in and out of school* (pp. 148-171). Washington, D.C.: Center for Applied Linguistics.

Ladner, Joyce A. (1998). *The ties that bind: Timeless values for African American families.*

Ladson-Billings, Gloria & William Tate (1995). Toward a critical race theory of education. *Teachers College Record,* Vol. 97, pp. 47-67.

Ladson-Billings, Gloria (1994). *The dreamkeepers: Successful teachers of African American children.* New York: Jossey-Bass.

Ladson-Billings, Gloria (2000). Racialized discourses and ethnic epistemologies. In Norman K. Denzin & Yvonna S. Lincoln (Eds.), *Handbook of qualitative research* (pp. 257-277). Thousand Oaks, CA: Sage (2d ed.).

Langlois, Judith H., Lisa Kalakanis, Adam J. Rubenstein, Andrea Larson, Monica Hallam, & Monica Smoot (2000). Maxims or myths of beauty? A meta-analytic and theoretical review. *Psychological Bulletin*, Vol. 126, pp. 390-423.

Lappin, Elena (2004, July 4). Your country is safe from me. *The New York Times Book Review,* Vol. 119, p. 11.

Lasch-Quinn, Elisabeth (2001). *Race experts: How racial etiquette, sensitivity training, and new age therapy hijacked the Civil Rights revolution.* New York: W.W. Norton.

Le Blanc, Paul (Ed.) (2003). *Black liberation and the American Dream: The struggle for racial and economic justice.* Amherst, NY: Humanity Books.

Lefkowitz, Mary & Guy MacLean Rogers (Eds.) (1997). *Black Athena revisited.* Chapel Hill, NC: University of North Carolina Press.

Lefkowitz, Mary (1996a). *Not out of Africa: How Afrocentrism became an excuse to teach myth as history.* New York: Basic Books.

Lefkowitz, Mary (1996b). Whatever happened to historical evidence? In Paul R. Gross, Norman Levitt, & Martin W. Lewis (Eds.), *The flight from science and reason* (pp. 301-312). New York: New York Academy of Sciences.

Levine, Lawrence W. (1977). *Black culture and black consciousness: Afro-American folk thought from slavery to freedom.* New York: Oxford University Press.

Levinson, Bradley A., Kathryn M. Borman, Margaret Eisenhart, Michele Foster, Amy E. Fox, Margaret Sutton (Eds.) (2000). *Schooling the symbolic animal: Social and cultural dimensions of education.* Lanham, MD: Rowman & Littlefield.

Levy, Andrew (2005). *The first emancipator: The forgotten story of Robert Carter, the Founder who freed his slaves.* New York: Random House.

Lewis, Amanda E. (2003). *Race in the schoolyard: Negotiating the color line in classrooms and communities.* Newark, NJ: Rutgers University Press.

Lieberman, Joel D. & Jamie Arndt (2000). Understanding the limits of limiting instructions, *Psychology Public Policy & Law*, Vol. 6, pp. 677-711.

Lieberman, Myron (1993). *Public education: An autopsy.* Cambridge, MA: Harvard University Press.

Lincoln, Abraham (1989). *Speeches and writings, 1859-1865.* New York: Library of America (Don Fehrenbacher, Ed.).

Lincoln, Yvonna S. (1995). In search of students' voices. *Theory Into Practice*, Vol. 34, pp. 88-93.

Lopez, Ian H. (1994). The social construction of race: Some observations on illusion, fabrication and choice. *Harvard Civil Rights-Civil Liberties Law Review*, Vol. 39, pp. 1-62.

Lovejoy, Paul E. (2000). *Transformations in slavery: A history of slavery in Africa.* New York: Cambridge University Press (2d ed.) (originally published 1983).

Lublin, David (2004). *The republican South: Democratization and partisan change.* Princeton, NJ: Princeton University Press.

Luma, Lydia E. (1983). *The education of African teachers.* Cameroon: SOPECAM.

Lyotard, Jean-François (1984). *The postmodern condition: A report on knowledge.* Minneapolis: University of Minnesota Press (Geoff Bennington & Brian Massumi, Trans.) (originally published 1979).

MacDougall, Walter A. (2004). *Freedom just around the corner: A new American history: 1585-1828.* New York: HarperCollins.

Macedo, Donaldo (1994). *Literacies of power: What Americans are not allowed to know.* Boulder, CO: Westview.

Macedo, Donaldo & Panayota Gounari (Eds.) (2005). *The globalization of racism.* Boulder, CO: Pardigm

Macedo, Stephen (2000). *Diversity and distrust: Civic education in a multicultural democracy.* Cambridge, MA: Harvard University Press.

MacLeod, Jay (1991). Bridging street and school. *The Journal of Negro Education,* Vol. 60, pp. 260-275.

Madhubuti, Haki R. & Safisha L. Madhubuti (1994). *African-Centered education: Its value, importance, and necessity in the development of Black children.* Chicago: Third World Press.

Mahler, Margaret, Fred Pine, & Anni Bergman (1975). *The psychological birth of the human infant: Symbiosis and Individuation.* New York: Perseus Books.

Majors, Richard (Ed.) (2001). *Educating our black children: New directions and radical approaches.* New York: RoutledgeFalmer.

Malcomson, Scott (2000). *One drop of blood: The American misadventure of race.* New York: Farrar, Straus and Giroux.

Malik, Kenan (1996). *The meaning of race: Race, history and culture in western society.* New York: New York University Press.

Mamdanie, Mahmood (1996). *Citizens and subjects: Contemporary Africa and the legacy of late colonialism.* Princeton, NJ: Princeton University Press.

Mann, Michael (1986). *The sources of power: A history of power from the beginning to A.D. 1760.* New York: Cambridge University Press.

Mannheim, Karl (1985). *Ideology and utopia: An introduction of the sociology of knowledge.* New York: Harcourt Brace (Louis Wirth & Edward Shils, Trans.) (originally published 1936).

Markowitz, Gerald & David Rosner (1996). *Children, race, and power: Kenneth and Macie Clark's Northside Center.* Charlottesville, VA: University of Virginia Press.

Marx, Anthony W. (1998). *Making race and nation: A comparison of the United States, South Africa, and Brazil.* New York: Cambridge University Press.

Massey, Douglas S. & Nancy A. Denton (1993). *American apartheid: Segregation and the making of the underclass.* Cambridge, MA: Harvard University Press.

Mbiti, John S. (1969). *African religions and philosophy.* New York: Heinemann.

McCarthy, Cameron (1998). *The uses of culture: Education and the limits of ethnic affiliation.* New York: Routledge.

McGowan, William (2001). *Coloring the news: How crusading for diversity has corrupted American journalism.* New York: Encounter Books.

McLaren, Peter (2002). *Life in schools: An introduction to critical pedagogy in the foundations of education.* New York: Allyn & Bacon (4th ed.).

McPhail, Mark Lawrence (1994). *The rhetoric of racism.* Lanham, MD: University Press of America.

McSorley, Richard T. (1960). *The causes of prejudice: A correlation of its causality as described by sociology and by philosophy.* Unpublished doctoral dissertation. University of Ottawa, Ottawa, Canada.

McWhorter, John (2000). *Losing the race: Self-sabotage in black America.* New York: Free Press.

Mead, Margaret (1959). *Race: Science and politics.* New York: Viking (rev. ed.) (originally published 1940).

Mead, Margaret (1989). *Patterns of culture.* Boston: Houghton Mifflin (originally published 1934).

Meredith, Martin (2005). *The fate of Africa: From the hopes of freedom to the heart of despair.* New York: Public Affairs.

Merelman, Richard M. (1995). *Representing black culture: Racial conflict and cultural politics in the United States*. New York: Routledge.

Merriam, Sharon B. (1998). *Qualitative research and case study applications in education*. San Francisco, CA: Jossey-Bass.

Mickelson, Rosalind A. (1990). The attitude-achievement paradox among black adolescents. *Sociology of Education*, Vol. 63, pp. 44-61.

Miele, Frank (Ed.) (2002). *Intelligence, race, and genetics: Conversations with Arthur R. Jensen*. Boulder, CO: Westview Press.

Miles, Robert & Malcolm Brown (2003). *Racism*. New York: Routledge (2d ed.).

Miller, William Ian (1997). *The anatomy of disgust*. Cambridge, MA: Harvard University Press.

Miller, William Ian (2003). *Faking it*. New York: Cambridge University Press.

Mills, Charles Wade (1997). *The racial contract*. Ithaca, NY: Cornell University Press.

Mills, Charles Wade (1998). *Blackness visible: Essays on philosophy and race*. Ithaca, NY: Cornell University Press.

Minow, Martha (1990). *Making all the difference: Inclusion, exclusion, and American law*. Ithaca, NY: Cornell University Press.

Moikobu, Josephine M. (1981). *Blood and flesh: Black American and African identification*. Greenwood Press.

Monaghan, E. Jennifer (2005). *Learning to read and write in colonial America*. Amherst, MA: University of Massachusetts Press.

Montagu, Ashley (1997). *Man's most dangerous myth: The fallacy of race*. New York: Oxford University Press (6th ed.) (originally published 1942).

Morgan, Edmund S. (2003). *American slavery, American freedom: The ordeal of colonial Virginia*. New York: W.W. Norton (originally published in 1975).

Morris, Thomas D. (1996). *Southern slavery and the law, 1619 – 1860*. Chapel Hill, NC: University of North Carolina Press.

Morrison, Toni (1992). *Playing in the dark: Whiteness and the literary imagination*. Cambridge, MA: Harvard University Press.

Moses, Michelle (2002). *Embracing race: Why we need a race-conscious education policy*. New York: Teachers College Press.

Moses, Wilson Jeremiah (1998). *Afrotopia: The roots of African American popular history*. New York: Cambridge University Press.

Mosha, R. Sambuli (2000). *The heartbeat of indigenous Africa: A study of the Chagga educational system*. New York: Garland Publishing.

Moya, Paula M. L. (2002). *Learning from experience: Minority identities, multicultural struggles*. Berkeley, CA: University of California Press.

Murrell, Peter C. (2002). *African-centered pedagogy: Developing schools of achievement for African American children*. Albany, NY: State University of New York Press.

Myers, Linda James (1988). *Understanding an Afrocentric worldview: Introduction to an optimal psychology*. Dubuque, IA: Kendall/Hunt.

Myrdal, Gunner (1996). *An American dilemma: The negro problem and modern democracy*. New Brunswick, NJ: Transaction (originally published 1944).

Nasaw, David (1979). *Schooled to order: A social history of public schooling in the United States*. New York: Oxford University Press.

Nash, Gary B. (2005). *The unknown American revolution: The unruly birth of democracy and the struggle to create America*. New York: Viking.

Nahshon, Edna (Ed.) (2005). *From the ghetto to the melting pot: Israel Zangwill's Jewish plays*. Detroit, MI: Wayne State University Press.

Nieto, Sonia (1992). *Affirming diversity: The sociopolitical context of multicultural education*. New York: Longman.

Nieto, Sonia (1999). *The light in their eyes: Creating multicultural learning communities*. New York: Teachers College Press.

Nisbett, Richard E. (2003). Response to President George W. Bush's question "What are the pressing scientific issues for the nation and the world, and what is your advice on how I can begin to deal with them?" Edge: The World Question Center, available at http://www.edge.org/q2003/q03_nisbett.html.

Nisbett, Richard E. (2005). Heredity, environment, and race differences in IQ: A commentary on Rushton and Jensen (2005). *Psychology, Public Policy, and Law*, Vol. 11, pp. 302-310.

Nobles, Wade W. (1991). Extended self: Rethinking the so-called negro self-concept. In Reginald L. Jones (Ed.), *Black Psychology* (pp. 295-304). Berkeley, CA: Cobb & Henry (3d ed.).

Nobles, Wade W. (2004). Utilizing culture in the achievement of educational excellence for African American adults: From cultural precepts to recurring themes. Challenging the genius: Excellent education for children conference, Sept. 10-12, 2004, Phila., PA. This paper, and others from this conference, is available at http://www.sankofapublishing.com/Final%20Conference%20papers.

Noguera, Pedro Antonio (2003). *City schools and the American dream: Reclaiming the promise of public education*. New York: Teachers College Press.

Nugent, Paul (2004). *Africa since independence*. New York: Palgrave Macmillan.

Nussbaum, Martha C. (1997). *Cultivating humanity: A classical defense of reform in liberal education*. Cambridge, MA: Harvard University Press.

Nussbaum, Martha C. (2004). *Hiding from humanity: Disgust, shame, and the law*. Princeton, NJ: Princeton University Press.

O'Connor, Carla (1997). Dispositions toward (collective) struggle and educational resilience in the inner city: A case analysis of six African-American high school students. *American Educational Research Journal*, Vol. 34, pp. 593-629.

Ogbu, John U. & Herbert D. Simons (1998). Voluntary and involuntary minorities: A cultural-ecological theory of school performance with some implications for education. *Anthropology & Education Quarterly*, Vol. 29, 155-188.

Ogbu, John U. (1974). *The next generation: An ethnography of education in an urban neighborhood*. New York: Academic Press.

Ogbu, John U. (1978). *Minority education and caste: The American system in cross-cultural perspective*. New York: Academic Press.

Ogbu, John U. (1983). Literacy and schooling in subordinate cultures: The case of black Americans. In Daniel P. Resnick (Ed.), *Literacy in historical perspective*. (pp. 129-153). Washington, DC: The Library of Congress.

Ogbu, John U. (1991). Immigrant and involuntary minorities: A comparative perspective. In Margaret A. Gibson & John U. Ogbu (Eds.), *Minority status and schooling* (pp. 3-33, 249-285, 383-399). New York: Garland Publishing.

Ogbu, John U. (1992, Autumn). Adaptation to minority status and impact on school success. *Theory Into Practice*, Vol. 31, 287-295.

Ogbu, John U. (1994a). Racial stratification and education in the United States: Why inequality persists. *Teachers College Record*, Vol. 96, 264-298.

Ogbu, John U. (1994b). From cultural differences to differences in cultural frame of reference. In Patricia M. Greenfield & Rodney R. Cocking (Eds.), *Cross-cultural roots of minority child development* (pp. 365-391). Hillsdale, NJ: Lawrence Erlbaum.

Ogbu, John U. (2003). *Black American students in an affluent suburb: A study of academic disengagement.* Mahwah, NJ: Lawrence Erlbaum Associates.

Ogletree, Charles (2004). *All deliberate speed: Reflections on the first half-century of* Brown v. Board of Education. New York: W.W. Norton.

Oliver, Melvin L. & Thomas M. Shapiro (1995). *Black wealth/white wealth: A new perspective on racial inequality.* New York: Routledge.

Olsen, Laurie (1997). *Made in America: Immigrant students in our public schools.* New York: New Press.

Omi, Michael & Howard Winant (1994). *Racial formation in the United States from the 1960s to the 1990s.* New York: Routledge (2d ed.).

Omotosho, Samson Akinloye (2005). *Being an African student: Stories of opportunity and determination.* Lanham, MD: University Press of America.

Orfield, Gary & Chungmei Lee (2004). Brown *at 50: King's dream or* Plessy's *nightmare?.* Cambridge, MA: The Civil Rights Project at Harvard University. Full text available at http://www.civilrightsproject.harvard.edu.

Orfield, Gary, Daniel Losen, Johanna Wald, & Christopher B. Swanson (2004). *Losing our future: How minority youth are being left behind by the graduation rate crisis.* The Civil Rights Project at Harvard University. Full text available at http://www.civilrightsproject.harvard.edu.

Ortiz de Montellano, Bernard R. (1996). Afrocentric pseudoscience: The miseducation of African Americans. In Paul R. Gross, Norman Levitt, & Martin W. Lewis (Eds.), *The flight from science and reason* (pp. 561-572). New York: New York Academy of Sciences.

Painter, Nell Irvin (2005). *Creating black Americans: African-American history and its meanings, 1619 to the* present. New York: Oxford University Press.

Parekh, Bhikhu (2000). *Rethinking multiculturalism: Cultural diversity and political theory.* Cambridge, MA: Harvard University Press.

Parham, Thomas A., Joseph L. White, & Adisa Ajamu (1999). *The psychology of blacks: An African centered approach.* Upper Saddle River, NJ: Pearson Education (3d ed.).

Patterson, Orlando (1982). *Slavery and social death: A comparative study.* Cambridge, MA: Harvard University Press.

Patterson, Orlando (1997). *The ordeal of integration: Progress and resentment in America's "racial" crisis.* New York: BasicCivitas.

Patterson, Orlando (1998). *Rituals of blood: Consequences of slavery in two American centuries.* New York: BasicCivitas.

Perea, Juan F. (1995). Los olivdados: On the making of invisible people. *New York University Law Review,* Vol. 70, pp. 965-991.

Perie, Marianne, Rebecca Moran, & Anthony D. Lutkus (2005). *NAEP 2004 trends in Academic progress: Three decades of student performance in reading and mathematics* (NCES 2005–464). U.S. Department of Education, Institute of Education Sciences, National Center for Education Statistics. Washington, D.C.: GPO. Text available at http://nces.ed.gov/nationsreportcard/pdf/main2005/2005464.pdf.

Perry, Theresa, Claude Steele, & Asa Hilliard III (2003). *Young, gifted, and black: Promoting high achievement among Africa-American students.* New York: Beacon Press.

Peshkin, Alan (2001). *Permissible advantage? The moral consequences of elite schooling.* Mahwah, NJ: Lawrence Erlbaum.

Peters-Davis, Norah & Jeffrey Shultz (2005). *Challenges in multicultural education: Teaching and taking diversity courses.* Boulder, CO: Paradigm.

Philogene, Gina (Ed.) (2004). *Racial identity in context: The legacy of Kenneth B. Clark.* Washington, D.C.: American Psychological Association.

Plous, Scott (2002). *Understanding prejudice and discrimination*. New York: McGraw-Hill Humanities.

Pokempner, Jennifer & Dorothy E. Roberts (2001). Poverty, welfare reform, and the meaning of disability. *Ohio State Law Journal*, Vol. 62, pp. 425-463.

Pollard, Diane S. & Cheryl S. Ajirotutu (2000). *African-centered schooling in theory and practice*. Westport, CT: Bergin & Garvey.

Pollock, Mica (2004). *Colormute: Race talk dilemmas in an American school*. Princeton, NJ: Princeton University Press.

Powers, Richard (2003). *The time of our singing*. New York: Farrar, Strauss and Giroux.

Quote of the Day (2002, May 26). *The Washington Post*, p. C3.

Rasmussen, Birgit B., Eric Klinenberg, Irene J. Nexica, & Matt Wray (Eds.) (2001). *The making and unmaking of whiteness*. Durham, NC: Duke University Press.

Ravitch, Diane (2000). *Left back: A century of battles over school reform*. New York: Simon & Schuster.

Reese, William J. (2005). *America's public schools: From the commons school to "No Child Left Behind."* Baltimore, MD: Johns Hopkins University Press.

Reich, Rob (2002). *Bridging liberalism and multiculturalism in American education*. Chicago: University of Chicago Press.

Reid, Karla S. (2001). Researchers probe achievement gap. *Education Week*, Vol. 20, No. 22, pp. 13-14.

Roberts, Dorothy E. (1997). *Killing the black body: Race, reproduction, and the meaning of liberty*. New York: Pantheon Books.

Robinson, James J. (1979). In Barbara Rowes, *Book of quotes* (p. 70). New York: Ballantine.

Robinson, Randall N. (2000). *The debt: What America owes the blacks*. New York: E.P. Dutton.

Robinson, Randall N. (2002). *The reckoning: What blacks owe each other*. New York: E.P. Dutton.

Rodriguez, Nestor (1995). The real "New World Order:" The globalization of racial and ethnic relations in the late twentieth century. In Michael P. Smith & Joe R. Feagin (Eds.), *The bubbling cauldron: Race, ethnicity and urban crisis* (pp. 211-225). Minneapolis, MN: University of Minnesota.

Roediger, David (1994). *Towards the abolition of whiteness: Essays on race, politics, and working class history*. New York: Verso.

Roediger, David (1999). *The wages of whiteness: Race and the making of the American working class*. New York: Verso.

Roediger, David R. (2002). *Colored white: Transcending the racial past*. Berkeley: University of California Press.

Rong, Xue Lan & Judith Preissle (1998). *Educating immigrant students: What we need to know to meet the challenges*. Thousand Oaks, CA: Corwin.

Rose, Mike (1990). *Lives on the boundary: A moving account of the struggles and achievements of America's educationally underprepared*. New York: Penguin.

Roth, Ann Macy (1996). Building bridges to Afrocentrism: A letter to my Egyptological colleagues. In Paul R. Gross, Norman Levitt, & Martin W. Lewis (Eds.), *The flight from science and reason* (pp. 313-326). New York: New York Academy of Sciences.

Rothenberg, Paula S. (2001). *White privilege: Essential readings on the other side of racism*. New York: Worth.

Rothstein, Richard (1998). *The way we were?: The myths and realities of America's student achievement*. Washington, D.C.: The Brookings Institute.

Rothstein, Richard (2004). *Class and schools: Using social, economic, and educational reform to close the black-white gap.* Washington, D.C.: Economic Policy Institute

Rothstein, Richard, Martin Carnoy, & Luis Buenveniste (1999). *Can public schools learn from private schools: Case studies in the public and private sector.* Washington, D.C.: Economic Policy Institute.

Rothstein, Stanley W. (1994). *Schooling the poor: A social inquiry into the American educational experience.* Westport, CT: Bergin and Garvey.

Rothstein, Stanley W. (1994). *Schooling the poor: A social inquiry into the American educational experience.* Westport, CT: Bergin and Garvey.

Rothstein, Stanley W. (Ed.) (1995). *Class, culture and race in American schools.* Westport, CT: Greenwood Press.

Rousmaniere, Kate (1997). *City teachers: Teaching and school reform in historical perspective.* New York: Teachers College Press.

Rowe, David C. (2005). Under the skin: On the impartial treatment of genetic and environmental hypotheses of racial differences. *American Psychologist,* Vol. 60, pp. 60-70.

Rushton, J. Phillipe & Arthur R. Jensen (2005a). Thirty years of research on race differences on cognitive ability. *Psychology, Public Policy, and Law,* Vol. 11, pp. 235-294.

Rushton, J. Phillipe & Arthur R. Jensen (2005b). Wanted: More race realism, less moralistic fallacy. *Psychology, Public Policy, and Law,* Vol. 11, pp. 328-336.

Russell, Kathy, Midge Wilson, & Ronald Hall (1992). *The color complex: The politics of skin color among African Americans.* New York: Harcourt Brace Jovanovich.

Rutstein, Nathan (1993). *Healing racism in America: A prescription for the disease.* Springfield, MA: Whitcomb Publishers.

Ryan, Desmond (1968, Feb. 29). Principal urges teaching Negro history to all pupils. *The Bulletin.*

Ryan, James (1999). *Race and ethnicity in multi-ethnic schools: A critical case study.* Toronto, Canada: Multilingual Matters.

Sachs, Jeffrey D. (2005). *The end of poverty: Economic possibilities for our time.* New York: Penguin.

Sagan, Eli (1991). *The honey and the hemlock: Democracy and paranoia in ancient Athens and modern America.* Princeton, NJ: Princeton University Press.

Said, Edward W. (1993). *Culture and imperialism.* New York: Alfred A. Knopf.

Sarich, Vincent & Frank Miele (2004). *Race: The reality of human differences.* Boulder, CO: Westview Press.

Schlesinger, Arthur M., Jr. (1998). *The disuniting of America: Reflections on a multicultural society.* New York: W.W. Norton (rev. ed.).

Schuck, Peter H. (2003). *Diversity in America: Keeping government at a safe distance.* Cambridge, MA: Belknap Press of Harvard University.

Sears, David O., James Sidanius, & Lawrence Bobo (Eds.) (2000). *Racialized politics: The debate about racism in America.* Chicago: University of Chicago Press.

Serequeberhan, Tsenay (2000). *Our heritage: The past in the present of African-American and African existence.* Lanham, MD: Rowman & Littlefield.

Seymour, Mike (Ed.) (2005). *Educating for humanity: Rethinking the purposes of education.* Boulder, CO: Paradigm.

Shapiro, Thomas M. (2003). *The hidden cost of being African American: How wealth perpetuates inequality.* New York: Oxford University Press.

Shipler, David K. (1998). *A country of strangers: Blacks and whites in America.* New York: Knopf.

Shipler, David K. (2004). *The working poor: Invisible in America.* New York: Knopf.

Shipman, Pat (2002). *The evolution of racism: Human differences and the use and abuse of science.* Cambridge, MA: Harvard University Press.

Shonkoff, Jack P. & Deborah A. Philips (Eds.) (2000). *From neurons to neighborhoods: The science of early childhood development.* Washington, D.C.: National Academy Press.

Shujaa, Mwalimu J. (Ed.) (1994). *Too much schooling, too little education: A paradox of black life in white societies.* Trenton, NJ: Africa World Press.

Shulman, Steven & William Darity, Jr. (Eds.) (1989). *The question of discrimination: Racial inequality in the U.S. labor market.* CT: Wesleyan University Press.

Sleeper, Jim (2002). *Liberal racism: How fixating on race subverts the American Dream.* Lanham, MD: Rowman & Littlefield.

Sleeter, Christine E. & Carl A. Grant (2002). *Making choices for multicultural education: Five approaches to race, class, and gender.* New York: Wiley (4th ed.).

Sleeter, Christine E. & Peter McLaren (Eds.) (1995). *Multicultural education, critical pedagogy, and the politics of difference.* Albany, NY: State University of New York Press.

Sleeter, Christine E. (1996). *Multicultural education as social activism.* Albany, NY: State University of New York Press.

Smedley, Audrey (1999). *Race in North America: Origin and evolution of a worldview.* Boulder, CO: Westview Press (2d ed.).

Smedley, Audrey & Brian D. Smedley (2005). Race as biology is fiction,, racism as a social problem is real. *American Psychologist*, Vol. 60, pp. 16-26.

Smith, Rogers M. (1997). *Civic ideals: Conflicting visions of citizenship in U.S. history.* New Haven, CT: Yale University Press.

Snyder, Susan (2005, June 12). Forces behind history mandate. *The Philadelphia Inquirer*, p. B01.

Socolar, Paul (Ed.) (2002, Fall). *Philadelphia public school notebook.* Philadelphia: Public School Notebook.

Solomon, R. Patrick (1992). *Black resistance in high school: Forging a separatist culture.* Albany, NY: State University of New York Press.

Somé, Malidoma Patrice (1998). *The healing wisdom of Africa: Finding life purpose through nature, ritual, and community.* New York: Jeremy P. Tarcher/Putnam.

Sowell, Thomas (1992). *Inside American education.* New York: Free Press.

Sowell, Thomas (1994). *Race and culture: A world view.* New York: Basic Books.

Soyinka, Wole (1975). *Death and the king's horseman.* New York: W.W. Norton.

Spengler, Oswald (1928). *The decline of the west, Vol. II: Perspectives of world history.* New York: Alfred A. Knopf (Charles Francis Atkinson, Trans.) (originally published 1922).

Speth, James G. (1996, Sept.). Global inequality: 358 billionaires vs. 2.3 billion people. *New Perspectives Quarterly*, Vol. 13, No. 4, pp. 166-168.

Spring, Joel (1998). *Wheels in the head: Educational philosophies of authority, freedom, and culture from Socrates to human rights.* Boston: McGraw-Hill (2d ed.).

Spring, Joel (2000). *American education.* Boston: McGraw-Hill (9th ed.).

Spring, Joel (2004). *Deculturalization and the struggle for equality: A brief history of the education of dominated cultures in the United States.* Boston: McGraw-Hill (4th ed.).

Steinberg, Stephen (1995). *Turning back: The retreat from racial justice in American thought and policy.* Boston: Beacon Press.

Steinhorn, Leonard & Barbara Diggs-Brown (1999). *By the color of our skin: The illusion of integration and the reality of race.* New York: E.P. Dutton.

Stephan, Walter (1999). *Reducing prejudice and stereotyping in schools*. New York: Teachers College Press.

Stern, Daniel N. (1985). *The interpersonal world of the infant: A view from psychoanalysis and psychology*. New York: Perseus Books.

Sternberg, Robert J. (2005). There are no public policy implications: A reply to Rushton and Jensen (2005). *Psychology, public policy, and law*, Vol. 11, pp. 295-301.

Sternberg, Robert J., Elena L. Grigorenko, & Kenneth K. Kidd (2005). Intelligence, race, and genetics. *American Psychologist*, Vol. 60, pp. 46-591.

Stewart, Julia. (1997). *African proverbs and wisdom: A collection for every day of the year, from more than forty African nations*. Secaucus, NJ: Carol Publishing.

Street, Paul (2005). *Segregated schools: Educational apartheid in post-civil rights America*. New York: Routledge.

Stuckey, Sterling (1987). *Slave culture: Nationalist theory and the foundations of black America*. New York: Oxford University Press.

Subotnik, Dan (2005). *Toxic diversity: Race, gender, and law talk in America*. New York: New York University Press.

Sutton, Margaret & Bradley A. U. Levinson (Eds.) (2001). *Policy as practice: Toward a comparative sociocultural analysis of educational policy*. Westport, CT: Ablex.

Suzuki, Lisa & Joshua Aronson (2005). The cultural malleability of intelligence and its impact on the racial/ethnic hierarchy. *Psychology, Public Policy, and Law*, Vol. 11, pp. 320-327.

Swain, Carol M. (2002). *The new white nationalism in America: Its challenge to integration*. New York: Cambridge University Press.

Sykes, Charles J. (1995). *Dumbing down our kids: Why American children feel good about themselves but can't read, write, or add*. New York: St. Martin's Press.

Talis, Sara J. (1987). *Oral histories of three secondary school students in Tanzania*. Lewiston, NY: The Edwin Mellen Press.

Tatum, Beverly Daniel (2003). *Why are all the black kids sitting together in the cafeteria? And other conversations about race: A psychologist explains the development of racial identity*. New York: Basic Books (5th ed.).

Taylor, Paul C. (2004). *Race: A philosophical introduction*. Malden, MA: Blackwell.

Tedla, Elleni (1995). *Sankofa: African thought and education*. New York: Peter Lang.

Terkel, Studs (1992). *Race: How blacks and whites think and feel about an American obsession*. New York: W. W. Norton & Co.

Thernstrom, Abigail & Stephan Thernstrom (2003). *No excuses: Closing the racial gap in learning*. New York: Simon & Schuster.

Thernstrom, Stephan & Abigail Thernstrom (1997). *America in black and white: One nation, indivisible*. New York: Simon & Schuster.

Thompson, Gail L. (2004). *Through ebony eyes: What teachers need to know but are afraid to ask about African-American students*. New York: Jossey-Bass.

Thornton, John (1998). *Africa and Africans in the making of the Atlantic world, 1400-1800*. New York: Cambridge University Press (2d ed.).

Thucydides (1972). *History of the Peloponnesian war*. New York: Penguin Books (Rex Warner, Trans.) (originally published 1954).

Todorov, Tzvetan (1993). *On human diversity: Nationalism, racism, and exoticism in French thought*. Cambridge, MA: Harvard University Press (Catherine Porter, Trans.).

Toepke, Alvaro & Angel Serrano (1998). *The language you cry in: The story of a Mende song*. California Newsreel Video.

Tougas, Francine, Jean-Claude Desruisseaux, Alain Desrochers, Line St-Pierre, Andrea Perrino, & Roxane De La Sablonnière (July 2004). Two forms of racism and their related outcomes: The bad and the ugly. *Canadian Journal of Behavioural Science*, Vol. 36, pp. 177-189.

Towles-Schwen, Tamara & Russell H. Fazio (2001). On the origins of racial attitudes: Correlates of childhood experience. *Personality and Social Psychology Bulletin*, Vol. 27, pp. 162-175.

Traoré, Rosemary L. (2002). *Implementing Afrocentricity: African students in an urban high school in America*. Unpublished doctoral dissertation, Temple University, Philadelphia, PA.

Tschannen-Moran, Megan (2004). *Trust matters: Leadership for successful schools*. San Francisco: Jossey-Bass.

Tsesis, Alexander (2004). *The thirteenth amendment and American freedom: A legal history*. New York: New York University Press.

Tyack, David (2004). *Seeking common ground: Public schools in a diverse society*. Cambridge, MA: Harvard University Press.

Tyack, David B. (1974). *The one best system: A history of American urban education*. Cambridge, MA: Harvard University Press.

Usdan, Michael D. (1998, Oct. 21). Is the grass that much greener? *Education Week*, Vol. 18, pp. 35-36.

Valencia, Richard R. & Lisa A. Suzuki (2001). *Intelligence testing and minority students: Foundations, performance factors, and assessment issues*. Thousand Oaks, CA: Sage.

Van Ausdale, Debra & Joe R. Feagin (2001). *The first R: How children learn race and racism*. Lanham, MD: Rowman & Littlefield.

Vaughan, Alden T. (1995). *The roots of American racism: Essays on the colonial experience*. New York: Oxford University Press.

Violence – for what? (1967, Nov. 19). *The Philadelphia Evening Bulletin*.

wa Thiong'o, Ngũgĩ (1986). *Decolonising the mind: The politics of language in African literature*. London: James Currey.

Wachtel, Paul L. (1999). *Race in the mind of America: Breaking the vicious circle between blacks and whites*. New York: Routledge.

Waldstreicher, David (2004). *Runaway America: Benjamin Franklin, slavery, and the American revolution*. New York: Hill & Wang.

Walker, Clarence (2001). *We can't go home again: An argument about Afrocentrism*. New York: Oxford University Press.

Walker, Sheila S. & Jennifer Rasamimanana (1993). Tarzan in the classroom: How "educational" films mythologize Africa and miseducate Americans. *Journal of Negro Education*, Vol. 62, pp. 3-23.

Ware, Vron (1992). *Beyond the pale: White women, racism and history*. New York: Verso.

Waters, Mary C. (1990). *Ethnic options: Choosing identities in America*. Berkeley: University of California Press.

Waters, Mary C. (1999). *Black identities: West Indian immigrant dreams and American realities*. Cambridge, MA: Harvard University Press.

Watkins, William H. (2001). *The white architects of black education: Ideology and power in America, 1865-1954*. New York: Teachers College Press.

Webber, Thomas L. (1978). *Deep like the rivers: Education in the slave quarter community, 1831-1865*. New York: W.W. Norton.

Weis, Lois & Michelle Fine (Eds.) (1993). *Beyond silenced voices: Class, race and gender in United States schools*. Albany, NY: State University of New York Press.

Weis, Lois (1992). Reflections on the researcher in a multicultural environment. In Carl A. Grant (Ed.), *Research and multicultural education: From the margins to the mainstream* (pp. 47-57). New York: Routledge/Falmer.

West, Cornel (1993). *Race matters*. Boston: Beacon Press.

White, Joseph L. & James A. Johnson, Jr. (1985). Awareness, pride and identity: A positive educational strategy for black youth. In Reginald L. Jones (Ed.), *Black Psychology* (pp. 409-418). Berkeley, CA: Cobb & Henry (3d ed.).

Wilentz, Sean (2005). *The rise of American democracy: Jefferson to Lincoln*. New York: W. W. Norton.

Williams, Eric E. (1994). *Capitalism and slavery*. Chapel Hill, NC: University of North Carolina Press (originally published 1944).

Williams, Linda Faye (2003). *The constraint of race: Legacies of white skin privilege in America*. University Park, PA: The Pennsylvania State University Press.

Williams, Heather Andrea (2005). *Self-taught: African American education in slavery and freedom*. Chapel Hill, NC: University of North Carolina Press.

Williams, Patricia J. (1991). *The alchemy of race and rights*. Cambridge, MA: Harvard University Press.

Williams, Patricia J. (1997). *Seeing a color-blind future: The paradox of race*. New York: Noonday Press.

Wilson, Amos N. (1992). *Awakening the natural genius of black children*. Trenton, NJ: Afrikan World Infosystems.

Wilson, Amos N. (1993). *The falsification of the Afrikan consciousness: Eurocentric history, psychiatry, and the politics of White supremacy*. Trenton, NJ: African World Infosystems.

Wilson, Midge, Ronald Hall, & Kathy Russell (1993). *The color complex: The politics of skin color among African Americans*. New York: Anchor.

Wilson, Robin (2001, July 27). A battle over race, nationality, and control at a Black university. *The Chronicle of Higher Education*, Vol. 48, p. A8.

Wilson, William Julius (1987). *The truly disadvantaged: The inner city, the underclass, and public policy*. Chicago: University of Chicago Press.

Wilson, William Julius (1996). The truly disadvantaged: The hidden agenda. In Susan S. Fainstein & Scott Campbell (Eds.), *Readings in urban theory* (pp. 191-206). Cambridge, MA: Blackwell.

Wise, Tim J. (2005). *Affirmative action: Racial preference in black and white*. New York: Routledge.

Wood, Peter (2003). *Diversity: The invention of a concept*. San Francisco: Encounter Books.

Woodall, Martha (2005, July 21). Text tapped for black history class. *The Philadelphia Inquirer*, p. B01.

Woodson, Carter G. (1990). *The mis-education of the Negro*. Trenton, NJ: Africa World Press (originally published 1933).

Woolman, David C. (2001). Educational reconstruction and post-colonial curriculum development: A comparative study of four African countries. *International Education Journal*, Vol. 2, No. 5, pp. 27-46.

Wright, Michelle M. (2004). *Becoming Black: Creating identity in the African diaspora*. Durham, NC: Duke University Press.

Yon, Daniel A. (2000). *Elusive culture: Schooling, race and identity in global times*. Albany, NY: State University of New York Press.

Young, Iris M. (1992). Five faces of oppression. In Thomas E. Wartenberg (Ed.), *Rethinking power* (pp. 174-195). Albany, NY: State University of New York Press.

Zangwill, Israel (1908). *The melting pot.* Full text of this classic drama is available at http://www.vdare.com/fulford/melting_pot_play.htm. Also in Edna Nahshon (Ed.) (2005), *From the ghetto to the melting pot: Israel Zangwill's Jewish plays.* Detroit, MI: Wayne State University Press.

Zehr, Mary Ann (2001, Mar. 21). The "lost boys" of Sudan find a home. *Education Week,* Vol. 20, pp. 34-35.

Ziegler, Dhyana & Molefi Kete Asante (1992). *The mass media in Africa.* Trenton, NJ: Africa World Press.

Ziegler, Dhyana (Ed.) (1995). *Molefi Kete Asante and Afrocentricity: In praise and in criticism.* Nashville, TN: James C. Wilson.

Zinn, Howard & Donaldo Macedo (2004). *Howard Zinn on democratic education.* Boulder, CO: Paradigm.

Index

About the Authors

Rosemary Traoré, Ph.D., is Assistant Professor, Urban Education, University of North Carolina at Charlotte.

Robert J. Lukens, Ph.D., J.D., is Co-Director of the Advocating on Behalf of Children Project at Community Legal Services in Philadelphia, Pennsylvania.